James Bentley

NLB

Between Marx and Christ

The Dialogue in
German-Speaking Europe
1870–1970

**British Library
Cataloguing in Publication Data**

Bentley, James
  Between Marx and Christ.
  1. Communism and Christianity
  I. Title
  261.2'1   HX536

  ISBN 0-86091-048-2 Cloth
       0-86091-748-7 Pbk

First published, 1982
© James Bentley

Verso Editions and NLB,
15 Greek Street, London W1

Typeset in Monophoto Sabon by
Butler & Tanner Ltd
Frome, Somerset

Printed and bound in Great Britain by
Butler and Tanner Ltd, Frome and London

Contents

For AWB

Preface

It is rare enough to find Christians and socialists relating to each other, let alone Christians and Marxists. When such a relationship occurs, the opponents of dialogue often feel the need to diminish it. At the beginning of this century the warden of New College, Oxford, was asked whether there was much Christian Socialism in the university. He replied that he knew of only two Christian Socialists in Oxford, himself and the theologian Dr Hastings Rashdall, adding immediately, 'and I'm not very much of a Socialist, and Dr Rashdall isn't very much of a Christian.'[1]

The warden's jest illustrates a widely held conviction: that those who take part in the Christian–Marxist dialogue are at best no more than lukewarm Christians or pseudo-Marxists; at worst they are involved in something sinister and subversive. Thus when the Czech Christian Jan Milic Lochman visited America in 1968 to speak about the Christian life in a Marxist society, the first comment at one of his public lectures was, 'I do not know who invited this gentleman into the United States. But it is clear that he is a Communist agent. There are no Christian theologians in Eastern Europe.'[2] Ironically, such Christians as Lochman have frequently found themselves equally suspect in socialist countries, stigmatized by the assertion of *The Communist Manifesto* that 'Christian Socialism is but the holy water with which the priest consecrates the heart-burnings of the aristocrat.' By the same token, Marxist atheists living in these countries who wish to engage in dialogue with Christians find themselves mistrusted by the authorities, and sometimes even disgraced.

My assumption throughout this book is that it is completely inadequate to respond to the Christian–Marxist dialogue in such ways.

1. R. A. Knox, *Literary Distractions*, 1958, p. 59.
2. J. M. Lochman, *Church in a Marxist Society. A Czechoslovak View*, 1970, p. 17.

The encounter between Christianity and Marxism was exhausted neither by the barbs of *The Communist Manifesto* nor by the passionate and sometimes polemical observations on religion made by the young Marx. Inevitably, as a result of these attacks, Christians and Marxists in German-speaking Europe regarded each other with considerable hostility in 1870, the year with which this study opens. But a hundred years later some of them were enthusiastically co-operating in an attempt to discover an ever more human form of socialism, an endeavour that reached such an intensity in Czechoslovakia in 1968 that its enemies decided to try to destroy it by force.

The aim of this book is to explore how that point was reached, principally by examining the lives and thought of six important German-speaking intellectuals—three of them Christians, three of them Marxist atheists: Christoph Blumhardt, Karl Kautsky, Karl Barth, Ernst Bloch, Dorothee Sölle, and Milan Machovec. Two of them (the Christian Karl Barth and the Marxist Ernst Bloch) must by any account be rated amongst the most creative thinkers of the twentieth century. All six influenced less important writers and theoreticians who nevertheless played significant roles in the Christian–Marxist dialogue. In the course of this dialogue very many of those taking part, and in particular five of the principal characters, suffered persecution, professional disgrace, or exile because of their beliefs.

To explore such a dialogue without also paying regard to the social conditions of the time would be inappropriate. German-speaking Europe was the context of this encounter between Christians and Marxists partly because in the early decades of the period it contained the largest urban proletariat in the world. In addition, the political upheavals of German-speaking Europe greatly affected the dialogue and those who participated in it.

But my subject is essentially the intellectual encounter between Christians and Marxists. I wish to consider what drew German-speaking Marxists and Christians together, and to show how (in spite of Marx and Engels's undoubted hostility to religion[3]) they continued to examine where Marxism and Christianity might converge as well as part. My aim too is to show how, as the dialogue developed, new insights altered traditional attitudes—with respect to rival models of

---

3. As Marx and Engels *On Religion*, Moscow 1957, amply demonstrates. Cf. D. B. McKown, *The Classical Marxist Critiques of Religion: Marx, Engels, Lenin, Kautsky*, The Hague 1975, pp. 10ff., and (for a cautionary word) O. Chadwick, *The Secularization of the European Mind in the Nineteenth Century*, 1975, p. 65.

humanity, to revolution, to atheism, to the notion of God itself, and (although only two of the six principal characters were ever practising politicians) to the political consequences of belief. If Marxism manifestly developed by opening itself to an encounter with Christianity, it is also clear that the dialogue could not have advanced as it did without massive shifts in Christian understanding brought about almost entirely by the theologians of German-speaking Europe. My study concludes at a point when participants on both sides (such as the Marxist Milan Machovec and the Christian Dorothee Sölle) had come to believe that the debate could no longer be confined to the concerns and traditions of that part of the world.

The subject of this book inevitably involves assessing a number of historical disputes (such as the validity of Marxist readings of the early church and the historical Jesus); but my chief aim is to explore and demonstrate continuity and development in the dialogue between Christians and Marxists over one hundred years of Central European history.

Acknowledgements

The principal sources on which this book is based are the published writings of the persons involved, as well as the writings of their critics. The most valuable unpublished source was the collection of Kautsky papers in Amsterdam (although his letters to his wife during the relevant period contain no mention of Kautsky's *Foundations of Christianity*[1]). These papers have an index neither of subjects nor of dates, but are classified according to correspondents.[2] I am therefore particularly grateful to Dr Götz Langkau and the staff of the International Institute of Social History in Amsterdam for helping me to find what I needed in them.

Much of the material relating to the young Karl Barth is now in print, including in particular his correspondence with Eduard Thurneysen. His political speeches are being edited by Friedrich-Wilhelm Marquardt under terms that do not make them available at present; but Professor Marquardt generously gave me of his time and hospitality to discuss them and Barth in general. Dr Eberhard Bethge confirmed that almost all the literary remains of Dietrich Bonhoeffer are now in print.[3]

In addition to these sources the book is based on interviews and correspondence with those who knew principal participants in the dialogue and were active in it themselves. As well as Professor F.-W. Marquardt, I must thank here Professor Eduard Goldstücker, Professor Helmut Gollwitzer, Professor Jan Milic Lochman, Professor Jürgen Moltmann and Bishop Albrecht Schönherr for invaluable help. I am grateful to Sir Robert Birley and Dr Visser 't Hooft for illuminating

1. Kautsky papers, Familienarchief, 1901 to 1909.
2. W. Blumenberg, *Karl Kautskys literarisches Werk. Eine bibliographische Übersicht*, 'S-Gravenhage 1960, is a short and sometimes inaccurate introduction to the archive.
3. Letter to the author, 17 November 1978.

conversations. It would be wrong not to thank Frau Lochman, Frau Marquardt, and Frau Schönherr for their kindness and food, and my own wife for so patiently driving me about Europe.

I am indebted to the staff of the libraries in which I worked, namely the library of the Evangelical Academy at Bad Boll, the Bodleian, the British Library, the John Rylands University Library in Manchester, the London Library, the University of Sussex Library, and the Library of the World Council of Churches in Geneva. The Christendom Trust enabled me to do some of the work for this book by appointing me Maurice Reckitt Research Fellow in Christian Social Thought at the University of Sussex and by making a grant towards the expense of my research abroad. Professor Geoffrey Best, the Revd Professor Owen Chadwick, the Revd Professor Duncan Forrester, and the Revd Professor Ronald Preston gave me much encouragement, as did the chairman of the Christendom Trust, Dr Robert Towler. I am deeply indebted to Professor John Röhl, who read a draft of the book in typescript and suggested many improvements.

Some of the material in this book has appeared in articles published in *Theology*, *The Expository Times*, the *Journal of Theological Studies*, and the *Journal of Church and State*, as well as in the *Papers in Religion and Politics* published by the Department of Government and Faculty of Theology in the University of Manchester. I am grateful to the editors of those journals for allowing me to use again the material here.

Finally I must thank Stephen Medcalf and Angela Lambert for generously allowing me to live in their homes when I was working in Sussex and London.

I
The Historical Background

The relations between Christians and Marxists in German-speaking Europe between 1870 and 1970 could not have developed as they did—from mutual hostility to intense dialogue—without the remarkable social, political, and intellectual conditions prevailing in that part of the world. The second German Reich arose in 1871 at a time when the country was experiencing profound social and economic changes. Industrial production, which was rising twice as fast as in Britain, increased by 4.2 per cent a year between 1873 and 1913.[1] By the end of the nineteenth century the population was twice that of 1850. Less than one person in five now lived and worked in the countryside. The German nation had to cope with a large and growing urban proletariat. By 1907 there were eight and a half million factory workers in the country, and by the outbreak of the First World War three million of these had joined trade unions.[2]

Seeking to represent these workers politically was the Social Democratic Party (SPD). The SPD had been created in 1875 (as the Socialist Workers Party) through the merger of the German Social Democratic Workers Party, led by Wilhelm Liebknecht and August Bebel (the 'Eisenach' party), and the General German Workers Union, founded by Ferdinand Lassalle in 1863. It was an unstable union. Though both founding groups were recognizably labour parties, the attitudes of the Eisenachers and the Lassallians differed considerably: over nationalism and internationalism, liberal democracy, and socialism itself.[3] Neither group managed long to retain the approval of Karl Marx, whose

1. N. Kaldor, citing an unpublished study by W. A. Lewis, in *De-Industrialization*, ed. F. Blackaby, 1979, p. 21.
2. See the statistics summarized in J. Joll, *Europe Since 1870*, 1973, pp. lff.
3. See R. Morgan, *The German Social Democrats and the First International, 1864–1872*, 1965, for these early quarrels.

prestige in the German labour movement had been immensely augmented by the publication of *Das Kapital* in 1867. Both groups, and their successor, the SPD, were open to what Marx regarded as dangerously heterodox opinions.

Socialist thought, socialist political parties, and the urban proletariat all formed part of the German 'Social Question'. Clergymen and politicians alike sought to grapple with and solve this question, often wishing to help the impoverished working classes while abhorring socialist beliefs.[4] When the distinguished Pastor Christoph Blumhardt decided to join the SPD in 1899, he provoked such outrage that the church authorities deprived him of his holy orders. Blumhardt and his fellow clergymen were concerned with socialism and the Social Question neither as theoreticians nor primarily as theologians; but their response (rather than any systematic attempt to deal with Marx's strictures on religion) marks the beginning of the Christian–Marxist dialogue in German-speaking Europe. And Blumhardt is the first major figure in this history.

As the reaction to Blumhardt indicates, criticism from Marx was not the only hazard faced by active German Socialists. In Bismarck's Germany the Social Democrats, brave honourable men (as Golo Mann has described them), were 'hounded by the public prosecutor and boycotted by middle-class industry', travelling about with limited resources in order to stir up their countrymen, working as artisans or small traders between periods in prison, sitting beside rich men as members of parliament while themselves dependent on food parcels and small contributions from party members. They found it difficult to articulate the political aims of the urban proletariat, which was, in the contemporary judgement of Max Weber, economically 'far more mature than the propertied classes will admit', but politically 'infinitely less mature than a journalistic clique which would like to monopolize its leadership wants to believe'.[5] Often debarred from real power, the Socialist leaders frequently disagreed among themselves. The Gotha programme adopted by the party in 1875 was savagely criticized by Marx. It took twenty-five years of argument and the severe persecution of the Bismarck era before the Socialists adopted, at Erfurt, a pro-

4. See K. E. Pollmann, *Landes-herrliches Kirchenregiment und Soziale Frage*, Berlin 1974. Johannes Messner, *Die Soziale Frage*, Vienna 1964. *Quellen zur Geschichte der sozialen Frage in Deutschland*, hrsg von E. Schappler, 2nd edn, 2 vols, Göttingen 1960–1964.

5. G. Mann *The History of Germany Since 1789*, tr. M. Jackson, Harmondsworth 1974, pp. 362 and 347.

gramme Marxist enough to be entirely approved by Engels. Even then, although the SPD was revolutionary in theory, it was committed to working through established parliamentary procedures in practice—a contradiction that ensured steady strife between revisionist Socialist politicians like Eduard Bernstein and more 'orthodox' Marxists like Karl Kautsky and Rosa Luxemburg. Nonetheless, until the unexpected success of the Bolshevik revolution in Russia in 1917, the left-wing politicians and Socialist intellectuals of Germany dominated European Marxism. At the same time, their failure to develop a monolithic party orthodoxy allowed some of them (including Kautsky himself) to explore avenues of thought that more rigid Marxists would have shunned.

One such avenue was the relationship between Marxism and Christianity. In the Russia of Lenin and his successors, even the acknowledgement that such a relationship might exist was officially condemned, and the church was vigorously persecuted.[6] Shortly before his death Lenin told a French Roman Catholic that 'Communism and Catholicism offered two diverse, complete, and inconfusable conceptions of human life.'[7] In any case, the leading figures of Russian Orthodoxy, by-passed by the Reformation and even by much of the Enlightenment, were ill-equipped for an intellectual encounter with Marxism. Under the Tsars the Russian church showed itself scarcely able to come to terms with the existence of other sorts of Christians, let alone with the atheist intellectuals who in 1917 set about destroying the old order.[8]

German Protestantism was different. 'When, at some future day', wrote Albert Schweitzer in 1906, 'our period of civilization shall lie, closed and completed, before the eyes of later generations, German theology will stand out as a great, a unique phenomenon in the mental and spiritual life of our time.'[9] Schweitzer did not believe himself to be exaggerating. His *Quest of the Historical Jesus* not only expounded the astonishing development of German theology, through industry,

6. T. Beeson, *Discretion and Valour*, 1974, chapters 2 and 3. N. Zernov, *The Russians and their Church*, 3rd edn, 1978, chapter 17.

7. Quoted, J. Hellman, 'French "Left-Catholics" and Communism in the Nineteen-Thirties', *Church History*, vol. 45, December 1976, p. 507.

8. E. Crankshaw, *The Shadow of the Winter Palace. The Drift to Revolution 1825–1917*, 1978, pp. 331f., for details of the persecution of other Christian groups by Russian Orthodoxy.

9. A. Schweitzer, *Von Reimarus zu Wrede* (1906), tr. W. Montgomery, *The Quest of the Historical Jesus*, 1910, p. 1.

polemic, and scholarly openness, from Hermann Samuel Reimarus in the eighteenth century to Wilhelm Wrede more than a hundred years later; as a *tour de force* in its own right it also helped to justify Schweitzer's high assessment of his own discipline. This discipline did not find Marxism intellectually daunting. And German Marxists might even enter into it. Schweitzer's paradoxical contention was that what he regarded as the greatest achievement of German theology, the critical investigation of the life of Jesus, served only to demonstrate that it is impossible to reconstruct a chronological and psychological account of Jesus's life: theologians who attempted this merely invested Jesus with their own thoughts and ideas. In the words of an Irish Catholic (writing under Schweitzer's influence), looking back through nineteen centuries of darkness they saw only the reflection of their own faces at the bottom of a deep well.[10] Yet notwithstanding the contention that the quest of the historical Jesus had come to nought, it now seemed possible to peer down the well and perceive a proletarian face. In 1908 Karl Kautsky observed that everyone presented in Jesus not what he taught but what they wished he had taught.[11] Kautsky then proceeded to describe the founder of Christianity as a quasi-mythical primitive communist.

In spite of (or perhaps because of) the intractable nature of some of the problems it had set itself, German theology retained its extraordinary vitality in the twentieth century. This remained especially true of German Protestant theology. As late as 1960 the philosopher Jürgen Habermas observed, 'In Germany, philosophy is so thoroughly imbued with the Protestant spirit that Catholics, in order to engage in philosophy, must almost turn Protestant.' For too long, Habermas contended, Roman Catholic philosophy had been imprisoned in the ivory tower of Thomism.[12] For many years, too, the Papal response to Soviet Communism helped to inhibit a Christian–Marxist dialogue involving German Catholics. In *Divinis Redemptoris* (March 1937) Pius XI took up an attitude similar to that of Lenin on the incompatibility of Christianity and communism. Even Paul VI's *Populorum progressio* referred to Marxist hopes as messianisms laden with promises that in

10. G. Tyrell, *Christianity at the Cross-Roads* (1906), edition of 1963, p. 49.

11. Karl Kautsky, *The Foundations of Christianity*, translation of the 13th German edition, 1925, p. 40.

12. J. Habermas, 'Ein marxistischer Schelling. Zu Ernst Blochs spekulativem Materialismus', in *Merkur. Deutsche Zeitschrift für europäisches Denken*, vol. 15, 1960, p. 1083.

truth fabricated illusions,[13] in spite of the progress towards dialogue and detente made by his predecessor, John XXIII.

In contrast, German philosophy continued to take the Hegelian and Marxist tradition seriously. (An English visitor in 1976 was surprised to discover that the Marxist-oriented were 'much the largest group among German philosophers.'[14]) The Hegelian tradition, Habermas observed with a slight air of self-congratulation, 'is likely to be more responsive to the spiritual quests of mankind than either Anglo-Saxon positivism or Soviet materialism.'[15] And steeped in what Karl Barth described as the 'peculiar greatness' of Hegel's philosophy,[16] German Protestant theologians coped more readily than others with the Hegelian aspects of Marxism.

Neither the philosophers nor the theologians could isolate themselves from German politics. The same forces that created the Social Question proved disastrously impossible to contain. 'The history of Europe in the hundred years since 1870 has been dominated politically by the German question', wrote James Joll, 'by the need, and the failure to absorb, the economic resources and the productive capacities of Germany into an acceptable European political framework.'[17] The consequences of this failure included two world wars and the Hitler Reich. Karl Barth considered his theological masters to have been 'hopelessly compromised' by their support of German war aims in 1914.[18] Equally compromised was German Social Democracy. As Stefan Zweig observed, 'the Social Democrats, who a month before had condemned militarism as the greatest evil, were if possible even noisier than the others in order not to be regarded, in Kaiser Wilhelm's words, as "fellows without a fatherland".'[19] As Rosa Luxemburg bitterly observed, ' "Workers of the world, unite!" has been changed on the battlefields into "Workers of the world, slit each others' throats".'[20]

13. Quoted J. Miranda, *Marx and the Bible. A Critique of the Philosophy of Oppression*, New York 1974, p. xiv.

14. A. Kenny, 'German Philosophy Today', in *The Listener*, 20 May 1976, p. 641.

15. Habermas p. 1091.

16. *Protestant Theology in the Nineteenth Century*, tr. B. Cozens, J. Bowden, *et al.*, 1972, p. 396.

17. J. Joll, p. 481.

18. E. Busch, *Karl Barth. His life from letters and autobiographical texts*, tr. J. Bowden 1976, p.81.

19. S. Zweig, *Die Welt von Gestern*, Frankfurt am Main 1970, p. 273.

20. R. Luxemburg, in April 1916, *Ausgewählte Reden und Schriften*, Berlin 1951, II. 534.

Yet the First World War also enabled Lenin to come to power in Russia, another development that profoundly affected Karl Barth.

It disturbed German Marxists that the revolution did not take place in their own country at the end of the war. (*The Communist Manifesto*, after all, had asserted that the bourgeois and proletarian revolutions would take place first in Germany and then in Britain.) The failure of their hopes forced them to look again at the subjective springs of human action. 'In the fateful months after November 1918', wrote Karl Korsch, 'when the organized political power of the bourgeoisie was smashed and outwardly there was nothing else in the way of transition from capitalism to socialism, the great chance was never seized because the *socio-psychological* preconditions for its seizure were lacking.'[21] Among these subjective springs of human action was Christianity. Some, such as Erich Fromm, presented Christianity as supremely a force for social control; but men like Ernst Bloch in particular began to discern in the messianic and utopian elements of Christianity a principle of hope and social change.

The increasing freedom with which some Christians and Marxists were able to explore their common ideals was helped by a greater understanding of Marx himself which can be traced back to the publication in 1932 of his *Economic and Philosophical Manuscripts*. These early writings proved invaluable to the members of the Frankfurt Institute for Social Research, who had begun to reconsider the whole nature of historical materialism.[22] Marx was now perceived to be a person of many moods and ambiguities, and a number of Marxists as well as Christians came to accept that, in Sidney Hook's words, 'there are many Marxs. There is Marx the revolutionary fighter ..., Marx the historical sociologist and political economist, ... Marx the social and moral prophet ..., and Marx the radical historicist for whom all moral ideals—freedom, equality, fraternity, integrity, independence— are deceptive abstractions, concealing the economic class interests at their roots.' Hook adds that 'to make the matter even more complicated, we must distinguish all these Marxs, embodied in what was published over a period of forty years, from the Ur-Marx of the so-called *Economic-Philosophic Manuscripts*, who quietly entered the world only in 1932, and was discovered almost a quarter century later

21. Quoted R. Jakoby, *Social Amnesia: A Critique of Conformist Psychology from Adler to Laing*, Hassocks 1975, p. 75.
22. See for instance the 1932 review by Herbert Marcuse, in *Studies in Critical Philosophy*, tr. J. de Beres, London 1972.

to be the most effective ally of the Communist opposition to Stalinism.'[23] For fear that dialogue with Christians (or existentialists, for that matter) might contaminate their ideological purity, a number of Western Marxists, led by Louis Althusser, attempted to make a radical distinction between Marx's early beliefs, which undoubtedly contain humanist notions, and the later theorist; but the publication of Marx's *Grundrisse* amply demonstrated the survival of this humanism in his mature writings.[24]

The rise to power of Hitler damaged both socialism and Christianity in Germany. Yet it ultimately helped to bring about a new phase in the Christian-Marxist dialogue. As one of Hitler's Christian opponents observed, 'The best and most reliable "resisters" were to be found among mature Christians—not among those who merely went along with the Christian convention—and among Communists.'[25] It was, indeed, scarcely possible to overlook the Communist opposition to Hitler. In 1932 the German Communist Party, the largest outside the Soviet Union, had won 17 per cent of the vote and returned some hundred members to the Reichstag. Its estimated membership was 300,000. By the end of 1933, some 130,000 of these were in concentration camps, and 2,500 had been murdered.[26] Some Communists came to acknowledge that Christians were in the same struggle. In 1936, noting that Hitler was setting up a *Reichskirche* with himself as Tsar-Pope, Ernst Bloch also noted the determined Christian opposition to this. He added: 'If religion is the opium of the people, fascism is its strychnine.'[27]

The outstanding leader of those in the churches who were trying to fight against the Nazi *Weltanschauung* was undoubtedly Karl Barth. 'We know how much we owe directly to him in the struggle for the purity of the Gospel', wrote an ally in December 1934.[28] But Barth's religious opposition had also decidedly political overtones. It revived

23. S. Hook, 'The Enlightenment and Marxism', in *Journal of the History of Ideas*, vol. 29, New York 1968, p. 93. For an example of the importance of these early Marxist writings after World War II, see J. M. Lochman, *Encountering Marx*, tr. E. Robertson, Belfast 1977, chapter 2: 'The Image of Man in the Young Karl Marx'.

24. For Althusser, see G. Gutierrez, *A Theology of Liberation*, 1974, p. 253n, and D. McLellan, *Marx*, 1974, p. 52, as well as Althusser's *For Marx*, London 1977.

25. H. Thielicke, *Between Heaven and Earth*, tr. J. W. Dobersteen, 1967, p. 153.

26. E. Matthias, *Das Ende der Parteien*, Düsseldorf 1960, pp. 162 and 694.

27. 'Hitlers "Kulturkampf", Herrenpfaffen und Christen' (1936), in *Politische Messungen, Pestzeit, Vormärz*, Frankfurt am Main 1976, pp. 126f.

28. Hans Asmussen to George Bell, 1 December 1934, in *Die Mündige Welt V*, ed. J. Glenthøg, Munich 1969, p. 239.

his socialist leanings, and after the Second World War brought him into practical co-operation with Communists for the first time. Other Christian opponents of Hitler were to reveal a new openness to Marxism. Pastor Martin Niemöller, imprisoned for nearly eight years after his arrest by the Gestapo in July 1937, was the first leading German Protestant to make a public visit to Russia after the war. (The German Chancellor, Konrad Adenauer, described the visit as a stab in the back for the German government, which prompted the Swiss Evangelical Press Service to ask whether churches in the West were expected to conform to government views on foreign policy.[29]) And sensitive communists were impressed that in a Nazi prison the martyr Dietrich Bonhoeffer had brooded on the special responsibility that would fall after the war on the German nation, lying as it did 'midway between East and West'.[30]

Bonhoeffer's attempt as a theologian to speak in a secular way about God (which was inspired in part by Karl Barth's criticism of 'religion'[31]) led him to analyse how the working classes interpreted Jesus. 'What does it mean', he wrote, 'when a proletarian in his suspicious world says, "Jesus was a good man"? He means that one need not distrust him. The proletarian does not say, "Jesus is God"; but in saying that Jesus was a good man he says in any case a great deal more than a bourgeois who says that Jesus is God. For him God is something that belongs to the church. But in the factories Jesus can be present as the socialist; in the political world as the idealist; in the proletarian existence as the good man. In their ranks he fights with them against the enemy—Capitalism.'[32] After his death, the thought of Dietrich Bonhoeffer helped many to work out a political theology adequate for dialogue between Christians and Marxists. Barth's leading disciple, Helmut Gollwitzer, used the above quotation to introduce *Jesus for Atheists*, by the Czechoslovakian Marxist Milan Machovec, in Germany.[33] The German Marxist Dorothee Sölle began her systematic outline of political theology by underlining Bonhoeffer's insistence that thinking is not the luxury of the spectator but must always be the

---

29. J. A. Hebly, *The Russians and the World Council of Churches*, Belfast 1978, pp. 57f.

30. D. Bonhoeffer, *Letters and Papers from Prison*, quoted R. Garaudy, *Marxism in the Twentieth Century*, tr. R. Hague, 1970, p. 161.

31. *Letters and Papers from Prison*, ed. E. Bethge, enlarged edition, 1971, pp. 280, 286 and 328.

32. *Gesammelte Schriften*, Munich 1959, III. 174.

33. Geleitwort to Milan Machovec, *Jesus für Atheisten*, 3rd edn, Stuttgart 1973, p. vii.

prelude to practical action.[34] At the beginning of his account of Marxism in the twentieth century, the French communist theoretician Roger Garaudy quoted Bonhoeffer's judgement that one must 'take the risk of saying things that are in dispute, provided that vital problems are thereby raised'.[35] And twenty-five years after a Communist state had been set up in East Germany, Bishop Albrecht Schönherr of Berlin-Brandenburg argued that the Christian's place in that society can be illuminated best by Bonhoeffer's notions of a church without privilege, of a church existing entirely for others, of the essential unity of loving God and one's brethren, of total 'this-worldliness', and of suffering with God in the world.[36]

After meeting Dietrich Bonhoeffer and his fellow conspirator Hans Schönfeld in Sweden in 1942, Bishop George Bell of Chichester predicted, 'The collapse of Hitler will leave a vacuum in Europe. Unless the problem of how that vacuum can rightly be filled is squarely and immediately faced, the last state of Europe may be worse than the first.'[37] After the Nazi capitulation and the subsequent division of Germany, it seemed to many Christians that Bell's gloomiest fears were justified: for the first time in history a large Protestant church (nominally comprising the majority of the population of East Germany) was obliged to live and witness entirely within the Marxist–Leninist version of socialism. Czechoslovakia too (including the four million 'Sudeten Germans' clumsily included within its borders) came under Russian hegemony, not entirely unwillingly: in the light of their treatment by the Nazis and in view of the earlier 'betrayal' of Czechoslovakia by the Munich agreement between Hitler and Neville Chamberlain, the Czechs initially conceived of the Russians as liberators. For the first time Soviet Russia came into contact with Protestant Christianity as a major force in society. In Czechoslovakia the comparatively small group of Protestants was led by Josef Hromadka, a Barthian of international standing who was willing to persuade his fellow Christians to co-operate in building a socialist humanism. And in the Soviet zone of Germany 82 per cent of the population declared themselves to be

34. D. Sölle, *Politische Theologie. Auseinandersetzung mit Rudolf Bultmann*, Stuttgart 1971, p. 9.

35. R. Garaudy, p.6.

36. A. Schönherr, 'The Christian's Place in East German Society as Illuminated by Aspects of Bonhoeffer's Theology', duplicated copy of the lecture delivered at the University of Durham, 15 November 1972, pp. 3, 13, 12, and 21.

37. In *The Christian Newsletter* No. 13, ed. J. H. Oldham, reprinted in *Die Mündige Welt* V, p. 307.

Protestant and were served by eight *Landeskirchen*.[38] In six East German universities theologians continued to teach and publish, among them old Christian socialists from the days before Hitler, such as Emil Fuchs of Leipzig.[39]

The military administration in Berlin established a central office for religious affairs to co-ordinate church policy in East Germany. A considerable amount of mutual tolerance and respect existed as a result of common opposition to Hitler. (Walter Ulbricht, the first East German head of state, had escaped from the Third Reich into the Soviet Union; but Erich Honecker, his far less rigid successor, had suffered ten years in Brandenburg prison, condemned by a Nazi treason trial.) In 1946 the German Communist Party and the SPD in East Germany were merged to form a single party, the SED;[40] but the Soviet military authorities also set up the Christian Democratic Union, which consisted mostly of bourgeois anti-fascist Christians.[41]

After the failure of Stalin's blockade of Berlin in 1948–1949, East Germany became the German Democratic Republic. In creating a new state, the Russians were to some extent reacting to the West, which had set up the Bundesrepublik under Konrad Adenauer. Dr Kurt Gust has shown that the East German authorities thereafter organized a fierce battle against the church, at times attempting to stamp it out by brute force.[42] After the rising of June 1953 oppression was terminated for a time. This was apparently far from the wish of Walter Ulbricht, who provoked fresh tension by proposing that a new city, Stalinstadt, should be built entirely without churches. The new Soviet leaders appear to have forced him to climb down.[43] But in 1957 persecution began again, partly in response to the Hungarian uprising of the previous year, and partly (it seems) because of the decision by West German Protestants to provide military chaplains for the West German army, a move strongly opposed by Martin Niemöller among others.[44] Finally, the East German authorities forced the eventual separation of East German Protestants from their Western brethren by refusing to

38. H. D. Brunotte, *Die Evangelische Kirche in Deutschland*, Hanover 1959, p. 17.

39. E. Fuchs published after World War II, *Marxismus und Christenglaube*, Leipzig 1953, and *Christliche und marxistische Ethik*, 2 vols, Leipzig 1959.

40. Socialist Unity Party.

41. In the first post-war elections (21 October 1949) the SED gained 249 seats in the provinces. The CDU came second with 121 seats.

42. K. Gust, 'East German Protestantism under Communist Rule, 1945–1961', Ph. D. thesis, University of Kansas, 1966.

43. J. Steele, *Socialism with a German Face*, 1977, pp. 84 and 86.

44. K. Gust, p. 202.

allow the synod of the United Evangelical Church of Germany to meet in East Berlin in 1961. All this ran directly counter to Articles 42 through 46 of the German Democratic Republic, which recognized freedom of belief (so long as this was not used for 'unconstitutional' or 'party political' purposes), permitted religious associations to levy taxes on their members (the state providing the tax lists), allowed the churches to hold property and even to receive state subsidies, and granted persons in hospital or prison the right to worship. The attempts of the church to proselytize were now hindered. The Soviet military administration had provided for religious broadcasting; but after 1959, 'For all practical purposes, the broadcasting system as a means of mass communication was closed to the church.'[45] The plight of East German Christians was not eased until Erich Honecker succeeded Walter Ulbricht in the 1970s.

Open-minded Marxists found the regime equally repressive. After the defeat of Hitler, Ernst Bloch returned from exile to East rather than to West Germany. In 1961, increasingly harassed by the authorities, he crossed to the West.

These developments were paralleled, with far greater viciousness, in Czechoslovakia. Partly because of the inclusion of German-speaking citizens when Czechoslovakia was created after the First World War, Czechoslovakian theologians had retained close contacts with their German counterparts. Hromadka's pupil Jan Milic Lochman followed his teacher's example and studied under Barth; in 1968 he took Barth's old chair in the University of Basle. Czechoslovakia had played a part in bringing together political praxis and theology in Barth's own lifetime: when the country was threatened by Hitler in 1938, Barth had written that 'every Czech soldier will stand and fall not only for the freedom of Europe, but also for the Christian church.'[46]

But Czechoslovakia also cherished its own traditions. Lochman singled out two as of particular importance in the Christian–Marxist dialogue.[47] First, the Czechs (and not solely the Czech Protestant brethren) self-consciously identified with the Hussite Reformation. The Czech Reformation developed a type of Christianity with which even communists might identify; it did not issue in capitalism but remained a popular movement. Hus was intensely socially-minded; he placed great emphasis on the social responsibility of the Gospel. When,

45. Ibid. p. 318.
46. Barth to P. Maury, 12 October 1938, in E. Busch, p. 289.
47. Personal conversation with the author, 28 March 1978.

therefore, Czech Marxists began to search history for their own roots, they found in Hus a social revolutionary. The notion of religion as opiate of the people did not fit the facts of Czech history. The fifteenth was the most progressive as well as the most religious century. One of the Marxist participants in the Czech dialogue (which reached its peak and tragic end in 1968) was Robert Kalivoda, who had written a volume on Hussite ideology, urging that Marxists ought to differentiate between religion that served as opiate and religion that did not.[48] As Lochman said elsewhere, 'No person was so much present and alive in the Prague spring of 1968 as Jan Hus.'[49]

Second, Lochman argued, of all the East European countries Czechoslovakia had best preserved the tradition of dialogue. Czechoslovaks regarded as supremely important the formula of the first president of their country, Thomas Masaryk: 'Democracy is discussion.' In this context the dialogue developed and began to flourish. The Stalinist pattern of imposing policy from above was alien to Czechoslovaks. Zdenek Mlynar, along with other reformist members of the Central Committee of the Czechoslovak Communist Party, drew up an *Analysis of the Party's Record*, which stated: 'For the Czechs and the Slovaks, traditionally intolerant of bureaucratic stupidity, of boorishness and bullying, of rigid hierarchies in the economic and political fields, socialism is acceptable only if it means a system that encourages an efficient and rational economy, that reinforces democratic rights and defends human freedom.'[50] On 5 January 1968 the Stalinist Antonin Novotny was replaced as first secretary by Alexander Dubcek, first secretary of the Communist Party of Slovakia.

Dubcek had no intention of leading his country into the Western bloc. The son of a Slovak Communist, he had been educated in Russia and spent three years in the Higher Party School in Moscow. But he favoured open debate. The largest public discussion between Christians and Marxists took place in April of that year. In August the Soviet leader Leonid Brezhnev ordered Warsaw Pact troops into Czechoslovakia to crush the Prague Spring. Few Christians were dismissed, but almost all Marxist intellectuals who had taken part in the dialogue lost their jobs. The Czechoslovak politicians, led by Dubcek and President Svoboda, were forced to renounce their planned reforms. As under the Third Reich, so again persecution stimulated mutual respect between

48. Information from J. M. Lochman, 28 March 1978.
49. J. M. Lochman, *Church in a Marxist Society. A Czechoslovak View*, 1970, p. 107.
50. Quoted K. Kyle, 'The Fall of Prague', in *The Listener*, 24 August 1978, p. 227.

Christians and Marxists. 'Dubcek and Svoboda became symbols of freedom', wrote Dorothee Sölle. '. . . In 1968 they set an example for humanity. They are Communists. But what does that mean? Christians could not have done better.'[51]

Yet the intervention of Soviet Marxism, though undoubtedly destructive of the dialogue, is in some respects an alien element in this story. Although often impressed by Russian achievements in 1917 and after, the Marxists and Christians who entered into dialogue in German-speaking Europe were those who did not capitulate to Lenin's ideological imperialism. Kautsky immediately condemned Lenin for introducing the dictatorship of the proletariat in revolutionary Russia. 'The future of the Russian proletariat lies not in dictatorship but in democracy', he wrote. He perceived that a dictatorship could not properly offer prosperity as an alternative to liberty, because without the fullest co-operation of the citizens the revolution faced impossible economic odds. He therefore argued that 'Democracy is the essential basis for building up a Socialist system of production.' He concluded: 'The essential achievement of the revolution will be saved, if dictatorship is opportunely replaced by democracy.'[52] This attack on dictatorship, Kautsky did not doubt, would have been supported by Karl Marx. For it Lenin dubbed him 'the renegade' and accused him of turning Marx into a 'hackneyed Liberal'.[53] Trotsky charged him with 'crawling capitulation before imperialism' and contemptuously classed Kautsky and Bernstein 'as the right and left boots on the feet of reformism'.[54]

In spite of denigration, Kautsky did not change his mind. Shortly before his death he wrote, 'Democracy is the shortest, surest, and least costly road to socialism, just as it is the best instrument for the development of the political and social prerequisities for socialism. Democracy and socialism are inextricably intertwined.'[55] This was the socialism of Rosa Luxemburg and Ernst Bloch. Only in such a socialist society could Bishop Albrecht Schönherr urge that life for a Christian 'is

51. D. Sölle, *Politische Nachtgebet in Köln*, Stuttgart 1969, I. 16f.
52. K. Kautsky, *The Dictatorship of the Proletariat*, tr. H. J. Stenning, 1920, pp. 134 (slightly altered), 42, and 149.
53. N. Lenin, *The Proletarian Revolution and Kautsky the Renegade*, 1920, p. 12.
54. Introduction to the second edition of L. Trotsky, *The Defence of Terrorism. Terrorism and Communism, A Reply to Karl Kautsky*, 1935, p.i; and 'What Next? Vital Questions for the German Proletariat' (1932), in *The Struggle against Fascism in Germany*, Harmondsworth 1975, p. 111.
55. Quoted S. H. Hook, *Marx and the Marxists: The Ambiguous Legacy*, New York 1955, p. 58.

something to be taken seriously and welcomed as an opportunity to be grasped, rather than just fatalistically accepted', for Schönherr conceived that it was the role of the church to call attention from time to time to developments within the Marxist state that 'might pose a threat to society, to human welfare, or to justice.' Within a Marxist dictatorship no such role would be possible.

Schönherr was speaking at the end of the period under study here, when the Christian–Marxist dialogue had developed far more than Kautsky would ever have envisaged. The bishop was consequently able to support his contention that life in a socialist society ought to be welcomed by Christians by pointing out that (even though Marxists often understand themselves to be in irreconcilable conflict with Christianity) there are elements within the Marxist outlook that can be related to the outlook of the Bible. Instead of merely co-existing, said Schönherr, Marxists and Christians ought to be ready 'to live in creative tension'. He held that this creative tension would be able to correct and inspire Christians as well as Marxists.[56]

56. A. Schönherr, pp. 3 and 13.

2

Christoph Blumhardt:
the Beginning

The response of German Protestantism to the problems of the working classes was not ungenerous. Many church leaders were deeply concerned about poverty and distress, as well as about the political manifestations of the Social Question. In the revolutionary year of 1848 Pastor Johann Hinrich Wichern of Hamburg observed that the struggle between the propertyless and the propertied was completely unacceptable in a Christian nation.[1] Wichern knew the situation at first hand, having worked initially in Hamburg, where the population had grown to one hundred and thirty thousand, and then in Berlin, when the city included nearly two hundred thousand inhabitants. He had, moreover, known hunger himself as a young man in Hamburg, on the death of his father. Wichern's first important practical response to the Social Question was to set up a school for vagrant boys in the village of Horn, three miles from Hamburg. Not only the character of the vagrants, but also the broken-down nature of the farmhouse in which they were taught suggested the name *Rauhes Haus* (Rough Haus). Wichern determined to teach orphans and castaways a trade or craft. He made a special study of the problems of great cities, visiting Paris and London as well as Berlin. But his aim was also the renewal of the Protestant churches. He wished to rouse the laity from apathy, to provide by voluntary effort that essential charity which the corporate state could not achieve, and to restore the lost confidence between church and people. In 1848 he founded the German 'Inner Mission', to work for the spiritual regeneration of the nation and to apply Christianity to every aspect of social and industrial life. He organized an annual *Kirchentag*, which met in a different German city every year between 1848 and 1871 in order to promulgate his social teachings. By 1865

1. J. H. Wichern, *Sämtliche Werke*, hrsg von P. Meinhold, Berlin and Hamburg 1958, I.152.

Wichern controlled thirty separate institutions throughout Germany—asylums, orphanages, *Rauhe Häuser*, youth hostels—all concerned with developing a new Protestant social ethic capable of dealing with the Social Question.[2]

Yet in spite of his wide knowledge of contemporary socialist literature (he had read Owen, Marx, Ruge, Feuerbach, and Proudhon), Wichern resolutely opposed both socialism and communism.[3] He analysed society differently. In Wichern's view, Germany's social problems derived from the loss of Christian faith, the decline of middle- and upper-class charity, the breaking of the natural bonds of society, and the gambling and drink that inevitably led to poverty. He believed in the efficacy of private charity as opposed to state intervention, though he did once seek legislation to prohibit work on Sundays. ('What is a people without Sunday?' he asked, 'and what will become of them if they have no Sunday? Whoever loses Sunday loses the blessing of his working days! That is a piece of godly national economics.'[4]) He was determined to preserve not only middle-class society but the monarchy and the aristocracy too.[5] He was thus able to gain influential support for his work. The Prussian royal family helped to finance the *Rauhe Häuser* and Wichern's great friend the aristocrat Moritz August von Bethmann-Hollweg served on the central committee of the 'Inner Mission'.

Wichern's decision to eschew politics and his preference for ethical rather than structural change were seen as errors by his chief protégé, Pastor Adolf Stöcker. Stöcker went so far as to describe himself as a Christian socialist. As a child in the 1830s and 1840s he had, like Wichern, known poverty and hardship. Ordained in 1862, he had seen the evils of the Social Question as pastor to miners and factory workers in Saxony (where he also began to read the works of Marx, Lassalle, and Adam Smith). In the early 1870s he became involved in the 'Inner Mission'.

The financial crisis of 1873 led many to question the moral and economic foundations of the social order. Stöcker persuaded another

2. M. Gerhardt, *Johann Hinrich Wichern. Ein Lebensbild*, Hamburg 1929, I.220.

3. G. Brakelmann, *Kirche und Sozialismus im 19. Jahrhundert. Die Analyse des Sozialismus und Kommunismus bei Johann Hinrich Wichern und bei Rudolf Todt*, Witten 1966, pp. 18-54. Cf. Wichern's essay 'Kommunismus und die Hilfe gegen ihn', in *Werke*, I.132-151.

4. K. Kupisch *Quellen zur Geschichte des deutschen Protestantismus 1871-1945*, Munich 1965, p. 66.

5. Brakelmann, pp. 62f.

pastor, Rudolf Todt, to try to examine the programme of the Socialists in the light of the New Testament. Todt took as his central text for the social gospel Ephesians 4.25: 'we are members one of another.' The whole community, he argued, and especially the church, was responsible for social sin. The teachings of Jesus made it clear that wealth is held only in stewardship from God.[6] To promulgate these views Todt and Stöcker formed an association for social reform 'on Christian and constitutional principles' in 1868. In the same year Stöcker founded the Christian Socialist Workers Party.

Unlike Wichern, he believed that structural changes as well as individual moral regeneration were necessary to solve the social problems of the time. He held that free, unrestricted capitalism, treating labour as a commodity, inevitably dehumanized and degraded the workers.[7] His party's programme proposed Sunday as a day of rest, shorter working hours, restrictions on child labour, and a complete ban on the employment of married women in factories. It also proposed state ownership of railways and other public utilities.[8] But this was as far as Stöcker would go in responding favourably to the socialist critique of society. He was totally opposed to Marxism (with which he identified Social Democracy). Marxism, he averred, was a false response and offered a demonic solution to serious social problems. Stöcker's Christian convictions were opposed to the atheism of the Marxists, and his nationalism conflicted with Marxist internationalism. So at the public meeting that set up his Christian Socialist Workers Party in 1878, the Berlin Social Democrats sang the *Marseillaise* and Stöcker's followers sang Luther's *Ein' Feste Burg*.[9] True socialism, in his view, worked not for social revolution but for pensions, the prohibition of child labour and Sunday work, an eight-hour working day, higher wages, and the like.[10] When Bismarck put into practice social insurance, Stöcker welcomed it as a move towards the Christian state.[11]

6. R. Todt, *Der radikale deutsche Sozialismus und die christliche Gesellschaft*, 2nd edn, Wittenberg 1878.

7. A. Stöcker, 'Der Hass der Sozialdemokratie' (18 January 1878), in *Christlich-sozial. Reden und Aufsätze*, 2nd edn, Berlin 1890, pp. 6–12. Cf. 'Zur Handwerkfrage', (3 March 1880) ibid. pp. 232–246.

8. Manifesto in Kupisch, pp. 72–74.

9. *Christlich-sozial*, pp. xv–xx.

10. R. L. Massanari, 'True and False Socialism: Adolf Stoecker's Critique of Marxism from a Christian Socialist Perspective', in *Church History*, vol. 41, December 1972, pp. 488 and 494.

11. W. Frank, *Hofprediger Adolf Stöcker und die christlichsoziale Bewegung*, 2nd edn, Hamburg 1935, p. 132.

In place of socialism Stöcker presented a 'Christian socialist' solution to social problems. Convinced that the huge gap between rich and poor was an affront to God, he called on the church to stimulate the state into remedial action. This, Stöcker believed, was infinitely preferable to impractical and utopian Social Democracy, continually preaching revolution while doing nothing about social reform.[12] Marxism, he argued, prospering on social injustice and class hatred, was bound to promote the destruction of both divine and human order.[13] He, in contrast, desired not class struggle but the solidarity of all classes. He wanted to lead a Christian-social and conservative party, believing that if society was to survive, loyalty was essential, including loyalty to the monarchy, the church, and the German nation. He summed up his political creed as 'Christianity, monarchy, the Fatherland, and social reform.'[14]

Stöcker served as an army chaplain during the Franco-Prussian War, and he saw the hand of God in Germany's victory. A patriotic speech made in 1874 led to his call as preacher to the Prussian court. When none of the candidates put up by his party in 1878 was elected, Stöcker changed its name to the Christian Social Party, omitting the word 'Workers' and adding a virulent anti-Semitic streak to its propaganda. In 1879 he was elected a member of the Prussian *Landtag*. In 1881 he joined the German Conservative Party and was elected a member of the *Reichstag*. As a publicist he appeared successful; but his anti-Semitism was not to the taste of Bismarck, who turned an initially sympathetic Prinz Wilhelm against Stöcker. In 1890 the Kaiser forced his resignation as court preacher. Six years later, his 'socialism' proved too much for the Conservative Party and Stöcker was expelled. He reconstituted his Christian Social Party, which gained three seats in the *Reichstag*. Stöcker served as a member from 1898 to 1908, the year before his death, his passionate anti-Semitism ensuring that he remained a controversial figure.

Stöcker has been described as 'part of a conservative political tradition that possessed a profound social awareness.'[15] But the truth is that

12. 'Sozialdemokratisch, sozialistisch, und Christlich-sozial', (30 March 1880), in *Christlich-sozial*, pp. 215-232.

13. Adolf Stöcker, *Dreizehn Jahre Hofprediger und Politiker*, Berlin 1895, p. vii.

14. 'Die Berliner Bewegung. Ein Stück deutscher Erweckung', in *Christlich-sozial*, p. 133.

15. R. L. Massanari, 'Christianity and the Social Problem: Adolf Stoecker's Christian Socialist Alternative to Marxist Socialism in Nineteenth Century Germany', Ph.D. dissertation, Duke University 1969, p. 215.

his attempt to woo back the workers into established society was essentially reactionary.[16] In spite of his willingness to engage in politics and to accept limited state intervention to right the ills of society, he remained true to his master Wichern in urging that, the 'most difficult aspect of the social question is the alienation of our people from the outlook of religion.'[17] Yet one of his disciples, Friedrich Naumann, was able to break out of this ecclesiastical strait-jacket, to emerge among the leading political figures of the next generation. In 1890 Stöcker had founded the Evangelical Social Congress, an annual meeting at which clergymen and laymen were to discuss the Social Question. Five years later, dissatisfied with its 'liberal' tendencies, he broke with the movement, leaving its leadership to Naumann, Adolf Harnack, and Ernst Troeltsch.

Naumann had known Stöcker since 1881 and shared his anti-Semitism,[18] as well as his concern for the poor; but he reacted against what he regarded as the essence of Stöcker's political philosophy. 'We were on the left', he wrote, 'and he was on the right.'[19] He acknowledged Stöcker's genuine attempt to persuade the Conservative Party to care for free workers' organizations, better houses for workers, Sunday rest, new mortgage laws, free speech, and so on; but he recognized, too, that Stöcker failed to keep any working-class support, simply because he was a man of the right.[20] And without working-class support, Stöcker had nothing to offer the Conservatives in return for their patronage.

Naumann also reacted against Wichern. He had grown to maturity working at the Hamburg *Rauhes Haus* and for the 'Inner Mission' in Frankfurt am Main. Soon, however, he began to find their philosophy too narrowly religious: 'It is not churchliness we thirst for, but brotherhood.'[21] In socialism he recognized 'a word signifying hope for thousands'.[22] From the 'Inner Mission' he did claim to have learned the importance of the community for political success. 'Whoever wants to

16. This is the judgement of K. Kupisch, *Durch den Zaun der Geschichte*, Berlin 1964, pp. 188-198.

17. 'Christlich-Konservative Ziele für die Gegenwart', in *Christlich-sozial*, p. 249.

18. T. Heuss, *Friedrich Naumann. Der Mann, Das Werk, Die Zeit*, 2nd edn, Stuttgart 1949, p. 67 (where this anti-Semitism is played down).

19. F. Naumann, *Werke*, hrsg von W. Usahdel and T. Schieder, vol. I, 'Religiöse Schriften', Cologne 1964, p. 762, from 'Stöcker', pp. 753-762.

20. 'Was wir Stöcker verdanken', in *Was heisst Christlich-sozial?*, vol. 2, Leipzig 1896, pp. 34-36.

21. *Werke*, I.357.

22. Ibid. p.172.

educate people must first form organizations', he insisted. 'An idea that acts individualistically flaps its wings helplessly; working in an organization, it becomes constructive.' Yet he soon began to place far less emphasis on the teachings of Wichern and Stöcker than on those of Marx, Engels, Bebel, Liebknecht, and Lassalle. In Frankfurt am Main in the early 1890s he began to attend meetings of the Social Democrats. Such an approach toward a Christian–Marxist dialogue, however cautious, was barely acceptable to most of Naumann's fellow churchmen. Convinced that the sole answer to the Social Question was political action leading to social reform, he soon found himself in trouble with the church authorities for helping to form a trade union.[23] He became convinced also that moral problems often had social and economic causes. In an economic free-for-all, he believed, even the good employer was bound to oppress the worker. In such a society it was an error to suppose that men and women were out of work or inadequately housed simply because of idleness or evil living. On the contrary, Naumann argued that inadequate housing and unemployment were often the cause of moral evils in the lives of both individuals and families.[24]

Yet although he renounced *laissez-faire*, he did not condemn either private property or free enterprise. Instead Naumann demanded that liberalism recognize the right of the proletariat to legal and political justice. This, he insisted, was not the same as the paradise promised by utopians: to expound a 'formula to master all difficulties' was 'mere deception'. Whether or not men welcomed the fact, Germany was moving toward a more socialistic corporate state; but this did not mean that free will, ethical idealism, or even authority were out of date.[25] In *Demokratie und Kaisertum* (1900) Naumann argued for a democratic monarchy that would serve the whole German nation.[26] And he claimed that his Christian socialism could offer all classes the benefits of the Christian faith, social reform, and the Prussian state. Unlike Marxism, he added, his philosophy also possessed an ethic and a *Weltanschauung* capable of inspiring men and women long after the improvements envisaged by socialists had come to pass.[27] Naumann held that 'the people and the monarchy, faith and religion, have a

23. Heuss, pp. 64, 49, and 83f.
24. *Werke*, vol. 5, 'Schriften zur Tagespolitik', pp. 153–162.
25. Ibid. vol. 1, pp. 345, 96.
26. Ibid. vol. 2, pp. 1–351.
27. *Was heisst Christlich-sozial?*, II.115.

longer life than political parties.' Even if Bebel came to power, he said, the sun would continue to shine on Germany![28]

Naumann's Christian socialism was by now clearly some considerable distance from Marxist socialism. He summed up the errors of Social Democracy, as he saw them, under four headings:

1. Socialism took an incorrect attitude to Christianity in regarding it as either false or irrelevant.

2. Socialism took a false position with regard to Jews, wishing to curb their spiritual influence, but not wishing to pass special legislation for them.

3. Socialism erred morally by stirring up hatred and bitterness in society.

4. Socialism preached a foolish pessimism about the present along with an absurd chiliastic optimism about the future.[29]

'O Lord Jesus', wrote Naumann, 'how little people know you!'[30] But Naumann's retreat from Social Democracy was accompanied by a marked diminution in his commitment to the political consequences of the Christian gospel.[31] The assertion that he 'replaced religion with Darwinism', perceiving that 'the "struggle for survival" among nations was not only inevitable but desirable as a means of proving Germany's greatness', is scarcely an exaggeration.[32] Neither at home nor abroad could politicians ignore the growth in Germany's population. Between 1870 and 1890 it increased from 40 to 50 million. By 1910 it had reached 65 million, and was nearly 70 million by 1914 (compared with 45 million in Britain and 40 million in France).[33] Naumann sought to sanction the burgeoning greatness of his country. In 1895 he had founded his own weekly, *Die Hilfe*. As one student has observed, 'the early years of the publication clearly document his transition from a concern for a Christian socialist programme to an almost exclusive

28. *Werke*, I.344. Cf. 'Das Schicksal des Marxismus' (1908), ibid. pp. 348–373.

29. *Was heisst Christlich-sozial?*, vol. 1, 2nd edn, Leipzig 1896, p. 89, from the section 'Das Irrtum der Sozialdemokratie', pp. 87–89.

30. Ibid. p. 97.

31. Partly under the influence of Rudolf Sohm and Max Weber, according to R. P. Chickering, 'The Peace Movement and the Religious Community in Germany, 1900–1914', in *Church History*, vol. 38, September 1969, p. 310.

32. J. D. Mote, 'Friedrich Naumann: The Course of a German Liberal', D.Phil. thesis, University of Colorado, 1971, p. 7.

33. F. Luetze, *Deutsche Sozial und Wirtschaftsgeschichte*, 3rd edn, Berlin p. 505.

interest in nationalism and liberalism.'[34] Naumann had ceased effec-
tively to be a Christian socialist in 1896 at the age of thirty-six. But the
final open break came with the publication of his letters on religion in
1903. These letters attempt to explain how Naumann could simultaneously support Christ, Darwin, and the German navy. He achieved
this by withdrawing Christ from the sphere of politics altogether. 'One
cannot wish to construct the whole of human development on sympathy and brotherly love. There are things that elude the grasp of the
Christian religion. The world remains the world and power comes
before compassion.' Naumann offered his energies in service of the
German navy, he said, not as a Christian but as a citizen of the German
state, for although Christians individually were called on to love their
enemies, 'the struggle for existence has taught the nations to be
armour-plated beasts.'[35]

Naumann left the Christian ministry in 1896 (though he never allowed that he had left the Christian church). His theology was not
equal to his politics. Referring specifically to Stöcker and Naumann,
K. S. Latourette concluded that in the nineteenth century 'Germany
had no one who gave such substantial theological basis for Christian
Socialism as did Maurice in England.'[36] Naumann, wrote Helmut
Thielicke, had been led to the seductive notion, 'dismissed as quickly
as it arises, but not very convincingly', that there are two gods: the god
of the world, who 'produces the morality of the struggle for existence',
and the Father of Jesus Christ, who 'produces the morality of mercy.'[37]
This was an odd result for the man who had early criticized Marxism
for its failure to develop an ethic, who had once declared that men
must feel God working in them as He formerly did in the prophets of
the Old Testament.[38]

K. S. Latourette rightly observed that neither Stöcker nor Naumann
could properly be called theologians, and both departed widely from

34. J. C. Fout, 'Protestant Christian Socialism in Germany, 1848-1896, Wichern,
Stoecker, Naumann: the Search for a New Social Ethic', Ph.D. thesis, University of
Minnesota, 1969, p. 213. The major essays in which Naumann worked out his attitude
to Social Democracy and Christian socialism are 'Was will die Sozialdemokratie?' (1899),
'Die inneren Wandlungen der Sozialdemokratie' (1906), in Werke, IV, 321-325, 339-48;
and 'Arbeiterkatechismus oder der wahre Sozialismus' (1889), 'Unsere Stellung zur
Sozialdemokratie' (1893), 'Gedanken zum Christlich-sozialen Programm' (1896) in
Werke, V.1-63, 73-101, 63-73.

35. 'Briefe über Religion,' in Werke, I.588 and 623.

36. K. S. Latourette, Christianity in a Revolutionary Age, 1960, II.127.

37. H. Thielicke, Theological Ethics, vol. 2, Politics, 1969, p. 99, quoting 'Briefe über
Religion', F. Naumann, Werke, I. 617.

38. Werke, I.509f.

their early faith.[39] Neither they nor Wichern came to terms with socialism. Their theology and their politics were essentially defensive against it.

Their contemporary Christoph Blumhardt was also no systematic theologian. He differed from them in most other respects. He derived his theology not from *Rauhe Häuser* or the 'Inner Mission' but from his father. He remained true to it for the rest of his life. It led him into politics, but as an ally, not an enemy, of the Socialists.

Christoph Blumhardt was born at Möttlingen in 1842, when his father, Johann Christoph Blumhardt, was already becoming known as a revivalist who seemed also to have the gift of healing. A year after Christoph's birth, the most remarkable act of healing in his father's career took place. On 28 December 1843 the elder Blumhardt, in the power of Jesus Christ, threw a demon out of a young woman named Gottliebin Dittus. As the demon left Gottliebin, her sister Katherina uttered a cry, 'almost inconceivable in a human throat',[40] which Johann Christoph Blumhardt took to be the cry of the devil itself. The words uttered were 'Jesus is victor'.

This miraculous healing altered the elder Blumhardt's attitude to the whole of life. His son recalled his explaining how, in the light of the sure victory of Christ, heaven and earth had become new and even the stars shone differently. It seemed as if he had seen the kingdom of God as it would be over the whole earth.[41] Christoph himself judged that 'with this cry hell was obliged to give way before a personality completely in Christ'.[42] Such theological speculations were quite uncharacteristic of the pietism in which both Blumhardts had been born. As Karl Barth observed, 'The contrast was not between Jesus and the unconverted heart of man, but between Jesus and the real power of darkness.' Barth quoted a sermon in which the elder Blumhardt strikingly put this point: 'Yes, dear Christians, make sure that you die saved! But the Lord Jesus wants more. He wants not only my redemption and yours, but the redemption of all the world. He wants to finish off the evil that dominates the world and to make the whole world free

39. K. S. Latourette.

40. F. Zündel, *Pfarrer Johann Christoph Blumhardt. Ein Lebensbild*, Heilbronn 1880, pp. 162f. Cf. C. Troebst, *Aussenseiter oder Wegbereiter, Christoph Blumhardt, der Prediger zwischen den Fronten*, Bad Boll n.d., p. 5.

41. C. Blumhardt, *Gottes Reich kommt! Predigten und Andachten aus den Jahren 1906 bis 1919*, Zürich 1932, p. 59.

42. Christoph Blumhardt's preface (1887) to J. C. Blumhardt, *Ausgewählte Schriften*, Zürich 1947, I.xv.

that occupies itself in sheer godlessness.'[43] The extraordinary event at Möttlingen had moved the Blumhardts from individualistic pietism towards a social gospel. 'Jesus is victor', wrote Christoph, 'over every devil, over hell and over death! And today he is likewise victor over all flesh, over the whole world, over all mankind in its earthly concerns.'[44]

The healing made the elder Blumhardt famous. Gottliebin Dittus became a permanent member of his community, which in 1852 moved to Bad Boll, into a large sanatorium at the foot of the Swiss Alps. The sanatorium soon became internationally renowned. So powerful was his conviction that God would soon decisively intervene in the world that the elder Blumhardt for a time supposed he would not die before the Second Coming. He wrote poetry on the theme 'Jesus is victor', which was quoted at his funeral in 1880 by his son.[45] Gottliebin Dittus had been buried in January 1872 with the words 'Jesus is victor' inscribed on the cross over her grave. The phrase dominated the preaching of the younger Blumhardt till the end of his own life.[46] Its implications for his thought and actions were subtle and increasingly pervasive.

And not only for Blumhardt. Over a hundred years after the miraculous healing Karl Barth took the phrase (or, as he put it, the 'challenge') 'Jesus is victor' to be the 'first, last, and decisive word' about the prophetic work of Christ the mediator. From this cry had arisen an understanding of Jesus that Barth described as 'new for Blumhardt, for his contemporaries, and for our modern world'.[47]

The alleged voice of the devil, however, is an unexpected source for a twentieth-century theology. The healing of Gottliebin Dittus had caused intellectual difficulties for the nineteenth century.[48] The elder Blumhardt fell foul of the medical profession, which censured him and

43. K. Barth, *Protestant Theology in the Nineteenth Century*, pp. 644f., and 651, quoting F. Zündel, *Pfarrer J. C. Blumhardt. Ein Lebensbild*, Heilbronn 1880, pp. 174 and 302.

44. C. Blumhardt, *Sterbet, so wird Jesus leben! Predigten und Andachten aus den Jahren 1888 bis 1896*, Zürich 1925, p. 53.

45. C. Blumhardt, *Jesus ist Sieger! Predigten und Andachten aus den Jahren 1880 bis 1888*, Zürich 1937, pp. 7f.

46. See for example 'Der Sieger', preached in May 1915, and 'Jesus ist Sieger', preached in March 1917, *Gottes Reich kommt!* pp. 388-392 and 427-431.

47. K. Barth, *Church Dogmatics*, IV/iii, 1st half, p. 170f. See H. Gollwitzer on Blumhardt's influence on Barth's doctrine of reconciliation: *Karl Barth. Kirchliche Dogmatik. Auswahl und Einleitung von Helmut Gollwitzer*, Frankfurt am Main 1965, p. 23.

48. T. H. Mandel, *Der Sieg von Möttlingen im Lichte des Glaubens und der Wissenschaft*, Leipzig 1895.

persuaded the church authorities to do the same.[49] In the twentieth century the theologian Rudolf Bultmann found the whole tale preposterous. 'No one can use the electric light and the radio or the discoveries of modern medicine and at the same time believe in the New Testament world of spirits and miracle.'[50] Barth's approach, by contrast, was much more sympathetic. The miracle seems to have fascinated him from his early days as a parish pastor. In June 1914 he finished reading Zündel's life of the elder Blumhardt. It left him mainly with a feeling of shame. 'Alongside such a man', he wrote, 'I see how very small I am.' He then recounted how the previous Saturday a local drunkard had greeted him with clenched fists from a first storey window, crying, 'Get out of here, you beast, you priest, you God-damn fool; where you go no grass will ever grow again.' Barth commented, 'The elder Blumhardt would at once have struck up a song of praise in that situation and would have driven the devil out of him.'[51]

He was still grappling with the problem of the miracle when he wrote his famous commentary on Romans.[52] Finally he came to think that it could be looked at in three ways. It could be explained 'realistically', in the sense of ancient and modern mythology. Or else it could be explained 'in terms of modern psychopathology or depth psychology'. Or, finally, making the assumption that the two former explanations are also possible and even justifiable in their own ways, the miracle is not to be explained at all, 'but can only be estimated spiritually'. In the end, Barth asserted, the only truly relevant aspect of the incident was its spiritual significance: what the saying 'Jesus is victor' means and what it summons us to do.[53] These too were the questions worked out in the life of the younger Blumhardt.

It has been rightly observed that one can as little systematically summarize Blumhardt's teachings as one can those of the Bible; both

49. F. Zündel, *J. C. Blumhardt*, pp. 166ff.

50. Quoted Heinz Zahrnt, *Die Sache mit Gott*, Munich 1972, p. 239. E. G. Rüsch 'Dämonenau streibung in der Gallus-Vita und bei Blumhardt dem Älteren', in *Theologische Zeitschrift*, March/April 1978, pp. 86-94, examines the healing in the light of biblical parallels (Mark 1.23-28, 5.1-20 and 9.14-29).

51. *Revolutionary Theology in the Making. Barth-Thurneysen Correspondence 1914-1925*, tr. J. D. Smart, 1964, p. 30.

52. *The Epistle to the Romans*, 1968, p. 312. The translator, E. C. Hoskyns, added a footnote misdating the episode and attributing the mysterious cry to the wrong person.

53. *Church Dogmatics*, IV/iii, 1st half, pp. 170f. Cf. Gaetano Benedetti, 'Blumhardts Seelsorge in der Sicht heutiger psychotherapeutischer Kentnisse', in *Reformatio*, 1966, pp. 474-487 and 531-539; Otto Bruder, 'Zu den Heilungen Blumhardts', in *Evangelische Theologie*, ix, 1949-50, pp. 478-480, and 'Johann Christoph Blumhardt als Seelsorger', in *Reformatio*, 1953, pp. 621-630.

he and his father were men who lived and experienced rather than philosophized.[54] Eduard Thurneysen tried to sum up his thinking in the word 'hope'. Blumhardt certainly hoped, as Thurneysen wrote, 'for a thorough renewal of everything on earth through the real power of God in Jesus Christ.'[55] Blumhardt characterized Jesus as one who 'exuded hope'.[56] But a word with equal claim to summarize Blumhardt's teaching is 'future'. Blumhardt's hope was based on a belief in what he called 'the future of Jesus Christ' (an expression he had picked up from the early church).[57] This belief decisively affected his attitude to the present. 'We cannot be swallowed up by the present age', he preached, 'because we are bound to the future and because we experience the future in the present.'[58] Blumhardt did not share Albert Schweitzer's view that Jesus's attempt to live eschatologically had been a tragic error. In Schweitzer's rhetorical analysis of the significance of the crucifixion, Jesus 'lays hold of the wheel of the world to set it moving on that last revolution which is to bring all ordinary history to a close. It refuses to turn, and He throws Himself upon it. Then it does turn; and crushes Him. Instead of bringing in the eschatological conditions, He has destroyed them.'[59] Since the promise of the kingdom of God had not been fulfilled, Schweitzer saw the whole of subsequent Christianity in terms of 'the abandonment of eschatology, the progress and completion of the "de-eschatologization" of religion'.[60] For Blumhardt and his father, on the other hand, the eschatology of the New Testament was what they lived by in the nineteenth and twentieth centuries. In many a situation Christoph Blumhardt would say one could do no more; 'then God would find a way forward, progress is made, and we have a scrap of the future of Jesus Christ'.[61] 'Make the future of Jesus Christ your own experience', he urged his followers, so that 'however poor we are or weak we feel, ever again we will hope and keep watch, till a moment comes when we can take hold of a piece of the future of Jesus Christ.'[62] If Jesus were truly victor, such moments would inevitably come.

54. *R.G.G.*, 3rd edn, Tübingen 1957, p. 1326.
55. E. Thurneysen, *Christoph Blumhardt*, 2nd edn, Stuttgart 1962, p. 5.
56. *Gottes Reich kommt!*, p. 57; cf. the whole sermon 'Hoffnung' (on II Peter 3. 13-15) pp. 57-62.
57. Ibid. p. 58. Cf. the sermon 'In der Zukunft Jesu Christi' (1911), pp. 230-238.
58. *Gottes Reich kommt!* p. 333.
59. *The Quest of the Historical Jesus*, p. 369.   60. Ibid. p. 358.
61. *Gottes Reich kommt!*, p. 334.
62. *Christoph Blumhardt und seine Botschaft*, hrsg von R. Lejeune, Erlangenbach 1968, p. 193.

Barth described the elder Blumhardt as one of the nineteenth century's outsiders; Protestant school dogmatics simply slept through such
a phenomenon.[63] Thurneysen found it strange that 'official' theology
had ignored both Blumhardts.[64] In fact, in the light of contemporary
de-eschatologizing of Christianity it is not at all strange that the nineteenth century found the Blumhardts difficult to assimilate. In addition,
an age that experiences acute embarrassment over the mythology of
the Bible would not find it easy to cope with the way the Blumhardts
took most of the New Testament literally. Barth himself was aston-
ished at this (especially as the elder Blumhardt had shared his basic
education in Swabia with the prophet of demythologizing, David Friedrich Strauss). There was a credible tradition at Bad Boll, Barth tells us,
that a coach was kept ready, year in, year out, with all its equipment,
in case the elder Blumhardt needed to set out for the Holy Land to
meet the returning Christ.[65]

One further consideration helps to explain why the influence of
Blumhardt has been strong in the twentieth century. Central to every
aspect of his preaching is the notion that the kingdom of God involved
power to transform this world. The early church, he asserted, 'understood in the future of Jesus Christ the prospect of an alteration in
heaven and earth'.[66] Such a notion would most gain assent in a time
when many people were seriously seeking to restructure society. So at
the beginning of the twentieth century the influence of Blumhardt is
seen in the work of the Swiss founders of Religious Socialism, Leonhard
Ragaz and Hermann Kutter. Ragaz believed the day would come
when Möttlingen, Bad Boll, and Blumhardt were considered more
significant than Wittenberg, Geneva, Luther and Calvin.[67] Karl Barth
confessed that had he not discovered Blumhardt and Kutter (as well
as Dostoevsky), he could never have written the first and second
drafts of his commentary on Romans.[68] Their influence is seen, I
believe, not only in the undoubted socialism of that commentary,
but also (as far as Blumhardt is concerned) in Barth's uncom-
promising eschatology. 'Christianity that is not entirely and altogether

---

63. *The Humanity of God*, Fontana 1967, p. 7; Church Dogmatics I/i, 1936, p. 321.

64. *Revolutionary Theology in the Making*, p. 16.

65. *Protestant Theology in the Nineteenth Century*, p. 647.

66. *Gottes Reich kommt!*, p. 58. On this see G. Sauter, pp. 91f.

67. L. Ragaz, *Der Kampf um das Reich Gottes in Blumhardt, Vater und Sohn-und
Weiter!*, Zürich 1922, p. 289.

68. *Revolutionary Theology in the Making*, p. 72.

eschatology', he wrote, 'has entirely and altogether nothing to do with Christ.'[69]

These two aspects of Blumhardt's legacy are neither separate nor in any sense contradictory. Some fifty years later, the theologian Jürgen Moltmann was still exploring the social consequences of Christian eschatology in the light of the preaching of Blumhardt. The de-eschatologizing of Christianity, Moltmann maintained, reveals itself in a 'loss of hope for the real outstanding future'; and he quoted Blumhardt's Easter sermon of 1899: 'If I must give up a man, or give up hope for an area or an earth, then Jesus is not risen for me. You are not the light of the world if I must give up hope anywhere.'[70]

That year Blumhardt took the most decisive step of his life in joining the SPD. After his father's death he had taken over the running of the sanatorium at Bad Boll, but he soon became impatient with the work, believing that a certain spiritual selfishness was afflicting the countless pious Christians who flocked there. Württemberg was now the centre of much industrial unrest, of anarchical, syndicalist, and radical-socialist politics. In 1899 the authorities brought out a law savagely punishing picketing strikers. For taking their side, Blumhardt was forced by the church to resign his orders.

In the circumstances of the time this was inevitable. Kaiser Wilhelm II had expressed the prevailing attitude to parsons who meddled in politics in a letter about Adolf Stöcker in 1896: 'Pastors should concern themselves with the souls of their parishioners, should promote charity, and should keep out of politics.'[71] Friedrich Naumann was frequently reprimanded by the church authorities for his political activities. He replied that either the church speaks for and endeavours to gain the trust of the propertyless classes, or else it must give up hope of winning them; but in 1897 he had come to the conclusion that the church as an institution was too limited in its outlook, and he abandoned his orders—though not, he said, his faith.[72] But neither he nor Stöcker had ever allied themselves with socialists. Blumhardt, by contrast, was now asserting that Jesus himself had been a socialist, with proletarian disciples. His nineteenth-century followers could no longer minister to

69. Carl E. Braaten, referring to *The Epistle to the Romans*, p. 314, observed that Barth had been quoted to this effect 'a thousand times, so once more won't hurt': in 'The Significance of the Future: An Eschatological Perspective', *Hope and the Future of Man*, ed. E. H. Cousins, 1973, p. 46.

70. J. Moltmann, *Hope and Planning*, tr. M. Clarkson, 1973, pp. 139 and 49.

71. W. Frank, *Hofprediger Adolf Stöcker*, p. 358.

72. T. Heuss, *Friedrich Naumann*, pp. 78 and 225.

the poor solely on a one-to-one basis, along the lines of the traditional 'cure of souls' (*Seelsorge*). What was needed was a corporate movement to improve people's lives.[73] Blumhardt ignored the fact that the hostile attitude of most Marxist intellectuals to contemporary Christianity was matched by a hostile political programme. (Not least alarming to the clergymen was the notion put forward in clause 6 of the Erfurt programme of 1891 that since religion was a private affair, the clergy should no longer be paid out of state funds![74] Atheism in practice could bite deep.)

Blumhardt's attitude to men of such views was bound to shock most churchmen. 'From every pulpit in every Mission', he asserted, 'it should be preached: you men belong to God. Whether you are godless or already pious, under judgement or grace, in bliss or in damnation, God is for you. And God is good and wants what is best for you. Whether you are dead or alive, whether you are righteous or unrighteous, whether you are in heaven or in hell, you belong to God.'[75] In 1899 he claimed that his alliance with the workers expressed what lived in him of Christ and what he had always desired of the kingdom of God and his righteousness. Although people were in the habit of equating Social Democracy with godlessness, the truth according to Blumhardt was that what was called 'godlessness' (along with attempts to subvert society and covetousness of the possessions of others) was to be found in every social class.[76]

The contrast with Stöcker and Naumann is again revealing. For Stöcker Social Democracy was the direct result of 'religious apostasy and the loss of morality'. Atheism went hand in hand with materialism and the worship of mammon.[77] Naumann was far more sympathetic to the programme of the Social Democrats, but he regarded their lack of faith as posing the greatest threat to Christianity since the Muslim invasions of Europe.[78] Blumhardt differed. He described a 'moral and industrious atheism in the world' and declared this to be dearer to him than a belief that does not comprehend God's will for the world and therefore opposes its progress.[79] In a sermon on 'the people of Zion' he

73. *Ihr Menschen seid Gottes! Predigten und Andachten aus den Jahren 1896 bis 1906*, Zürich 1936, p. 459f.

74. W. Treue, *Deutsche Parteiprogramme 1861–1961*, 3rd edn, Göttingen 1961, p. 76.

75. E. Thurneysen, *Christoph Blumhardt*, p. 97.

76. *Ihr Menschen seid Gottes!*, p. 472.

77. A. Stöcker, *Christlich-sozial*, pp. 216 and 494.

78. F. Naumann, *Werke*, I.112, from his 1889 address to the 'Inner Mission': 'Was tun wir gegen die Glaubenlose Sozialdemokratie', ibid. pp. 112–141.

79. *Christoph Blumhardt und seine Botschaft*, p. 35.

concluded, 'The greatest sin is to doubt that you are one of God's people, for every creature belongs to God.'[80] Blumhardt believed that if the church had attempted to use violence against the heathen or force against unbelievers in the past, 'the future of Jesus Christ would have been lost.'[81]

Blumhardt was closer to Wichern and Naumann in his disappointment with the institutional church. Wichern believed that he had failed to renew the 'crippled' and 'tired' institutional church. Had the church been a true *Volkskirche* it could have become a force to avert revolution by revealing the proper solution to social problems: the spirit of love.[82] Blumhardt went further in condemning the church, declaring once that 'the rich church creates the social problem, namely the misery of mankind.'[83]

Few other Christians went as far as Blumhardt in accepting the possibility of revolution. Naumann's *Jesus als Volksmann* presented a figure of Jesus entirely sympathetic to working men but seeking change by completely non-violent means. He argued that no revolutionary movement had ever perfectly achieved its ideals, and that in the Germany of his own day a struggle between the bourgeoisie and the working class would destroy the entire nation.[84] Blumhardt joined the SPD before it was forced to choose whether or not it was a revolutionary party; yet on joining he received many letters expressing his correspondents' fears of bloody revolution. He wrote open letters striving to reassure them. The Reformation of the sixteenth century had been bloodier than the French revolution, but had it not ushered in religious freedom? Was the French revolution to be hated because it initiated political freedom? And in any case, Blumhardt argued, 'the principles of Social Democracy will bring such revolutions to an end', inaugurating the freedom of mankind by a bloodless revolution. Changes were necessary, even subversion; but 'Fear not!' he urged. 'Believe all the more that this time more than any other is called to bring us nearer to the kingdom of God.'[85]

Few were reassured. Blumhardt's action in 1899, according to one biographer, was simply a 'sacrifice'.[86] In the words of another, his

---

80. Ibid. p. 137, on the text Isaiah 54.4.
81. *Gottes Reich kommt!*, p. 235.
82. Martin Gerhardt II.352.
83. *Ihr Menschen seid Gottes!*, p. 487.
84. *Werke*, I. 323 and V.48.
85. *Ihr Mensch seid Gottes!*, pp. 443, 449f., and 472.
86. E. Jackh, *Christoph Blumhardt. Ein Zeuge des Reich Gottes*, Stuttgart 1950, p. 212.

home at Bad Boll became the 'spittoon of the nation'.[87] The attack came chiefly from the religious. (In the election at Bad Boll 230 voted for and 29 against Blumhardt. 'At Göppingen also my election was triumphant', he wrote, 'in spite of the anger of all the clergy and their sectaries.'[88]) Since that time, Protestant theologians and historians have consistently tried to play down the whole affair. Gerhard Sauter described it as 'a relatively isolated episode'. Otto W. Heick observed that Blumhardt associated with Social Democrats, not 'because he equated Marxism with Christianity, but rather because he saw in Marxism a demonstration of the fact that God's love truly extends to all men.' And according to Eduard Thurneysen, Blumhardt had no political aspirations when he joined the SPD. His action was essentially a 'demonstration' of theological significance, pointing to the Saviour who was 'the friend of publicans and sinners'.[89]

Such attempts to minimize the shock of Blumhardt's behaviour should drive us back to his own interpretation of what he was doing. Blumhardt said that the socialist movement was like a fiery sign in the sky proclaiming justice. When Christian society perceived itself to be in a state of opposition to justice, its proper role, he believed, was not to continue defiantly in its old ways, but to pull itself together and ask what the new movement was bringing to it of truth.[90] 'In the aspiration Social Democracy represents, which everywhere enkindles thousands of hearts', he wrote, 'I see a sign of Christ, for Christ too wants a humanity penetrated by justice and truth, love and life. In the spirit of Christ I ally myself with this aspiration.' He also perceived a growing spirit of persecution against the workers and felt compelled to extend them a hand.[91] In the light of Blumhardt's own words, Gerhard Sauter was obliged to concede that at least initially he fully believed that a revolution achieved by Social Democracy could once and for all do away with the great gulf that existed between the powerful and the impotent.[92]

Blumhardt spent six years of intense political activity as one of the

87. C. Troebst, p. 23.

88. C. Blumhardt, 'Lettres à un missionnaire en Chine', in *Études théologiques et religieuses*, no. 3, 1976, p. 280.

89. G. Sauter, p. 131; cf. the whole section 'Blumhardts Verhältnis zur Sozialdemokratie', pp. 131-215. O. W. Heick *A History of Christian Thought*, Philadelphia 1966, II.271 n.6. E. Thurneysen, pp. 104 ff.

90. *Gottes Reich kommt!*, pp. 451f.

91. *Ihr Menschen seid Gottes!*, p. 472.

92. G. Sauter, p. 144.

five opposition deputies in the Stuttgart *Landtag*. He by no means confined his speeches to religious affairs.[93] And because he was principal spokesman for the opposition deputies, their weight (as Christian Troebst put it[94]) far exceeded their number. He has been accused in all this of sharing the cultural optimism of many contemporary liberal Protestants: the notion that the kingdom of God was coming progressively nearer. According to one critic, he had 'absorbed the prevailing optimism which followed the Enlightenment. He, too, was looking for the continuing progress of mankind toward a grand ideal.'[95] Some things he said and wrote make this charge plausible. At the turn of the century he believed that men were in 'the last stage of the evolution of the kingdom of God.'[96] 'We Christians must be people of progress in accord with God who wants to make something new', he preached; 'we must be people who see the beginning of the kingdom of God today, expect progress tomorrow and fulfilment the day after tomorrow.'[97] Some of the Religious Socialists directly inspired by Blumhardt (such as Johannes Müller) instantly fell for the next-but-one German political development, National Socialism.[98]

But the charge of cultural optimism is in the end unfair. After 1906 Blumhardt clearly no longer believed that German Social Democracy could usher in the kingdom of God. In that year, feeling the need to put some distance between himself and the world, he undertook a long journey to Palestine, and on his return refused to enter the *Landtag* for a second term. Thenceforth he would compare himself with Moses (who did not enter the Promised Land).[99] In any case, his concern had always been to attack not liberal Protestantism but inward-looking church pietism. And he never doubted that men needed some redemption from outside themselves. 'The new is revealed in the flesh', he wrote, 'but what is to become new is also locked away in the flesh.' For Blumhardt, therefore, the coming of Christ involved 'a judgement upon all flesh—albeit a judgement of redemption, just as properly speaking every judgement is.'[100] He remained adamant that only Jesus

93. See, for example, his opinions on education and grain tariffs, in *Ihr Menschen seid Gottes!*, pp. 463–466.

94. C. Troebst, p. 21.

95. J. Regehr, 'The Preaching of Christoph Blumhardt', Th.D. thesis, Southern Baptist Seminary, 1970, p. 20.

96. Letter of 21 January 1901, in 'Lettres à un missionnaire en Chine', p. 279.

97. C. Troebst, p. 24.

98. K. Barth *Church Dogmatics*, II/i, 1957, p. 633.

99. *Christoph Blumhardt und seine Botschaft*, pp. 33f.

100. *Sterbet, so wird Jesus leben!*, p. 396. *Ihr Menschen seid Gottes!*, p. 222f.

could deal with human sinfulness and that man is ineffective without the power of God. In January 1889, during a serious illness of his wife, he began to develop the notion of dying so that Jesus might live.[101] 'Wherever there is an end', he came to believe, 'there is a new beginning.' Such maxims, rather than the idea of progress, helped him to accept the need for some sort of revolution in the ordering of society. He specifically applied the maxim 'die, so that Jesus might live', to his own 'year of battle', 1899.[102]

Blumhardt sometimes spoke as if he knew of many times when Christ had already come. Every experience of helping another or of being helped was an experience of Christ's coming.[103] In a sermon on Kaiser Wilhelm I's ninetieth birthday in 1887 he declared that the kingdom of God had partly come in social provisions for the aged and invalid, and in the lessening of class distinctions.[104] But he was careful to distinguish such advances from the ultimate coming of Christ. The last day would see not a new great reformer or philosopher or sovereign, but a lightning flash that would transform the whole earth.[105] Because he held that men cannot bring about their own salvation, he also insisted that there is no real hope for the world apart from the personal activity of the Son of God.[106] 'The kingdom of God', he once said, 'is God's own objective, which shapes history and enables us to live until the Day of the Lord comes.'[107] This is what Thurneysen called the 'Copernican revolution', whereby Blumhardt replaced the pietistic insistence that everything depends on my relationship to God by the Pauline realization (based on Romans 3.22) that what counts is God's relationship to me. Thurneysen commented: 'God's kingdom must come upon earth, but in such a fashion as to remain *God's* kingdom. . . . Blumhardt was no utopian. There was a reason for his hope. It was anchored in the perception—central to both Blumhardts—of the actuality of God: the reality of God, God himself, God alone, God entire.'[108] Against the church-centred pietists with their purely individual hope of a future life for the soul, Blumhardt set what Karl Barth

---

101. *Sterbet, so wird Jesus leben!*, pp. 102–106 and R. Lejeune's note, p. 592. Cf. E. Zellweger, *Der jüngere Blumhardt. Was verdenken wir ihm?*, Basle 1945, p. 25.
102. *Christoph Blumhardt und seine Botschaft*, pp. 179 and 46.
103. *Sterbet, so wird Jesus leben!*, p. 556. *Gottes Reich kommt!*, p. 334.
104. *Jesus ist Sieger!*, p. 35. Cf. *Gottes Reich kommt!*, pp. 69–72.
105. *Gottes Reich kommt!*, p. 251, from 'Das Reich Gottes in der Welt,' pp. 243–252.
106. *Gottes Reich kommt!*, p. 181.
107. E. Thurneysen, pp. 38f.
108. Ibid. pp. 54f., and 48.

called 'the confidence and unsettlement of the expectation of the kingdom of God which will rectify the whole world and all life even to its
deepest recesses.' Both he and his father gave a central position to the
Biblical prayers 'Thy kingdom come' and 'Even so, come Lord Jesus'.[109]

Holding such views Blumhardt inevitably took up an ambiguous
stance toward the church that had deprived him of his orders. After his
journey to Palestine he moved away from Bad Boll, though he often
returned to preach there until his death in 1919. There was no church
funeral service, simply the reading (at his own request) of Psalm 46.
Working men may have covered his coffin with the red flag.[110]

By chance, and quite unexpectedly, Friedrich Naumann died in the
same year. Karl Barth took the opportunity of writing a joint obituary
of the two men.[111] Barth was then a pastor in the Aargau, labelled
already 'the red priest of Safenwil' because of his socialist leanings.[112]
He turned this joint obituary into a eulogy of Blumhardt and a savage
attack upon Naumann. Barth urged that for both men socialism was
the decisive question of the day; but they had responded to it so
differently that others were obliged to choose uncompromisingly
between them. Naumann, Barth observed, had found in the New
Testament 'a message so radical, so *revolutionary*, directed so precisely
to a transformation of the world, that as a result the church's pretty
balance between God and the world seemed to him to threaten to fly
apart.' The contrast between this Naumann and the later Naumann,
dedicated to democracy, industry, and German world power was so
great that Barth could only attribute it to a second conversion. 'Con-
fronted by the choice between the visible and the invisible, between the
possible and the impossible, with a heavy heart, but finally, deliberately
and resolutely, he grasped the visible and possible', wrote Barth. 'The
stormy conflict between God and the world was solved in a sensible
arbitration, a *both-and* that gave both sides their due. Naumann was
back where he started—with the God who acts inscrutably, with the
religion of the soul which may seek comfort and power in the world,
but does not seek victory *over* the world.'[113]

109. Karl Barth, *Church Dogmatics*, II/i, 1957, p. 633.
110. C. Troebst, p. 24.
111. In *Neuer Freier Aargau*, 14, 1919, issues 204 and 205, ET 'Past and Future:
Friedrich Naumann and Christoph Blumhardt', in *The Beginnings of Dialectic Theology*,
ed. James M. Robinson, Richmond Virginia 1968, I.25–45.
112. E. Thurneysen, *Karl Barth. 'Theologie und Sozialismus' in den Briefen seiner
Frühzeit*, Zurich 1973, p. 7.
113. J. M. Robinson, pp. 35–37 and 39.

Naumann had affected to perceive Christ in the age of the machine.[114] But in the moment of conflict, Naumann's Christ retired. 'Every age has had its own particular struggles', he wrote. 'In ours we are experiencing the battle of titans, the machine against the olympiad of the old ideas.'[115] So in the brutal world of politics, industry, and war, the uncompromising demands of Christ were suspended.

In contrast, Blumhardt's gravestone at Bad Boll reads: 'That Jesus is victor remains for ever true. His is the whole world.' For Blumhardt, that world included Marxists and socialists as well as Christians. His Christianity, in response to Marxism and socialism, forced him out of pietism into politics. The eschatological, even chiliastic theology he had inherited from his father was given a political context. He made the connection between the kingdom of God and the socialist hope, a connection which was to be refined and explored by his twentieth-century heirs. And seeing a sign of Christ in Social Democracy, this believer allied himself with it to the unprecedented extent of ascribing value even to its moral and industrious atheism.

114. In K. Kupisch, *Quellen zur Geschichte des deutschen Protestantismus 1871-1945*, pp. 83-87.
115. F. Naumann, *Werke*, I.150f.

3
Karl Kautsky:
the Marxist Approach
to Christianity

The experiences of Christoph Blumhardt revealed the hostility of the church establishment to the Christian–Marxist dialogue. The world of academic theology was equally hostile. In 1899 Adolf Harnack's famous series of lectures to the University of Berlin on the essence of Christianity described as newest among the 'clatter of contradictory voices' purporting to explain the faith, those that 'assure us that the whole history of religion, morality, and philosophy is nothing but clothes and finery; that what at all times underlies them, as the only real motive power, is the history of economics; that, accordingly, Christianity, too, was in its origin nothing more than a social movement and Christ a social deliverer—the deliverer of the oppressed lower classes.'[1] Harnack's objection to this Marxist analysis was not based simply on the unrivalled learning of his own researches into Christian history; it stemmed also from his intense personal belief that Christianity was essentially non-political. In 1906 he defined the gospel of Jesus as 'the joyous news to the poor and with them to the peaceable, the meek, and those who are pure in heart; it is the news that the kindom of God is near, that this kingdom will soothe the sorrows of the distressed, bring justice and establish their childhood in God in addition to giving all good things.' This gospel, he immediately added, brought with it a new order of life 'above the world and politics'.[2] Since, in Harnack's view, the sphere of faith was 'pure inwardness', for him the gospel, though in a sense 'profoundly socialistic', could bring no political programme but aimed instead at transforming 'the socialism which rests on the basis of conflicting interests into the

1. A. Harnack *What is Christianity?*, tr. T. B. Saunders, 3rd and revised edn, 1904, pp. 2f.
2. A. Harnack, 'Das doppelte Evangelium in dem Neuen Testament', (Giessen 1906) in *Aus Wissenschaft und Leben*, Giessen 1911, ii.215.

socialism which rests on the consciousness of a spiritual unity' among men.[3]

Harnack's views were widely shared. They contrasted not only with those of Blumhardt but also with the teachings of the Lutheran pastor Albert Kalthoff, who in 1904 declared that the primitive church had given the world 'the widest communist manifesto that was ever framed'.[4]

Kalthoff was unable to attribute this communism to Jesus himself, since his Marxist analysis led him to the view that Jesus never existed at all. The figure in the gospels he saw as a mythical embodiment of the needs and desires of the economically and socially deprived in the ancient world. Christianity he described 'as only the religious synthesis of the factors controlling the historical development of that time'.[5] The life of Jesus he dubbed a 'theological fiction'; and although Philo and Josephus did mention someone with that name, Kalthoff insisted that there is no trace in their writings of anyone identifiable with the Jesus of the evangelists.[6] Those who still maintained that Jesus was a real man were condemned by Kalthoff as indulging in 'theological hypnotism'. He believed that 'The obstinacy with which the critical school insists on ascribing *Galatians*, *Romans*, and *Corinthians* to Paul would soon cease, if it were not for the fact that these Epistles give a certain support, it is thought, to the hypothesis that Jesus was historical.'[7]

Kalthoff held that primitive Christianity reflected not the activity of a personal founder but the communistic clubs that he believed to have existed everywhere except in the synagogue ('the organization of commercial capital'). Some of these clubs he envisaged as paramountly apocalyptic, especially among Jews; others preached a 'philosophy of poor men', especially among Greeks; and Rome itself had developed the fully-fledged spirit of a metropolitan proletariat.[8] Small wonder, then, if the gospels record that 'To him that hath shall be given' (Mark 4.25 and parallels), for according to Kalthoff, 'no political and social, and certainly no religious or ethical, resistance was possible to the great concentration of capital' in the Roman empire. He considered the statement in Matthew 8.20 that 'Foxes have holes and the birds of

3. *What is Christianity?*, pp. 190 and 102f.

4. A. Kalthoff, *Die Entstehung des Christentums*, Jena 1904; tr. J. McCabe, *The Rise of Christianity*, 1907, p. 181.

5. Ibid. pp. 3 and 30, slightly altered.

6. A. Kalthoff, *Modernes Christentum*, Berlin n. d. (1906), p. 20.

7. *The Rise of Christianity*, pp. 10, 14 and 16f.

8. Ibid. pp. 113, 99, 71 and 158.

the air nests, but the Son of Man has nowhere to lay his head', and concluded that it referred to the economic problems of the Roman proletariat. As early communists, the Christians responded to this situation by deciding that 'no one will call anything his own, but all things are in common'.[9]

Holding such views, Kalthoff looked upon himself as a loner: as he lay dying of a weak heart in 1906 (supposing himself to be suffering from bronchial catarrh) he took a friend's hand for the last time with the words, 'I can no longer bear this isolation.'[10] Yet in spite of his startling theology he was in many ways typical of his age. Born in 1850, he had been ordained in 1874 to a pastorate at St Mark's church in Berlin, moving from there to Bremen. His published writings reflect the interests of a thousand contemporary German clergymen. Sermons on Zarathustra, a volume on Nietzsche and the cultural problems of the age (which was said to have won him many friends outside Bremen[11]), another on the religious problems in Goethe's *Faust* (subtitled 'Serious Answers to Serious Questions'), and so on, stand alongside his books on social questions.[12] In practice he was cautiously progressive. In 1898 he founded an association for the social sciences which later became a society for social reform. His plan to set up an inter-confessional body under the standard of 'living religion' failed to get off the ground.[13] As president of the Monist Society he achieved some prominence among those preaching the devotional mysticism that before the outbreak of the First World War became known in Germany as 'the secret religion of the educated'.[14]

Similarly, even when promulgating his apparently more outlandish beliefs Kalthoff drew in part on the common theological currency of contemporary German Protestantism. By the time he came to publish his *Rise of Christianity* in 1904, he believed that, quite apart from

9. Ibid. pp. 37, 36, and 134.

10. F. Steudel in the biographical introduction to A. Kalthoff, *Zukunftsideale, mit einer Lebensskizze von Friedrich Steudel*, Jena 1907, p. xxvii, cf. pp. xxiii and xxvi. For the details of his life which follow, see pp. v–xxxiv.

11. Ibid. p. xx.

12. *Zarathustrapredigten*, Jena 1904; *Friedrich Nietzsche und die Kulturprobleme unserer Zeit*, Berlin 1900; *Die religiösen Probleme in Goethes Faust*, Braunschweig 1901; *An der Wende des Jahrhunderts. Kanzelreden über die sozialen Kämpfe unserer Zeit*, Braunschweig 1898; *Christusproblem. Grundlinien zu einer Sozialtheologie*, Jena 1902.

13. Steudel in *Zukunftsideale*, pp. xxiiif., and xxv.

14. Heinrich Weinel in *Die Religion in Geschichte und Gegenwart*, 2nd edn, Tübingen 1927–1932, tr. R. A. Wilson in *Twentieth Century Theology in the Making*, ed. J. Pelikan, 1970, ii. 399.

whether Jesus existed or not, the attempt by liberal theologians to reconstruct his biography from the gospel records had encountered insuperable difficulties.[15]

Here Kalthoff was supremely influenced by Bruno Bauer, a notorious theologian who had died in 1883. In the 1830s Bauer had taken up the notion put forward by D. F. Strauss that the gospels expressed in symbolic form the deepest desires of those who created them. Bauer then declared this notion to be insufficiently critical. His own studies led him to believe that neither the fourth gospel nor the three synoptic gospels possessed any historical validity. St Mark, which he regarded as the earliest surviving gospel, was in his opinion full of lies and inventions.[16] Indeed, he soon came to believe that Christianity preached nothing but hypocrisy and falsehoods. Not surprisingly, in March 1842 the theological faculties of Prussia voted that he should be dismissed by the University of Bonn. Nonetheless, Albert Schweitzer later considered Bauer's work by no means contemptible. He had compiled, said Schweitzer, 'the ablest and most complete collection of the difficulties of the Life of Jesus which is anywhere to be found.'[17] These difficulties persuaded Albert Kalthoff that Jesus never existed.

Bauer's critique of the gospels and of Christianity also drew Kalthoff closer to Karl Marx. For a time Bauer had been Marx's closest friend. Paradoxically, his connection with Marx lowered his reputation still further. As Professor Owen Chadwick has observed, 'In English-language history Bauer usually appears as a comic figure of scholarship, a man with bizarre theories of New Testament documents, the eccentric academic of his generation. Marxist historians dismissed him equally, because Karl Marx at last turned against him and confuted him at length. But we have lately been learning more about Bauer, and what we learn makes him less contemptible though not more attractive.'[18] Bauer taught Marx to be radical about religion. Together they planned a journal devoted to atheism. They worked together on a satirical pamphlet advocating atheism, which lost Bauer his university post.[19] Although Marx was to turn against his friend, the arguments

15. *The Rise of Christianity*, pp. 1ff, 11ff, 123ff., and 186ff.

16. B. Bauer, *Kritik der evangelischen Geschichte des Johannes*, Bremen 1840; *Kritik der evangelischen Geschichte der Synoptiker*, 3 vols, Leipzig 1841–1842.

17. A. Schweitzer, *Von Reimarus zu Wrede*, 1906; tr. W. Montgomery, *The Quest of the Historical Jesus*, 1910, p. 159.

18. O. Chadwick, *The Secularization of the European Mind in the Nineteenth Century*, 1975, pp. 52f.

19. Ibid. p. 53.

with which Bauer had convinced him that the Christianity of the gospels was academically indefensible proved equally compelling to the Marxist Kalthoff.

Kalthoff had a further, non-Marxist reason for wishing to do without the historical Jesus. He was quite certain that the spirit of his own time would not allow 'a man who lived at a certain time and place to be made the absolute law of its own life'.[20] This was an odd variant of the 'ugly broad ditch' that Lessing had found it impossible to cross in the eighteenth century: the famous argument first expressed in Lessing's pamphlet of 1777 that *'accidental truths of history can never become the proof of necessary truths of reason'*.[21] On the basis of this argument, Kalthoff refused to look for political formulas applicable to the twentieth century in the communism of the primitive church. Whereas earlier Christian socialists sought to find norms of economic life in the Bible or the Fathers, in order (as Kalthoff put it) 'to combat certain economic dogmas with weapons taken from the ecclesiastical arsenal', he saw the communism of primitive Christianity as an economic necessity for its own time, not an argument for or against any modern form of economic life.[22]

Kalthoff's biographer described *The Rise of Christianity* as his 'first great attempt at a solid historical foundation' for his beliefs.[23] Unfortunately, his historical resources were meagre. His book had the misfortune to appear just in time to be savaged in Albert Schweitzer's *Quest of the Historical Jesus*. As Schweitzer pointed out, Kalthoff had combined Bauer's assertion that no Jew could possibly have claimed to be the Messiah with the contradictory statement that there had been many Jewish Messiahs before anyone called Jesus was connected with the title. Again, Kalthoff asserted that the apocalyptic of Daniel arose under Platonic influence. Schweitzer commented, 'The Platonic apocalyptic never had any existence, or at least, to speak with the utmost possible caution, its existence must not be asserted in the absence of all proof.'[24]

Clearly Kalthoff was more important as a phenomenon of his time

20. *The Rise of Christianity*, p.8.
21. 'On the Proof of the Spirit of Power', in *Lessing's Theological Writings*, ed. H. Chadwick, 1956, pp. 55 and 53.
22. *The Rise of Christianity*, pp. 157 and 166.
23. Steudel, p. xxiii. Apart from Bauer, Kalthoff drew on L. Stein, *Die soziale Frage im Licht der Philosophie*, Stuttgart 1897, and A. Brentano *Untersuchungen über das wirtschaftliche Leben des christlichen Altertums* (which I have been unable to trace).
24. *The Quest of the Historical Jesus*, pp. 315-317.

than for his learning or acumen. Although a number of other Marxist students of early Christianity entirely eliminated the historical Jesus,[25] few do so today. In Kalthoff's own day this aspect of his thinking was meticulously and trenchantly demolished by Johannes Weiss.[26] Yet Kalthoff's hermeneutic, though extreme, has not been totally discredited among Marxists. One so sensitive to Christianity as Milan Machovec continues to believe that the noblest ideas of Christianity are primarily socio-economic in origin and only secondarily the result of the personalities of Jesus and his apostles. And although Machovec accepts the existence of and warmly responds to the historical Jesus, he finds it impossible to believe in him as a saviour, because in his view the ideals of 'salvation' and 'redemption' (and hence of a 'saviour' and a 'redeemer') were thrown up by the deprived as a result of the socio-economic conditions in which they lived at the time of the early church.[27]

Even as Schweitzer and Weiss were setting down their criticisms of Kalthoff, a far more scholarly and important Marxist, Karl Kautsky, partly under Kalthoff's influence, was also considering the origins of Christianity. Born in Prague in 1854, the son of a Czech father and a German mother, Kautsky had studied at Vienna, where he took up social Darwinism.[28] At the time of the Paris Commune he was converted to socialism (while not losing all traces of this social Darwinism). In 1883, the year of Marx's death, he founded *Die Neue Zeit*, which he edited for thirty-four years, making it the leading Marxist theoretical journal in the world, with himself as the dominant theoretician. His commentary on the Erfurt programme of the SPD became accepted as the classic exposition. Engels had rejected the programme drafted by the party executive at Erfurt; the one approved by him and eventually accepted by the party was Kautsky's. Kautsky became Engels's private secretary, and after Engels's death the editor of Marx's literary remains.

Kautsky's commentary on the Erfurt programme exhibits both the democratic and the revolutionary aspects of his socialism. Marxist

25. E. g. A. Drews, *Die Christusmythe. Verbesserte und erweiterte Ausgabe*, 2 vols, Jena 1910.

26. J. Weiss, *Jesus von Nazareth, Mythus oder Geschichte? Eine Auseinandersetzung mit Kalthoff, Drews, Jensen*, Tübingen 1910, esp. pp. 13-15 and 125-129.

27. M. Machovec, *Jesus für Atheisten*, 2nd edn, Stuttgart 1972, p. 8. Cf. p. 284, where Machovec comments on Marxist dismissals of the historical Jesus.

28. See 'The Ethics of Darwinism', chapter 4, pp. 70-104, of Karl Kautsky, *Ethics and the Materialist Conception of History*, tr. J. B. Askew, Chicago 1918.

theory, he wrote, aimed at 'supporting the class struggle of the proletariat by deepening its insight and helping its political and economic organizations', not by bringing 'salvation from proletarian misery from above.' [29] He aimed to bring about 'a government of the proletarian party guaranteeing all rights and liberties in a democratic state.'[30] Such a programme could not include a doctrinaire attempt to crush members of the state calling themselves Christians. Nor, in Kautsky's view, could even the revolution be imposed from above. The inexorable laws discovered by Marx and Engels (and already apparently vindicated by the developing capitalist structure and class-ridden nature of Germany) would, he believed, automatically lead to revolution. So, as he put it, the SPD, under his guidance and by virtue of its background, was a revolutionary but not a revolution-making party.[31] 'We know that our goal can be attained only through revolution', he wrote, adding immediately, 'We know that it is just as little in our power to create that revolution as it is in the power of our opponents to prevent it.' [32] Kautsky therefore attacked both the revisionists led by Eduard Bernstein, who wished to minimize the revolutionary aspects of Marxism, and those who sought to hasten the revolution by what he considered to be needless violence.

Naturally, he was attacked by both sides; but between 1900 and 1914 Kautsky was at the peak of his activity and influence.[33] He was as esteemed in Russia (where some Marxists had begun to hope for a revolution that would touch off uprisings elsewhere in Europe [34]) as in Germany. Thus in 1900 Nicolas Berdjajev wrote in connection with his forthcoming articles in Die Neue Zeit, declaring how much 'We Russian Marxists' admired Kautsky, and adding (underlined), 'I am not a Bernsteiner'.[35]

In this most productive period of Kautsky's life appeared his Foun-

29. Karl Kautsky, Das Erfurter Programm, Stuttgart 1892, p. 230.

30. Die soziale Revolution, Berlin 1907, pp. 46f.

31. 'Ein sozial-demokratischer Katechismus', in Die Neue Zeit, Jahrgang xii/i, 1893, p. 368.

32. S. H. Hook, Marx and the Marxists: The Ambiguous Legacy, New York 1955, p. 57.

33. Werner Blumenberg, Karl Kautskys literarisches Werk, 'S-Gravenhage 1960, p. 691.

34. Karl Kautsky, Rosa Luxemburg, Karl Liebknecht, Leo Jogiches. Ihre Bedeutung für die deutsche Sozialdemokratie, Berlin 1921, p. 4f.

35. Kautsky papers, D IV, 133, Berdjajev to Kautsky, 6 May 1900. The letter is in German, since Kautsky did not speak Russian. The articles, on 'Friedrich Albert Lange und die kritische Philosophie in ihren Beziehungen zum Sozialismus', appeared in Die Neue Zeit, Jahrgang 18, 1900, pp. 132-140, 164-174, and 196-207.

dations of Christianity, written, he said, in hours snatched from political activity between the start of the Russian revolution of 1905 and the outbreak of the Turkish revolution of 1908.[36]

Its impact was immediate. Kautsky's press-cutting agency sent him no less than twenty-three reviews of the book. (Only three of the many books he wrote received more.[37]) A translation appeared in Finnish in 1909, one year after the appearance of the German edition. From America the editor of the socialist journal *The Coming Nation* wrote to say that he had heard the German version 'very highly spoken of' and wished to translate it.[38] The book was evidently so widely discussed that even before an American version appeared, Kautsky's US publisher was writing anxiously to complain that although he had been granted exclusive American rights to *The Foundations of Christianity*, W. H. Kerr and Co. were planning to put him out of business by bringing out a pirated edition.[39] Within twenty-five years, the book (or parts of it) had been translated into Dutch, Hungarian and Greek; there had been two English and two Russian editions. German editions of the book proliferated. Neither Kautsky's denigration by Lenin nor his death in 1938 seems to have diminished the book's popularity. Indeed, the success of communism in Eastern Europe after the Second World War stimulated fresh translations. Though no new edition was published in East Germany, *The Foundations of Christianity* was translated into Polish and Romanian, as well as Japanese, in 1944, for a second time into Hungarian in 1945 and into Serbo-Croat in 1954. New American versions appeared in 1945 and 1953.[40]

According to the Czech Marxist Milan Machovec, Lenin himself admitted that Kautsky's book belonged to the abiding achievements of socialist culture. *The Foundations of Christianity* was the first systematic presentation of primitive Christianity based on Marxist methodology, written in the spirit of strict determinism.[41] As the continual

36. *Der Ursprung des Christentums*, Stuttgart 1908; tr. from the 13th edn, *The Foundations of Christianity*, 1925, p.8.

37. According to the catalogue to the Kautsky papers, these should be filed, with numerous other reviews, in the collection H2, 1901-1911. Unfortunately, the file containing reviews of *The Foundations of Christianity* has been mislaid.

38. Kautsky papers, D. XX, 668 letter of A.M. Simons to Kautsky, 21 July 1909. Simons's *The America Farmer* was reviewed by Kautsky, 'Bauernagitation in Amerika', in *Die Neue Zeit*, Jahrgang 20, 1902, pp. 453-463.

39. Kautsky papers, D VI, 64, letter of 6 January 1909. (This letter, one of the few cited in W. Blumenberg, p. 15, is there misdated 6 April 1909.)

40. The International Institute of Social History in Amsterdam holds copies of all these transalations.

41. *Jesus für Atheisten*, pp. 287f.

re-publication of the book indicates, Kautsky's assessment of Christianity remained extremely important in shaping the attitudes of later generations of Marxists (with the exception of those living in East Germany, where the authorities simply repeated and re-published the 'old' polemic of Marx, Feuerbach, Lenin, and Bebel [42]). And in spite of its ultimate hostility to Christianity, the work gained Kautsky the respect of a number of contemporary Christians, including not only those with Marxist leanings (such as his intermittent correspondent Pfarrer Schütz of Neukirch [43]) but also such notable scholars as Rudolf Otto (who in 1924 wrote to congratulate Kautsky on his seventieth birthday, regretting that the publisher they shared, J. W. Dietz, had gone out of business, and adding that it was a particular injustice that Social Democracy was not more esteemed).[44]

In assessing Kautsky's importance in the Christian–Marxist dialogue it is therefore essential to set aside his later poor reputation among the Bolsheviks. Denigration of his abilities had in fact begun with Marx himself, who described Kautsky in a letter of 1881 as 'small-minded and a mediocrity, far too clever (at the age of twenty-six), hard-working in one sort of way, greatly busying himself with statistics though unable to work out anything intelligent from them, deriving by nature from the stock of the Philistines.'[45] Marx's description was astute enough to indicate Kautsky's strengths and weaknesses, which were to appear in his *Foundations of Christianity*. But any examination of Kautsky's surviving papers reveals that Marx had grotesquely underestimated his disciple. Only 772 of Kautsky's letters survive in the International Institute of Social History in Amsterdam. (Kautsky seldom had time to make copies or condensations of his own correspondence.) But the surviving letters of those who wrote to him reveal him as a prodigious correspondent and a tireless organizer. Twenty-three volumes contain more than twelve and a half thousand letters (566 from Eduard Bernstein, 268 from August Bebel, and 731 from the publisher J. W. Dietz, for as well as editing the weekly *Die Neue Zeit*, Kautsky produced a stream of influential books and pamphlets). He remained in touch with many of these correspondents over many years.

42. K. Gust, pp. 66, 283, and 285f., gives details.

43. Kautsky papers, D XX, 479–482, letters of 14 October 1919, 7 January 1920, 21 July 1922, and 13 October 1924. Kautsky's letters to Schütz are referred to in the correspondence, but are not in the archive.

44. Kautsky papers, D XVIII, 338, letter of 16 October 1924.

45. Letter of 11 April 1881, in K. Marx and F. Engels, *Werke*, vol. 35, Berlin 1967, p. 178.

But the inadequacy of Marx's analysis of Kautsky's intellectual abilities is revealed above all by surviving voluminous notebooks in which Kautsky summarized and quoted from his enormous reading. [46] These notebooks display both his lifelong interest in the phenomenon of Christianity and how remarkably he qualified himself to write about it (and about much else, too). One notebook in particular, containing analyses of only three books, reveals the peculiar quiddity of his mind. Seven pages of notes on Strauss's notorious *Life of Jesus* are immediately followed by forty-eight pages analysing the second volume of *Capital*, which precedes another seven pages on G. F. Daumen's *Secrets of Christian Antiquity*.[47]

It is not always possible to assign a single date to each notebook, for although he was invariably systematic in his notes and references, Kautsky used several volumes at different times over several decades. Thus one notebook begins with a seventeen-page analysis of the *Histoire de Thomas More* by Thomas Stapleton. (Stapleton was professor of theology at Louvain in the sixteenth century, and his book had been republished in Paris in 1879.) Kautsky began this analysis in August 1886. This is followed by an eleven page summary of G. T. Rudhart's *Thomas More*, [48] and three pages of quotations from Gilbert Burnet's *History of the Reformation in England*. In September of the same year Kautsky started at the other end of the notebook with a page on Thomas Carlyle's *Chartism*, followed by a quotation on *Utopia* from Erasmus.[49]

Thirty years later he took up this notebook again and filled the middle pages with an analysis (almost seventy pages long) of Otto Pfleiderer's history of the primitive church.[50] He was now working intently on his *Foundations of Christianity*. In November 1906 he used the same notebook for a seventeen-page analysis of Wünsche's edition of the *Didache*,[51] carefully hunting down quasi-communistic elements

46. Kautsky papers. B-12 Dicke Kladden exzerpte. No analysis of the Kautsky papers has yet been published and there is no subject index to their contents. None of the notebooks is numbered, though this chiefly creates difficulties simply over adequately referring to them.

47. D. F. Strauss, *Das Leben Jesu kritisch bearbeitet*, 4th edn. 2 vols, Tübingen 1840; G. F. Daumen, *Die Geheimnisse des christlichen Altertums*, 2 vols, Hamburg 1847.

48. G. T. Rudhart, *Thomas Morus. Aus den Quellen bearbeitet*, Nuremberg 1829.

49. *Chartism*, 2nd edn 1870. *Epigrammatica Des. Erasmi Roterdami*, Basle 1519.

50. *Das Urchristentum, seine Schriften und Lehren in geschichtlichem Zusammenhang beschrieben*, 2nd edn, 2 vols, Berlin 1902. Kautsky analysed this in December 1906.

51. A. Wünsche, *Die Lehre der zwölf Apostel*, 2nd edn, Leipzig 1884. For a more recent assessment of the communist tendencies of the *Didache*, see G. Walter, *Les origines du communisme*, 2nd edn, Paris 1975, pp. 68–72.

in this early Christian document. (He found them in cap. I: 'Give to every one that asketh of thee, and ask not again; for the Father wishes that from all his gifts there should be given to all', and in cap IV: 'Thou shalt not turn away from him that is in need, but shalt share with thy brother in all things, and shalt not say that things are thine own; for if ye are partners in what is immortal, how much more in what is mortal?')

This is followed by an important section on the second edition of a work by Bruno Bauer from whose subtitle Kautsky took the title of his own book on Christianity.[52] Next come detailed analyses of Seneca's religion, of Christianity under Trajan, of Hadrian and gnosis, of the age of Marcus Aurelius, and of the formation of the New Testament literature. Finally Kautsky set down a summary of the article on angels in the *Dictionnaire de Théologie Catholique*,[53] a page on Suetonius and thirty pages drawn from volume 7 of *The Romans under the Empire* by Charles Merivale.[54] The last page of this is written upside-down.

Thus the leading Marxist of his time industriously prepared his analysis of primitive Christianity. Kautsky affected modesty about his knowledge of the early church compared with that of men who had made it their life's study. He boasted, however, that his intensive share in the class struggles of the proletariat possibly offered him 'precisely such glimpses of the essence of primitive Christianity as may remain inaccessible to the professors of Theology and Religious History!'[55] Yet Machovec is surely correct in insisting that the bulk of later Marxist propaganda on the subject remained at a level far below that achieved by Kautsky, 'because almost all lacked what was decisive about him, namely learning.'[56] When he came to write *The Foundations of Christianity*, Kautsky was able to draw on material he had pondered and researched over many years.

Kautsky's dependence on Bauer and his warmness toward D. F. Strauss clearly located his place in the quest of the historical Jesus. Indeed, the problem of the historicity of Jesus drove him to write his book in the first place. He had first written about Christianity more than twenty years earlier.[57] He took up the subject again, he said,

---

52. *Christus und die Caesaren. Der Ursprung des Christentums aus dem römischen Griechentum*, 2nd edn, Berlin 1875.
53. Paris 1848.   54. London 1862.
55. *The Foundations of Christianity*, p.8.
56. Machovec, p. 8.
57. 'Die Entstehung des Christentums', in *Die Neue Zeit*, Jahrgang 3, 1885, pp. 481–499 and 529–545.

because of criticisms that his previous work did not stand up to the findings of subsequent research and in particular to the claim that recent scholarship had rendered obsolete the notion first put forward by Bauer and accepted by Kautsky that 'there is nothing certain we can say about the person of Jesus and that Christianity can be explained without introducing this person.' Re-examining his former ideas in the light of the most recent literature, he arrived at the 'gratifying conclusion' that he had nothing to alter.[58]

Kautsky quoted Bauer throughout *The Foundations of Christianity*, always with approval.[59] In the spirit of his theological master he considered the gospels and Acts to be of incalculable value for studying the social conditions of their time, but assessed their historical value as probably no greater than that of Homer or the Nibelungenlied.[60] Kautsky classified study of the Old Testament as a branch of anthropology or ethnology more than historical truth, and he consigned most of his learned and extensive notes on it to the folio and octavo sheets usually reserved for his studies of eskimos, Indians, primitive marriage rites, oriental lore, and so on. [61] As for the historical Jesus, Kautsky reasserted his original conviction that the gospels leave us 'not even certain that he ever lived.'[62]

Oddly enough, when it suited him Kautsky could write as if he did believe there had once lived a man, Jesus, with quite definite characteristics. For example, he took the episode in Matthew 26.51ff., where Simon Peter cut off the ear of the high priest's servant, as embodying an earlier story of a planned coup d'etat in which Jesus was captured. He criticized later Christians for trying to suppress the fact that the historical Jesus had been a rebel.[63] And only by positing a historical Jesus could he observe that (unlike Marx and Engels) the one who presided over the cradle of Christianity was quite obviously not 'a person with a deep scientific training.'[64]

His basic aim, however, was to exhibit early Christianity as the

58. *The Foundations of Christianity*, foreword, p. 7.
59. Ibid. pp. 7, 32f. 40, 365, 385n, and 387 n.   60. Ibid. pp. 15, 17, 40f., and 80f.
61. Kautsky papers, I Kladde Postausgang 1915-1917, folio and 8vo, contain his notes on, for instance, G. Ebers *Aegypten und die Bücher Moses*, Leipzig 1868, and *Durch Gosen zum Sinai*, Leipzig 1872, and on J. Wellhausen *Geschichte Israels*, vol. 1, Berlin 1878. They occasionally contain material relevant to his Christian studies, e.g. an analysis of the article on 'Slavery and Christianity', in *Kirchenlexikon oder Encyklopädie der kattholischen Theologie*, hrsg von H. J. Wetzer and B. Welte, Freiburg im Breisgau 1853.
62. *The Foundations of Christianity*, p. 42.
63. Ibid. pp. 366 and 309ff.
64. Translation of H. F. Mins, New York 1953, p. 383; cf. the 1925 translation, p. 442.

product of revolutionary forces. The earliest Christians, he asserts, were proletarian, with the fierce hatred of the rich revealed in the parable of Dives and Lazarus (Luke 16.19ff.), the Blessings on the poor in the Sermon on the Mount (Matthew 6.20ff.), and the curses in the Epistle of James (5.1f.). (At one point Kautsky described Matthew as a 'revisionist' for weakening the vigour of the statement in Mark and Luke that it is easier for a camel to pass through the eye of a needle than for a rich man to enter into the kingdom of God.) He cited the gospel commands to sell one's goods and give to the poor (for instance, Luke 12.33), as well as the financial arrangements described in the Acts of the Apostles (2.42f., and 4.32f.) as evidence of the communistic character of the early Christian communities.[65] Christianity, he maintained, undoubtedly began as a movement of impoverished classes of the most varied kinds, a movement of proletarians. He quoted with approval Kalthoff's judgement (in *Das Christusproblem*) that 'From the social-theological point of view, the image of Jesus is therefore the most highly-sublimated religious expression of all the social and ethical forces operative in the era in question.'[66] His image, on this reading, represents not what a particular person actually did and taught, but what his followers and disciples projected onto him; and because of the social and economic conditions under which they lived, they inevitably projected an image of communism.

Yet Kautsky was careful to insist that this communism was not the mature kind he perceived in Marx and Engels and spent his life propagating. In its attitude to liberty, equality and property, primitive Christianity was not the same as Social Democracy. Whereas, Kautsky maintained, the former understood equality of property as 'equal division for the purpose of the consumption for all', Social Democracy demands not the division of property but its 'socialization'. Whereas primitive Christianity understood freedom as 'the emancipation from all work, as is the lot of the lilies of the field who neither toil nor spin and yet enjoy their life', Social Democracy brings not freedom from work 'but equal rights for all in the products of social labour.'[67] 'Enjoyment without labour', the early Christian communism mirrored in the lilies of the field and the ravens, was no longer possible.[68]

65. *The Foundations of Christianity*, translation of 1925, pp. 323–336.
66. *The Foundations of Christianity*, pp. 9 and 40.
67. Karl Kautsky, *Ethics and the Materialist Conception of History*, pp. 196f., where the word 'lilies' appears as 'toilers'.
68. 'Der Heilige Franz von Assisi,' in *Die Neue Zeit*, Jahrgang 21, 1904, p. 261.

Failure to perceive such distinctions sometimes misled Kautsky's academic critics. Adolf Deissmann's *Primitive Christianity and the Lower Orders*[69] contested Kautsky's interpretation (in *Die Vorläufer des Neueren Sozialismus*) of Christianity as 'a proletarian freedom movement with communist tendencies'. Kautsky argued in response that Deissmann himself provided the evidence that early Christianity was a proletarian movement. He had wrongly understood Kautsky as contending that the early Christians were modern Social Democrats. 'The facts brought forward by Deissmann', Kautsky concluded, 'bolster rather than contradict my interpretation of Christianity.'[70]

Yet a number of other distinguished scholars also questioned Kautsky's views. Ernst Troeltsch, for instance, maintained that the supposed relationship between primitive Christianity and communism was based on a misunderstanding of the idea of the kingdom of God, which was given political and social significance only much later.[71] It is important to consider the extent to which Kautsky's conclusions have stood up to later scholarship (leaving aside his extravagant belief that Jesus never existed at all). It is perfectly possible to find modern scholars both contesting and assenting to portions of Kautsky's thesis. Professor G. D. Kilpatrick has agreed with Kautsky's contention that the church tried to conceal the fact that Jesus died a rebel. He argues that the society represented in Luke consisted of men and women whose welfare and prosperity were linked with the Empire so closely that they were hardly prepared to support anyone crucified as a rebel against it. So Luke gives a revised version of the death of Jesus. 'Jesus is no longer a rebel setting out to subvert the Empire, but he is crucified by a species of lynch law.'[72] On the other hand, many modern scholars have doubted whether the community of goods in the primitive Jerusalem church (Acts 2.42) ought to be interpreted as some sort of communism, rather than an idealization based particularly on the promises of the Old Testament.[73]

The most thorough examination of property and riches in the early church was published by Professor Martin Hengel of Tübingen in 1973.

69. *Das Urchristentum und die unteren Schichten*, Stuttgart 1910.

70. *Die Neue Zeit*, Jahrgang 27, 1909, I. 649f.

71. Ernst Troeltsch, *Die Soziallehren der christlichen Kirchen und Gruppen* (1911), Tübingen edn of 1922, p. 17n.

72. G. D. Kilpatrick, 'The New Testament and History', in *St Mark's Review*, no. 85, Canberra, September 1975, p. 7.

73. There is a useful bibliographical discussion of this position in Marcello Del Verme, 'La Comunione dei beni nella Comunità di Gerusalemme', in *Rivista Biblica*, Paideia-Brescia, October–December 1975, pp. 353-382.

Referring to St Paul's remark (I Cor. 1.26) that not many of the Corinthian Christians were of noble birth or wise according to worldly standards, Hengel warned that the apostle had written 'not many', not 'none at all'. We cannot therefore infer that the Pauline mission communities were composed solely of proletarians and slaves. Hengel contended that the majority of early Christians actually belonged to the 'middle class' of antiquity, with the possible adherence of women from the upper classes. 'From the beginning', he wrote, 'early Christianity was essentially a petty bourgeois movement. . . ,' composed of 'manual workers and craftsmen, small businessmen and workers on the land, all of whom had a great respect for honest labour.'[74]

Hengel also asserted that in the biblical description of 'love-communism', the author of Acts combined the primitive Christian ethos with universal ideas of antiquity about the ideal state of man. Yet in the end Hengel ranged himself firmly with those who refuse to consider this 'love-communism' as nothing more than an idealistic invention. It derived from the teaching of Jesus about the eschaton; it appears to have been voluntary and spontaneous; it was related to Jesus's preaching about unrighteous Mammon and the folly of worldly anxiety, as well as to his radical criticism of property (which, Hengel insisted, was only one side of his ministry and preaching). [75] Hengel summed up his main conclusion in these words. 'The argument over the question of property, which already emerged in a radical way in the preaching of Jesus, was not settled in the early church, nor was there any clear and comfortable solution. The social demands associated with it introduced new stimuli to the ancient world which can be described without exaggeration as revolutionary.'[76]

Thus Hengel's researches both draw attention to a number of serious inadequacies in Kautsky's analysis of primitive Christianity and vindicate his contention that the primitive church preached a revolutionary social gospel. By the nineteenth century, Kautsky maintained, the church was preaching something completely different. 'The Christian Church has become an organization of domination', he wrote, 'either in the interests of its own dignitaries, or the dignitaries of another organization, the state.'[77] Whenever Kautsky detected early communism in Christian history, he invariably insisted that ultimately

74. M. Hengel, *Property and Riches in the Early Church*, tr. J. Bowden, 1975, pp. 36f., and 60.

75. Ibid. pp. 5, 8, and 31ff.

76. Ibid. p. 82.

77. *The Foundations of Christianity*, p. 21.

the church in general had turned against it. So he argued that the communism of the thirteenth-century Franciscans not only failed to destroy the established order but in the end came to uphold it. Unlike 'heretical communists', such as the Waldensians, who lived in open warfare with the church (which Kautsky characterized as being at that time the organization of the ruling classes), St Francis hoped to exploit the church in order imperceptively to reform it. 'Of course, the rules of the order forbade it to hold property, not only individually but also corporately', Kautsky commented; 'but they did not forbid the useful enjoyment of the property of the churches.' In consequence, the society flourished in the shade of Papal palaces. In spite of the communism that Kautsky believed St Francis had begun to preach in the year 1207, Kautsky likened the saint's followers to the English trade-union officials and French socialist politicians of his own day, whose chief function was to transform the workers into conservatives. St Francis himself he dubbed the Jean Jaurès of the thirteenth century.[78]

The Kautsky papers shed interesting light on how he reached such conclusions, and in doing so also illuminate his limitations as a historian. Kautsky's manuscript notes on *The Lives of English Popular Leaders in the Middle Ages*, by C. E. Maurice,[79] contain the observation, 'The work of the Franciscans in England in the early part of the thirteenth century was to knit the poor to the church, by living among them and sharing their way of life rather than by inciting in them that dislike of property as an institution which was so often produced by the preaching of the friars in the fourteenth century.'[80] On the same page Kautsky noted evidence that the later Franciscans were certainly found to be stirring up peasants against their rulers in a quite revolutionary fashion. But this observation did not find its way into his published writings.

Kautsky was in truth not so much a historian as a journalist, with a case to prove and a journalist's ability to gut sources toward this end. The limitations (and strengths) of his technique are clearly apparent in his account of the Tudor reformer Thomas More, though they affect all his historical writings. Kautsky considered More's *Utopia* important enough to write a lengthy book on the subject. *Utopia* sketched out a form of socialism that involved the equal obligation of all to work, the equal right of all to enjoyment, and an end to private

78. 'Der Heilige Franz von Assisi', p. 262f.
79. London 1875.
80. Kautsky papers, B–1 Kladde Postausgang 1915–1917.

property. Kautsky argued that this pattern of socialism had not been achieved in More's own time principally because there was no party or class to champion it.[81]

Kautsky researched his book on More with customary vigour. In October 1886 he analysed, with impeccably noted page-references, part of Henry Morley's *Ideal Commonwealths*, which had been published in London the previous year. But he knew what he was looking for before he began work. He was interested solely in Thomas More, and not even all of Thomas More. Morley's *Ideal Commonwealths* is 284 pages long, and deals (along with More's *Utopia*) with Plutarch's *Lycurgus*, Bacon's *New Atlantis*, Campanella's *City of the Sun*, and a *Fragment* of Hall— all of which Kautsky ignored, content with a twenty-page analysis of More's *Utopia*. The notebook[82] continues with fifteen pages of quotations from Erasmus on More, and then four pages on Raphe Robinson's sixteenth-century translation of *Utopia* and Hearne's edition of Roper's life of More.[83] These are followed by two pages on *The Life of Thomas More, Kt.*, by his great grandson,[84] and another twenty-five pages of quotations on Colet, Erasmus, and More from Frederic Seebohm's *Oxford Reformers of 1498*.[85]

The energy on display is prodigious,[86] but Kautsky's gutting was ruthless. In another notebook, [87] he wrote down two pages of quotations from the second edition of Seebohm's *Oxford Reformers*,[88] thus making a total of only 27 pages of notes from a book 557 pages long. The same notebook contains a mere 4 pages of notes on a 364-page American selection from More's works,[89] 3 pages on an edition of More's memoirs,[90] and 7 pages on a sixteenth-century edition of his

81. Karl Kautsky, *Thomas Morus und seine Utopie*, Stuttgart 1890; tr. H. J. Stenning *Thomas More and his Utopia*, 1927. Kautsky took great care over this translation. Thirty-six letters from Stenning, dating from 1920 to 1936, survive among the Kautsky papers: D XXI 405–440.

82. The notebook is in the Kautsky papers, B–12 Dicke Kladde exzerpte.

83. These had been published together as *Utopia and Roper's More*, ed. J. R. Lumby, 1879.

84. London 1726.   85. London 1867.

86. Kautsky later took up this notebook again and, starting a fifth of the way from the end, worked backwards through it, adding information on Elizabethan trade from J. A. Froude's *History of England* and two pages of notes about the Catholic martyrs from the same source (2 vols 1876), fourteen pages on Henry VIII from J. Lingard's *History of England* (5th edition 1849), and four pages on J. Wade's *History of the Middle and Working Classes* (vol. X, 1835).

87. In the same file as n.82 above.

88. 2nd edn, 1869.

89. *Sir Thomas More, a selection from his Works*, ed. W. J. Walter, Baltimore 1841.

90. *The Memoirs of Sir T. More*, ed. A. Cayley, 2nd edn, 1868.

writings.[91] Lastly, in this notebook Kautsky devoted no more than three or four pages to summarizing what he considered important about each of the protagonists of Désiré Nisard's *Renaissance et Réforme, Erasme, Thomas Morus, Melanchthon.*[92] In spite of the remarkable number of books he consulted in preparing his life of More, it cannot be said that Kautsky was immersing himself in his sources.

It becomes clear that Kautsky knew from the start what he thought about *Utopia*, and for ideological reasons considered the rest of More's writings irrelevant. 'His political, religious, and humanist writings are today only read by a small number of historians. Had he not written *Utopia*', Kautsky judged, 'his name would scarcely be better known today than that of the friend who shared his fate, Bishop Fisher. His socialism made him immortal.'[93] Kautsky may well have been correct in describing More's *Utopia* as his greatest work. He came to this decision and consigned the rest of More's writings to oblivion without for the most part even reading, let alone studying, them. This historical technique vitiated his historical conclusions. And it ensured that he made no major attempt seriously to encounter Christianity as it had developed in history.

His judgements on contemporary Christianity, however, though no doubt ideologically inspired in part, were based on observation, not historical research. Kalthoff agreed with him. In his view Christianity had become 'a pillar of society, a guardian of order. It told men that things as they are are good and reasonable; men should calm down and extinguish every great longing, every consuming restlessness of spirit.'[94] How had this happened? Kalthoff never explained. Kautsky put it down to the inevitable dialectic of history, which is barely an explanation, though he added at one point the suggestion that because the limited area covered by primitive Christianity prevented it from abolishing the class system, it 'necessarily' became a new form of aristocracy.[95]

It was left to a third Marxist, Erich Fromm, to make use of his astonishing blend of Freudianism and Marxism in an attempt to explain how this social revolutionary movement was transformed into

91. *The Works of Sir Thomas More, Knight,* 1557.
92. 3rd edn, Paris 1871.
93. *Thomas More and His Utopia,* p. 159.
94. A. Kalthoff, 'Die Religion der Zukunft,' in *Zukunftsideale,* p. 117.
95. *The Foundations of Christianity,* p. 467.

acceptance of the status quo. Fromm was then a leading member of the Frankfurt Institute of Social Research. His importance there can be judged by the number and weight of his contributions to the Institute's journal in the 1930s.[96] In the light of Germany's failure to develop into a truly socialist sate when the old order collapsed in November 1918, Fromm was one of those Marxists identified by Karl Korsch as seeking the psychological as well as social conditions that kept the workers in chains.[97] Fromm argued that psychoanalysis 'can show in what manner particular economic conditions influence the psychic apparatus of men and produce particular ideological results.'[98] He sought to relate Marx's analysis of the alienation produced by capitalist society to the mechanics of alienation in man's unconscious, in order to uncover the repressive character of whole civilizations. Although he was to describe Marx as 'a figure of world historical significance, with whom Freud cannot even be compared',[99] he remained convinced that the Marxism he encountered in the 1920s was greatly impoverished by its hostility to psychoanalysis.

This conviction underlay his sharp criticism of Kautsky's attempt to explain the development of Christianity. Fromm's essay on *The Dogma of Christ*, first published in Vienna in 1931, frequently refers to Kautsky and quotes with approval his statement that 'Rarely has the class hatred of the modern proletariat attained such forms as that of the Christian proletariat.' Fromm accepted Kautsky's description of primitive Christianity and defended him against his critics. 'Although Kautsky misses the real problem', he wrote, 'the class foundations of early Christianity are nevertheless so clear that the tortuous attempt, especially of Troeltsch (in his *Social Teaching of the Christian Churches*), to explain them away and weaken them betrays all too plainly the political tendencies of the author.' But for the most part Fromm found Kautsky's Marxism, and consequently his Marxist

96. 'Uber Methode und Aufgabe einer analytischen Sozialpsychologie', and 'Die psychoanalytische Charakterologie und ihre Bedeutung für die Sozialpsychologie,' in *Zeitschrift für Sozialforschung*, Jahrgang 1, 1932, pp. 28–54 and 253–277. 'Robert Briffaults Werk über das Mutterrecht', ibid. Jahrgang 2, 1933 (published 1934), pp. 382–387; 'Die sozialpsychologische Bedeutung der Mutterrechtstheorie', ibid. Jahrgang 3, 1934 (published 1935), pp. 196–227; 'Die Gesellschaftliche Bedingtheit der psychoanalytischen Therapie', ibid. Jahrgang 4, 1935, pp. 365–397; 'Zum Gefühl der Ohnmacht', ibid. Jahrgang 6, 1937, Heft I, pp. 95–118.

97. For Korsch, see above p. 6.

98. *Psychoanalitische Bewegung*, 1931, p. 444, quoted Jakoby, p. 91. Cf. Jakoby chapter 4: 'Negative Psychoanalysis and Marxism', pp. 73–100.

99. *Beyond the Chains of Illusion*, New York 1962, p. 12.

analysis of Christianity, inadequate, indeed 'completely banal'.[100] Kautsky, he wrote, had not understood the importance of fantasy satis- faction within the social process. In contrast Fromm argued that although the early Christian message had failed to relieve hunger, it 'brought a fantasy satisfaction of no little significance for the oppressed' in response to their need of hope and desire for revenge on their oppressors.[101]

At this point Fromm began to discuss theology, and it might be argued that some of the fantasies of contemporary psychoanalysis started to take over.[102] He was able to speculate all the more freely since, in the fashion of both Kalthoff and Kautsky, he felt no need to root early Christian theology in the historical Jesus. (The problem of the historical Jesus 'need not concern us', he wrote. 'Even if the primitive Christian message were the work of a single personality, its social effect is to be understood only on the basis of the classes to which it was directed and by which it was accepted.'[103]) Fromm con- tended that the first-century adoptionist notion of a man becoming God expressed the hostility of early Christians towards authority: it was an Oedipal 'expression of an unconscious wish for the removal of the Divine Father'. At the same time, this belief, 'born of the masses', was 'an expression of their revolutionary tendencies, and offered satis- faction for their strongest longing'. When, however, Christianity came under the leadership of the ruling classes, the 'decisive element' in theology 'was the change from the idea of man becoming God to that of God becoming man'. By the fourth century, hope of overthrowing the ruling class was futile. Authority was accepted and, according to Fromm, the Christians redirected resentment inwardly on themselves. As a means of psychic escape they preferred to submit, to learn to love authority and to receive love back. Fromm concluded, 'The ideologists of the dominant classes strengthened and accelerated this development by suggesting symbolic satisfactions to the masses, guiding their

100. *Die Entwickelung des Christusdogma*, Inter. psychoanalyt. Verlag, Vienna 1931; tr. J. L. Adams, *The Dogma of Christ and Other Essays*, 1953, pp. 15 n. 1, 26 n.1, 27 n. 2., 34 and n. 1. Kautsky based his assertion about the class hatred of the early church on James 5. 1 (cf. G. Walter *Les origines du communisme*, pp. 62-67, 'Un appel à la lutte de classes: l'épître de saint Jacques').

101. Ibid. p. 34.

102. Apart from Freud's *Totem and Taboo*, *The Future of an Illusion* and *Civilization and its Discontents*, Fromm was chiefly influenced by T. Reik, 'Dogma und Zwangsidee,' in *Imago*, 12, 1927, and by E. Jones *Zur Psychoanalyse der christlichen Religion*, Berlin 1913.

103. *The Dogma of Christ*, p. 27n.

aggression into socially harmless channels.' Christianity was now a religion for both the leaders and the led, the rulers and the ruled. Recreated and reformulated by the ruling class and its intellectual representatives, its new function was 'the integration of the masses into the absolutist system of the Roman Empire'.[104]

Fromm expressed with clarity judgements with which most contemporary Marxists would have agreed about the malign influence of religion. 'God is always the ally of the rulers', he alleged. 'When the latter, who are always real personalities, are exposed to criticism, they can rely on God, who by virtue of his unreality only scorns criticism and, by his authority, confirms the authority of the ruling class.' From the point of view of a social revolutionary, religious fantasies were harmful since they offered the masses a measure of satisfaction that made life tolerable and tended to prevent any attempt at rebellion. The refinement of these judgements by means of Freudian psychiatry served only to strengthen them in Fromm's view. Religion, he declared, 'has the task of preventing any psychic independence on behalf of the masses, of intimidating them intellectually, of bringing them into socially necessary infantile docility toward the rulers'.[105]

Later in life Fromm considerably distanced himself from this essay: he had ceased to be a strict Freudian, and in addition had come to believe that far more research into Christian origins was needed. [106] But in the early 1930s his colleagues regarded Fromm's work as a major advance in theoretical Marxism. Reviewing *The Dogma of Christ* on behalf of the Frankfurt Institute, Franz Borkenau described it as 'the first attempt to demonstrate by means of a concrete example the connection between Marxism and Freudian psychoanalysis'. Borkenau went on to disabuse his readers of the notion that contemporary Christianity might be of value in renewing Marxism. Christianity, he alleged, offered 'the fantasy of the collapse of the Father symbol—God—combined with passive messianic hopes for a collapse of the rulers of the world, instead of the real battle against the power of the state'. [107] However implausible some of these arguments, in *The Dogma of Christ* Fromm was attempting to account for an undoubted sociological fact: Christianity had become the ally of the status quo, relegating hopes for a better life to the hereafter. The church no longer

104. Ibid. pp. 35, 37, 47, 49, and 94.

105. Ibid. pp. 10 and 11.

106. Ibid. preface of 1953, pp. viif. Others have criticized him both as an analyst and as a Marxist, for example M. Schneider *Neurose und Klassenkampf*, Hamburg 1973.

107. *Zeitschrift für Sozialforschung*, Jahrgang 1, 1932, pp. 174f.

posed a threat to the state. And this was seriously reducing both its relevance and its credibility among the German proletariat. In 1906 Max Weber had observed that only a minority of proletarians attributed their disbelief to the rise of science; the majority explained it by referring to the injustice of the social order and their desire for 'a revolutionary settlement in this world'. [108]

Neither Fromm nor Kautsky was disturbed by this contemporary dismissal of Christianity. Kalthoff, on the other hand, wanted a reconstituted Christianity to play its part in reconstituting society. What had begun simply as a reflection of first-century social movements might itself become a force for social change in the twentieth century. 'The older Christ-ideal of the Churches', he wrote, 'will have fresh power imparted to it by the acceptance of a secularized Christ as the type of human autonomy, of the man who remains strong amid struggle and suffering, in order to offer the infinite fulness of life that is in him for the service of humanity.'[109] Such hopes earned Kalthoff further sarcasm from Albert Schweitzer, who asked what was so new about all that? An infamous method, he judged, had produced an extremely dull result. In Schweitzer's opinion, Kalthoff was passing off as a novelty a Christ exactly like the Christ of his liberal opponents, except that it was drawn in red ink on blotting paper, so that it appeared 'red in colour and smudgy in outline'.[110]

Here Schweitzer was unjust. Kalthoff's vision of a reconstituted Christianity was in fact fully set out not at the end of The Rise of Christianity but elsewhere. Moreover, this vision corresponded closely to the transformation of theology brought about in part by Schweitzer himself. In 1892 Johannes Weiss had shown that Jesus, far from spiritualizing contemporary Jewish apocalyptic (as the liberal theologians maintained), preached doctrines of the kingdom of God and the Messiah that were identical to those found in later Judaism. Schweitzer went further, asserting that eschatology not only coloured the thoughts of Jesus but also decisively determined his actions.[111] Theologians found such notions extremely difficult to assimilate. Rudolf Bultmann

---

108. Gesammelte Aufsätze zur Religionssoziologie, Tübingen 1920, I. 247.

109. The Rise of Christianity, p. 157.

110. The Quest of the Historical Jesus, p. 318.

111. J. Weiss, Die Predigt vom Reich Gottes, Göttingen 1892. A. Schweitzer Das Messianitäts-und Leidensgeheimnisse, 3rd edn, Tübingen 1956. Cf. Schweitzer's late essay, 'Die Idee des Reiches Gottes im Verlaufe der Umbildung des eschatologischen Glaubens in den uneschatologischen,' in Schweizerische Theologische Umschau, xxiii/i, February 1953.

recalled Julius Kaftan (professor of dogmatics at Berlin) as saying, 'If Johannes Weiss is right and the concept of the Kingdom of God is an eschatological one, then it is impossible to make use of this conception in dogmatics.'[112] As for Harnack, Bultmann observed that since he never clearly understood the eschatological consciousness of Jesus or the early church, it never worried him how Christian eschatology could remain valid once the immediate expectations of the first Christians had come to nothing.[113]

Schweitzer himself failed to work out what the eschatological Jesus might mean for twentieth-century Christians. His own belief that Jesus had been in error in adopting contemporary apocalyptic greatly affected the course of his life. Recognizing that the evidence of the New Testament had destroyed the notion of Jesus as the 'decent' man, the teacher of humility and obedience, Schweitzer nonetheless rejected the consistent eschatology he perceived in Jesus and turned instead to work for culture and the underdeveloped peoples of the world. Yet it was impossible to ignore the revolution in political theology implied in his writings. As Dr Frank Gillies has observed, 'Until Schweitzer it was possible to be a) a Kantian and a christian, b) a Hegelian and a christian, or c) a sentimental socialist and a christian. After Schweitzer, it was impossible to uphold any of these positions. . . , because none of them was eschatological.'[114]

Christians needed the stimulus of Marxism in order to perceive the social and political implications of eschatology. These implications are absent from the analyses of Schweitzer, and indeed of Kautsky.[115] They were seen by Blumhardt and by Kalthoff. Kalthoff looked to 'the Christianity of the future' to provide strength for social action in the present. 'The Lord comes!' he wrote. 'He stands at the door! He will establish his kingdom!' Since there are still 'new possibilities in religion', Kalthoff believed Christians should look forward rather than back. 'Before me is the day', he said; 'behind me is the night.'[116] Here

112. R. Bultmann, *Jesus Christ and Mythology*, 1960, p. 13.

113. R. Bultmann, preface to A. Harnack, *Das Wesen des Christentums*, Siebenstern-Taschenbuch edn, Munich 1960, pp. 9f.

114. F. Gillies, 'The Eschatological Structures of Marxism', University of Sussex, D. Phil. thesis, 1975, p. 19. But is there not a covert eschatological element in Hegelianism?

115. No such implications are mentioned in B. Rigaux's recent assessment of Schweitzer and his followers, 'La redécouverte de la dimension eschatologique de l'Evangile', in *Revue d'Historie de Philosophie Religieuse*, 1967, pp. 3–27.

116. This slogan concludes his sermon, 'Das Papstum', *Zukunftsideale*, p. 117. With it Steudel ended his account of Kalthoff's own life, ibid. pp. 237 and xxiv.

is an embryonic political 'theology of hope': the notion that faith in the future kingdom of God must realize itself in concrete action today. It may be (as Troeltsch asserted [117]) that Kalthoff's preaching had not the slightest political effect, either in Bremen in his lifetime or among his later followers. But in the thinking of other men and women, the 'theology of hope' has proved to be one of the most fruitful intellectual concepts of the twentieth century.[118] Fifty years after the death of Kalthoff, Jürgen Moltmann, in a direct imitation of Marx's famous eleventh thesis on Feuerbach,[119] drew out the political implications of Christian eschatology. 'The theologian', he wrote, 'is not concerned merely to supply a different *interpretation* of the world, of human history and of human nature, but to *transform* them in expectation of a divine transformation.' In Moltmann's understanding, reconciliation with God involves not merely salvation of the soul, the rescue of the individual from the evil world and comfort for the troubled conscience; the 'other side' of reconciliation involves 'the realization of the eschatological *hope of justice*, the humanizing of man, the *socializing* of humanity, *peace* for all creation.' [120] The conceptual inadequacies of Kalthoff's theology ought not to obscure the fact that, as a Marxist and a Christian, these were his ideals too.

117. 'Die Kirche im Leben der Gegenwart' (1911), in *Zur religiösen Lage, Religionsphilosophie, und Ethik*, Tübingen 1922, p. 103.

118. J. Macquarrie, 'Theologies of Hope', in *Expository Times*, 1971, pp. 100-105.

119. 'The philosophers have only *interpreted* the world, in various ways; the point, however, is to *change* it.': in Karl Marx and F. Engels *On Religion*, Moscow 1957, p. 72.

120. J. Moltmann *Theology of Hope*, tr. J. W. Leitch, 1967, pp. 84 and 329.

4
The Socialism of Karl Barth

If the First World War and its aftermath deeply affected German-speaking Marxists, its effect on German-speaking theologians was no less striking. It decisively altered both the theology and the politics of Karl Barth, by many accounts the outstanding theologian of the twentieth century.

Barth was outraged by the way his fellow theologians and clergy in Germany supported the war effort. As he bitterly observed in September 1914, 'The unconditional truths of the Gospel are simply suspended for the time being, and in the meantime a German war-theology is put to work, its Christian trimming consisting of a lot of talk about sacrifice and the like.'[1] A meeting between Barth and Friedrich Naumann early the following year revealed how sensitive Barth had become about the church's response. Naumann, possibly deliberately to provoke the younger man, observed that religion was at least proving a useful ally of the war effort. Barth left in anger.[2]

In a review of some of Naumann's meditations, Barth had already accused him of relegating the absolute to the sphere of personal morality, thus allowing politics to be pursued 'under the presupposition that there is no God'. At that time Barth was maintaining that the one political movement that 'took the absolute with political seriousness' was socialism, which, he naively believed, had 'completely finished with the realities of the present age, namely capitalism, nationalism, and militarism.'[3] Later that year the German Social Democrats voted to support the Kaiser's war credits. Barth made Naumann the scapegoat for this. 'Untiringly he preached reason, moderation, and oppor-

1. *Revolutionary Theology in the Making*, p. 26.
2. E. Thurneysen, *Karl Barth. 'Theologie und Sozialismus' in den Briefen seiner Frühzeit*, p. 8.
3. 'Die Hilfe, 1913,' in *Christliche Welt*, 28, 1914, pp. 777f.

tunism to the Social Democrats', Barth alleged, 'and August 4, 1914, the dark day on which the German Social Democrats betrayed socialism, was the fateful symbol of the character of his own life's work.'[4]

Barth's reluctance to lay the blame for this 'betrayal' where it belonged—on the Social Democrats themselves—must be compared with the fact that, in spite of his deep distress at their capitulation to patriotic fervour in 1914, on 26 January 1915 he became a member of the SPD for the first time. His revulsion at the war fever, permanent with respect to Naumann, was overcome with regard to the SPD by his commitment to socialism. He had already made this commitment clear enough.[5] Barth had come as a young pastor to Safenwil in the Aargau in 1911. Almost all the workers in his parish were ill paid. He wrote that the class war was going on before his very eyes and that almost for the first time he had been introduced to the real problems of life. The result was that he directed his main studies toward factory legislation, insurance, and trade-union affairs. And his energies were absorbed by disputes, within and without his congregation, sparked off by the support he gave to workers in the immediate neighbourhood and throughout the canton.[6]

In 1916 Barth was still convinced that the war and the capitalist order were 'the greatest atrocities of life'.[7] In 1914 both Christianity and Social Democracy had failed to combat these two evils. Barth therefore committed himself to their mutual reformation. Although he held that both had shown themselves inadequate, Barth nevertheless convinced himself that the one could reform the other. His first lecture

4. J. M. Robinson, p. 39.

5. *Pace* W. R. Ward, 'The Socialist Commitment in Karl Barth', in *Religious Motivation, Studies in Church History 15*, ed. D. Baker, 1978, pp. 455-459. Ward's article is directed against F.-W. Marquardt, *Theologie und Sozialismus. Das Beispiel Karl Barths*, 2nd edn, Munich 1972. The article, pp. 455f., plays down Barth's trade-union activity and his clash with the president of his church council in whose factory most of the workers of the parish were employed. Ward ignores, for example, Barth's 1911 lecture, 'Jesus Christ and the Movement for Social Justice', and the subsequent exchange of letters with W. Hüssy (tr. in G. Hunsinger *Karl Barth and Radical Politics*, Philadelphia, Pa, 1976, pp. 19-45), with the result that he stresses only one side of Barth's complex nature. Hunsinger's own conclusion is more just: 'Marquardt is not wrong to stress that there is a lasting socialist dimension to Barth's thought. He is wrong rather in stressing this dimension to the exclusion of all else, and at the same time subordinating all else to this dimension' (p. 190). Cf. Max Geiger's conclusion, printed in E. Thurneysen, *Karl Barth. 'Theologie und Sozialismus' in den Briefen seiner Frühzeit*, that at Safenwil 'Socialism was an essential influence on his theological development. But it was not the only one' (p. 441).

6. *The Word of God and the Word of Man*, 1928, p. 40.

7. E. Busch, pp. 69f.

as a party member, on 'War, Socialism, and Christianity', declared, 'A real Christian must become a socialist (if he is to be in earnest about the reformation of Christianity). A real socialist must be a Christian, if he is in earnest about the reformation of socialism.'[8] In December 1918 he made the remarkably unqualified assertion that 'Jesus *is* the social movement and the social movement today *is* Jesus.'[9] Yet he did not feel completely at ease in the SPD. Shortly before joining he had written of the difficulty he found in addressing its members: 'either one strengthens them in their party loyalty by providing a religious foundation and all manner of Christian aims for their political ethos, or one tries to lead them out beyond themselves and thereby, as I had the impression yesterday, one lays upon them a burden that is too heavy for many of them to bear.' After joining he wrote: 'The Socialists in my congregation will now, I hope, have a right understanding of my public criticisms of the party.'[10]

Both the impetus toward socialism and the theological basis for these misgivings came in part from Christoph Blumhardt. As a student Barth had travelled from Tübingen to Bad Boll to hear Blumhardt preach. Indeed, they had once met in Barth's student days. But their most decisive meeting was on the day of Barth's quarrel with Naumann. On that occasion Blumhardt had observed cryptically, 'The world is the world, but God is God', a phrase which (as Eduard Thurneysen observed) 'Barth later took up and expounded in his own fashion'.[11] In fact Blumhardt's remark re-inforced one Barth had long remembered from an address by his early teacher Wilhelm Hermann in 1908: 'A God who has been proven to exist is of the world, and a God of the world is an idol.'[12]

The publication of the first edition of Barth's commentary on Romans (1919) showed his determination to keep hold of the distinction between God and the world, in spite of his conviction that God was on the side of the revolution. One of his later pupils, Friedrich-Wilhelm Marquardt, has suggested that the section of the commentary devoted to chapter 13 of Paul's epistle was written in response to Lenin's *State and Revolution* and is commentary on that work as much as on the words of the apostle. Marquardt suggests that this part of the

8. E. Busch, p. 83.

9. Quoted from the lecture 'Jesus Christus und die soziale Bewegung,' Helmut Gollwitzer, *Reich Gottes und Sozialismus bei Karl Barth*, Munich 1972, p. 7n.

10. *Revolutionary Theology in the Making*, pp. 27f.

11. *Karl Barth. 'Theologie und Sozialismus' in den Briefen seiner Frühzeit*, p. 8.

12. Quoted, K. Barth *Theology and Church* (1928), ET New York 1962, p. 243.

Römerbrief was written in November 1918, by which time Lenin's tract had been translated into German. He observes that the function of the dictatorship of the proletariat as expounded by Lenin is replaced in Barth's commentary by the notion of the revolutionary activity of God, who, Barth considered, was even more radical than Lenin in his call for an upheaval in society.[13] Yet, Barth insisted, the revolutionary God not only goes further than all human revolutions but also discloses the evil in them. Whatever Barth's own political preferences, he did not believe that God merely served to reinforce them. 'Pacifism and Social Democracy represent not the kingdom of God', he wrote, 'but the old kingdom of man in new forms.'[14]

Nonetheless, in the same commentary Barth made clear his belief that Christians in politics ought to stand 'on the extreme left'. Marxist dogma, he said, was dying; but he believed it would blaze anew, 'when the socialist church will be raised from the dead in a socialist world'.[15] Barth himself described his commentary as a symptom of 'a kind of cultural awakening through the achievement of an improved socialistic philosophy or theology'.[16] And in the year of its publication, he was present at the first post-war International Socialist Conference at Bern.[17] The second edition of *Der Römerbrief* (1921), though completely revised, revealed a Barth still committed to the left. Christianity, he wrote, 'displays a certain inclination to side with those who are immature, sullen and depressed, with those who "come off badly" and are, in consequence, ready for revolution. There is, for this reason, much in the cause of Socialism which evokes Christian approval.'[18]

Marquardt argues that Barth never retreated from his early commitment to socialism, and that in Barth's most important work, the *Church Dogmatics*, the central notions of alienation and the revolutionary God were derived not from religious and theological debate but from Barth's response to the Bolshevik revolution in Russia and the attempted socialist revolutions in Germany and Switzerland.[19] But

13. *Theologie und Sozialismus*, pp. 126-149. B. Wielanga, *Lenins Weg zur Revolution*, Munich 1971, pp. 433ff., had already drawn attention to parallels between Lenin's tract and Barth's commentary.

14. *Der Römerbrief*, 1st edn, Bern 1919, p. 24.

15. Ibid. pp. 381 and 332.

16. *Revolutionary Theology in the Making*, p. 95.

17. F.-W. Marquardt 'Sozialismus bei Karl Barth', in *Junge Kirche*, January 1972, p. 5.

18. *The Epistle to the Romans*, tr. E. C. Hoskyns, 1968 edn, p. 463.

19. 'Exegese und Dogmatik in Karl Barths Theologie', in Karl Barth, *Die Kirchliche Dogmatik*, hrsg von H. Krause, Zürich 1970, p. 673.

the received opinion is that from the early 1920s Barth's interest in socialism declined rapidly. According to one historian, 'Barth distanced himself from the position of 1921, and from 1933 onwards he became the leading theologian of the so-called *Bekenntnisfront*.'[20] The French dominican Jerome Hamer suggests that Barth's early political activity was nothing more than youthful impetuosity. During the first years of his ministry, 'Barth recklessly devoted himself to the theory and practice of socialism. The impotence of German Social Democracy must have disappointed him and caused him steadily to abandon this activity.'[21] According to Hamer, the failure of both liberalism and socialism forced Barth to return 'without prejudice' to the Bible, abandoning his former beliefs.

Barth certainly did for a time distance himself not only from the thinking of Christoph Blumhardt but also from the Swiss Religious Socialists, Ragaz and Kutter. But as far as the latter two were concerned, he had never been in close agreement with them. (Indeed, in the years between 1914 and 1925 his attacks on them were often so pointed that as late as 1956 Thurneysen did not think fit to publish them.[22]) He soon became aware not only of where he differed from them but also of their own growing differences. In September 1915 he set down some of these schematically in a letter to Thurneysen:

Ragaz	*Kutter*
Experience of social needs and problems.	Experience of God.
Ethical demand.	The kingdom of God as promise.
Belief in development.	Insight into the enslaved condition of man without God.
Optimistic evaluation of Social Democracy.	The Social Democrats can never understand us!!
Opposition to the church.	Religious responsibility *in* the church in continuity with the pietistic tradition.

20. K. Heuss, *Kompendium der Kirchengeschichte*, 12th edn, Tübingen 1960, p. 522. Cf. T. F. Torrance, *Karl Barth, an Introduction to His Early Theology, 1910–1931*, 1962, p. 31, and P. Tillich, *Perspectives on Nineteenth and Twentieth Century Theology*, ed. C. E. Braaten, 1967, p. 237.

21. J. Hamer, *Karl Barth*, ET 1962, pp. 218f., slightly altered. (I am indebted to the Bishop of Oxford for drawing my attention to a mistake in the original translation.)

22. *Revolutionary Theology in the Making*, p. 16.

Ragaz	*Kutter*
Religious-socialist party with conferences and 'new ways'.	Circles of friends for *spiritual* deepening and for work.
Emphasis upon sympathy ᾽ith workers and other 'laymen'.	Concentration primarily on the pastors.
'They talk about us!'	The building of dams for a much more distant future.
Martyrdom hoped for and sought.	
Protest against war.	

Barth's conclusion was, 'The religious-socialist concern is finished, the talking of God in earnest is at its beginning.'[23] Yet for a time he tried, vainly, to reconcile the two men.[24] He was eventually forced to the conclusion that what in Kutter had been a laudable attempt to interpret the signs of the times had in Ragaz been transformed into a socialist programme that was falsely presented as a preliminary manifestation of the kingdom of God.[25] In Barth's own account, he and his friends, in the light of the First World War, 'felt compelled to put behind us the views of the younger Blumhardt, Kutter, and Ragaz, which combined the Christian expectation of the kingdom of God and the Socialist expectation of the future. It was far too easy for them to understand this, not as a combination, but as an identification, and in fact this is just how they did understand it.'[26]

For a decade Barth's political activities declined markedly. His un-published papers contain no political speeches after 1921.[27] But it is too simple to attribute this merely to a slackening in socialist commit-ment. In 1921 Barth had taken a professorial chair in Germany. As a Swiss citizen he may have felt reluctant to indulge in too much overt political activity on foreign soil. (Some of his German contemporaries undoubtedly resented it when he did.[28]) And, as he later admitted, the pressure of his early academic work forced him to draw back a little from the concerns that had prompted him to join the SPD in 1915 and

23. Ibid. p. 31. Barth's schema was partly based on a lecture given by the Zürich religious socialist pastor Hans Bader.

24. E. Busch, pp. 86 and 91f. F.-W. Marquardt, *Theologie und Sozialismus*, pp. 81ff.

25. K. Barth, *Church Dogmatics* I/i, ET (revised edn) 1975, p. 74.

26. *Church Dogmatics*, II/i, (1940), ET 1957, p. 634.

27. F.-W. Marquardt to the author, 2 April 1978.

28. E.g. Otto Dibelius, as he admitted in 'Karl Barth, a Birthday Tribute', in *The Listener*, 17 May 1956, p. 639.

that informed his *Römerbrief*. This aspect of his thinking was violently revived by the rise of National Socialism and the accession to power of Adolf Hitler. Barth maintained that he knew exactly where to stand in 1933 because he had always remained a man of the left.[29]

The truth is that even in the 1920s Barth never completely abandoned his earlier interests. In 1923 he was organizing university open evenings at which he read devotions by Christoph Blumhardt and Kutter's sermon of 1906 on 'The Social Question'. The following year he was staging ethical discussions on recent political biographies, beginning with those of Tirpitz and Liebknecht.[30] In the 1928 elections he voted socialist.[31] He deplored the survival into the Weimar Republic of what he dubbed 'Wilhelmine Germany', that is, Germany in its nationalist-racial aspect; and in spite of his admiration for the Hanseatic cities, he felt in Danzig in November 1924 what he had already sensed in Lübeck: 'anxiety about the connection of the *old* middle-class society with the church'.[32] As he wrote to Dietrich Bonhoeffer in 1936, basically Barth never doubted that the social gospel was correct; he only wondered whether in practice its materialism was a return to the flesh-pots of Egypt.[33] He came to admit that his reaction against Blumhardt and the Religious Socialists had gone too far. They had first enabled him to perceive the inadequacies of the theology of his first teachers and thus had brought him to a 'better understanding of the theology of the Old Testament, the New Testament and the Reformers'.[34]

Marquardt's assertion that Barth never left the socialist movement is therefore fundamentally correct. He also asserts that Barth never became a revisionist socialist.[35] Two considerations, however, forced Barth into the revisionist camp, so that (as his disciple, Helmut Gollwitzer admitted)[36] he no longer saw reformism and revolution as in total opposition. First, his commitment to the *Soli Deo gloria* of the Reformers made him recognize the possibility of making an idol even of the lowly and humble of this world. 'It may therefore be that those

---

29. *Letzte Zeugnisse*, Zürich 1969, pp. 21f. and 43. Cf. Barth's letter to E. Bethge in *Fragments Grave and Gay*, ed. M. Rumscheidt, tr. E. W. Mosbacher, 1972, pp. 120f.

30. *Revolutionary Theology in the Making*, pp. 143 and 184.

31. K. Barth and E. Thurneysen, *Briefwechsel*, Band II, 1921-1930, Zürich 1974, p. 607.

32. *Revolutionary Theology in the Making*, pp. 193ff.

33. Barth to Bonhoeffer, 14 October 1936, in D. Bonhoeffer, *Gesammelte Schriften*, II.289.

34. *Church Dogmatics*, II/i, pp. 636-638. E. Thurneysen, *Karl Barth. 'Theologie und Sozialismus' in den Briefen seiner Frühzeit*, pp. 13f.

35. 'Sozialismus bei Karl Barth', p. 8.

36. *Reich Gottes und Sozialismus bei Karl Barth*, p. 14.

whom we think to be *lowly* have long ago become in fact exalted', he wrote. 'It may be that their humility has been turned long ago to horrid pride.' He made this judgement in a specifically socialist context. Even the proletariat, he believed, 'may have become blunderingly and coarsely dogmatic'. Because of this the second edition of *Der Römerbrief* could ask whether the solid Western agricultural labourer was not nearer the kingdom of God than the 'Russian Man'.[37] Second, Barth turned to Immanuel Kant as a defence against the apparent immoralism of Marxism.[38] This introduction of Kantian ethics into Marxism was typical of revisionist socialism. It appears at the end of Bernstein's *Evolutionary Socialism*,[39] among French revisionists like Jaurès and Léon Blum,[40] and, in Barth's Germany, in the writings of the men connected with *Die Weltbühne*: Kurt Hiller, Hermann Cohen, Carl von Ossietsky, and Heinrich Mann.[41] It was condemned by Karl Kautsky,[42] and Rosa Luxemburg declared that Kant was a suitable interest for a retired gentleman, but not for an active Social Democrat.[43]

These considerations did not lead Barth to turn against Marxism. On the contrary, he continued to regard historical materialism as 'a necessary weapon and an indispensable apologetic and polemical ally'.[44] He used Marxism to expose the faults of the church, including its theological deficiencies. 'Has it not always stood on the side of the "ruling classes"? At any rate, has it not always been the surest guarantee of the existence and continuance of an order of classes which technically cannot be understood otherwise than as the order of superiority of the economically strong? And has it not with its doctrine of soul and body at least shown a culpable indifference towards the problems of matter, of bodily life, and therefore of contemporary economics? Has it not made a point of teaching the immortality of the soul instead of attesting to society, with its proclamation of the resurrection of the dead, that the judgement and promise of God compass

---

37. *The Epistle to the Romans*, p. 464.

38. Ibid. p. 468.

39. E. Bernstein, *Die Voraussetzungen des Sozialismus und die Aufgaben der Sozialdemokratie*, tr. E. C. Harvey, 1909, pp. 222f.

40. J. Joll, *Three Intellectuals in Politics*, New York 1965, pp. 13f.

41. G. L. Mosse, *Germans and Jews*, 1971, pp. 172ff.

42. 'Kant und der Sozialismus', in *Die Neue Zeit*, Jahrgang 28, 1900, pp. 1–4; *Ethics and the Materialist Conception of History*, pp. 55f.

43. Letter to Kurt Eisner, 22 April 1905, in J. P. Nettl, *Rosa Luxemburg*, 1966, II.136f., n. 2. Eisner's closest friend was Hermann Cohen: G. L. Mosse, p. 180.

44. *Church Dogmatics*, III/ii, ET 1960, p. 387. Cf. 'Marxistische Elemente bei Barth', in F.-W. Marquardt *Theologie und Sozialismus*, pp. 313–333.

the whole man, and therefore cannot be affirmed and believed apart from material and economic reality, or be denied or pushed aside as ideology in contrast to material and economic reality?'[45] 'In the materialism of Marxism', he declared, 'some part of the resurrection of the flesh lies hidden.'[46]

Barth also used Marxism to illuminate the defects of nineteenth-century Christian social action. He believed that the nineteenth-century church had 'needed the competition of Godless Marxist Socialism with its evangelization and diaconate.'[47] He lamented the constricting attention Christians had paid to the individual life of faith, reducing Christianity simply to a private matter.[48] Barth maintained that this limitation could be transcended only by a 'Christian alteration of general relationships achieved in the light of the Gospel'.[49] These are the accents of the Barth who had learned from and lamented the death of Christoph Blumhardt. In 1919 Barth had observed that the sole effect of Blumhardt's rejection by the church authorities had been to confirm his belief that when he spoke of 'God' he meant something other than what the church meant. His rejection had helped him to perceive more clearly than his father that the concerns of the church— its missions and societies, its experiments and successes, its theological erudition—were far less important than the 'worldly' concerns of men's daily lives.[50] So, half a century later, still under the influence of Blumhardt, Barth urged Christians to take the risk of singing 'a political and unwelcome tune', since, he believed, the needs of individuals are 'decisively, though not exclusively, grounded in certain disorders of the whole of human society'. Barth remained convinced that the pre-vailing social, economic, and political conditions set certain limits to what the Christian diaconate could achieve. Blumhardt had been one to show him the possibility of a Christian social criticism that would open up a new place for and give fresh meaning to Christian social action.[51] As late as 1959 he still refused to minimize the work of the men first introduced to him by Thurneysen: 'we must recognize the

45. *Church Dogmatics*, III/ii, pp. 389f.
46. Marquardt, ibid. p. 15.
47. *Church Dogmatics*, IV/iii, 2nd half, ET 1962, p. 893. Cf. Barth's comments on Marx, Engels and Feuerbach in 1920, in the essay 'Ludwig Feuerbach', in *Theology and the Church*, tr. L. P. Smith, 1962, pp. 233f.
48. *Church Dogmatics*, IV/iii, 2nd half, p. 569.
49. Ibid. p. 29.
50. J. M. Robinson, pp. 40 and 42.
51. *Church Dogmatics*, IV/iii, 1st half, ET 1961, p. 29.

continuing impact of the Religious Social movement', he wrote, 'which was stimulated by the preaching of the younger Blumhardt concerning the kingdom of God, which found in Hermann Kutter and Leonhard Ragaz its most important leaders and teachers.'[52]

Immediately after this passage Barth went on to speak of the German resistance to Hitler. Church historians (Marquardt excepted[53]) have tended to see his fight against Hitler as an entirely theological and religious matter, unconnected with political ideas. It is asserted that 'the heart of the German Church struggle lay in the confessing of Jesus Christ. This is the contribution, the decisive contribution, that Barth was enabled to supply from his understanding of the Gospel. Long before 1933 and quite independently of political considerations, he had learned that man's way consists in following God's way.'[54]

Barth's opposition was, however, political enough to lead him to join the SPD again in 1931, precisely because he recognized the dangers of National Socialism. Gollwitzer, who was far more left-wing than Barth at that time, wrote asking why he had joined a 'stinking corpse' (a phrase borrowed from Rosa Luxemburg).[55] Barth replied that he did so as 'a practical political decision', because, in spite of the defects in its *Weltanschauung*, he identified the party as most aware of the requirements of a healthy politics.[56] By the end of 1931 he was leading four other colleagues in defence of Dr Günther Dehn, whose leftist views were causing him trouble with Nazi students in the University of Halle. Ironically, in view of the way Adolf Stöcker's anti-Semitism later endeared him to the Nazis, Dehn had taken up left-wing Christianity partly under Stöcker's intellectual influence (though he carefully distinguished the Stöcker of the Christian Socialist Workers Party from the Stöcker who had allied himself to the Conservatives[57]). Dehn's troubles began when an anti-militarist speech he had delivered in 1928 was published three years later.[58] Barth defended him in the face of the attacks by the Nazi students, demanding publicly that the fight be

52. *Church Dogmatics*, IV/iii, 1st half, p. 29.

53. 'Theologische und politische Motivation Karl Barths im Kirchenkampf', in *Junge Kirche*, May 1973, pp. 283-303.

54. T. H. L. Parker in K. Barth, *The German Church Conflict*, ed. A. M. Allchin, M. E. Marty and T. H. L. Parker, 1964, p. 10.

55. Information from Helmut Gollwitzer in conversation with the author, 30 October 1979.

56. E. Busch, p. 217.

57. 'Adolf Stöcker,' in *Zwischen den Zeiten*, 1924, pp. 26-48.

58. 'Kirche und Völkerversöhnung,' in *Christliche Welt*, 45, 1931, pp. 194-204.

carried to the utmost limits.[59] In May 1932 the SPD itself, recognizing the extremity of the situation in Germany, recommended that left-wing academics who wished to retain their jobs should resign their party membership and remain socialists privately. Paul Tillich resigned, defending himself by arguing that socialism was going through a phase in which the organization of its existence was changing and no longer required a party.[60]

Barth refused to resign. He seems not to have forgiven Tillich's apostasy, describing him in 1940 as 'an incomparably more bloodless and abstract thinker than Kutter or Ragaz'.[61] Tillich later felt able publicly to regret Barth's supposed indifference to social questions and socialism.[62] This, as we shall see, was unfair to Barth. But Barth was equally unfair to Tillich, whose commitment to socialism made him an obvious target for the Nazis. Along with Dehn and Carl Mennicke, Tillich had edited the *Blätter für religiösen Sozialismus* in the 1920s. He perceived and proclaimed that it was impossible to seek 'to reconcile socialism and the Protestant church without changing either'.[63] In 1933 he published *The Socialist Decision*, which rejected both the materialism of Marxism and the hatred preached by National Socialism. The book affirmed a socialism based on faith in man's future and in the human potential. The Nazis banned it and burned as many copies as they could lay hands on.[64] Three years later Tillich wrote that through his contacts with the labour movement and the de-christianized masses he had reached the conclusion that 'The church's attempt to frame an apologetic message without considering the class structure was doomed to failure at the outset. Defending Christianity in this situation required active participation in the class struggle. Only religious socialism could carry the apologetic message to the proletarian masses. Religious socialism, not "inner mission", is the necessary form of Christian activity and apologetic among the working classes.'[65] By this time, however, Tillich had been dismissed as

59. 'Warum führt man den Kampf nicht auf der ganzen Linie?', *Frankfurter Zeitung*, 15 February 1932; E. Busch, p. 218.
60. F.-W. Marquardt, *Theologie und Sozialismus*, p. 48.
61. *Church Dogmatics*, II/i, p. 82.
62. *Auf der Grenze*, Stuttgart 1962, p. 54.
63. *Die religiöse Lage der Gegenwart* (1926), tr. H. R. Niebuhr, *The Religious Situation*, New York 1956, p. 197.
64. *Die sozialistische Entscheidung*, Potsdam 1933, tr. F. Sherman, *The Socialist Decision*, New York 1977.
65. *The Boundaries of Our Being*, Fontana edition 1973, p. 328.

Professor Ordinarius of Philosophy at Frankfurt, one of the first seven university professors to be thrown out by the Nazis. (The other six were Jews.)

It is difficult, therefore, to regard Tillich's resignation from the SPD in 1933 as a manifestation of weakness or cowardice. Others of impeccable socialist credentials took the same course. Ernst Fuchs, who remained committed to Christianity and Marxism before, throughout, and after the Hitler Reich, supposed that the Nazi regime would soon pass (as did many of his Christian socialist colleagues[66]) and became a member of the SPD only later.[67] Their error here serves only to highlight Barth's perspicacity.

Barth's party membership, he said, was a form of praxis, not a theory of religion and society. He proceeded to convey his views on the German political and religious situation to Hitler's minister for Prussian cultural affairs, Bernhard Rust. Rust (who had read Barth's *Römerbrief*) agreed that Barth should retain his chair provided that he carried out no 'cell building' (by which remark, commented Friedrich-Wilhelm Marquardt, Rust revealed that he knew what Barthian 'praxis' involved[68]).

Marquardt maintained that this socialist stance, far more than Barth's refusal to take the full oath of loyalty to Hitler, led to his dismissal by the Nazis from his professorial chair. It is, however, scarcely possible to separate out such matters. What is remarkable is the affinity between Barth's much earlier attack on the opportunism of Friedrich Naumann and the way he castigated those who chose to support or at least go along with Hitler in the thirties. Barth's onslaught even made use of the same biblical text. Observing in 1919 that many had spoken of Naumann as a possible president of the new Germany, Barth had savagely applied to him the promise of the devil tempting Jesus (Matthew 4.9): 'All these things will I give thee, if thou wilt fall down and worship me.'[69] Twenty years later, as an exile from Nazi Germany, Barth put to those who would welcome Hitler the question,

---

66. Aurel von Jächen, for instance, described fascism as a colossus with feet of clay, 'Der Faschismus nackt', in *Zeitschrift für Religion und Sozialismus*, Band III, 1931, Heft 5, p. 354.

67. Helga Krüger Day, 'Christliche Glaube und Gesellschaftliches Handeln: Eine Studie der Entwicklung der Theologie Helmut Gollwitzers', D.Theol. dissertation, Union Theological Seminary, New York, 1973, p. 29. For Ernst Fuchs in the 1920s, see his article 'Von Friedrich Schleiermacher zu Karl Marx', in *Zeitschrift für Religion und Sozialismus*, Band II, 1929, Heft 1, pp. 26-34.

68. 'Sozialismus bei Karl Barth,' p. 2.

69. J. M. Robinson, p. 39.

'May one sacrifice truth to a glorious opportunity?' He maintained that in 1933 the church in Germany had been offered a unique chance to evangelize the masses, on the one condition that Hitler's seizure of power be acknowledged as a divine revelation. The Confessing church had refused this offer; the *Deutsche Christen* had accepted it; and the neutrals had followed the policy of the ostrich. To the last two Barth again applied the words of the devil: 'All this will I give thee, if thou wilt bow down and worship me.'[70]

Barth's stance against Naumann was politically and theologically the same as that against Hitler. He returned to his native Switzerland politically committed. He became a member of the Swiss Soviet Union Society, asserting that he had long distrusted the fear of Bolshevism and communism rampant in his native land. 'A nation with a good conscience, whose social and democratic life is in order', and a church sure of the gospel of Jesus Christ, had nothing to fear, he said, from the communists.[71] Towards the end of the war he served on the Moscow Committee for Free Germany, alongside such Communists as Hans Teubner, Bruno Fuhrmann, Wolfgang Langhoff, and Dr Karl Mode.[72] This was the first time Barth had become personally acquainted with leading Communists, and (as he wrote) 'what was less pleasing—with Communist methods'.[73] His politics thus serve as a link between the *Kirchenkampf* and the opposition to Hitler from trade-union leaders (such as Wilhelm Leuschner and Julius Leber, who, along with Barth's friend Dietrich Bonhoeffer, were executed for their part in the July 1944 plot).

In 1939 Barth wrote, 'Despite the fact that even today many in the Confessing Church will not see and admit it, there could have been no other outcome than that this truth of the freedom of the church, despite the claims of National Socialism, should come to signify not only a "religious decision", not only a decision of church policy, but also and *ipso facto* a political decision.'[74] The man who in 1933 had asserted that 'Church and Theology are the frontiers of the State' could in the Czechoslovak crisis of 1938 readily write to Professor Josef Hromadka in Prague that the Bohemian frontier was to be defended not only for the freedom of Europe, but also for the freedom of the church.[75] This

70. *Trouble and Promise in the Struggle of the Church in Germany*, Oxford 1938, pp. 18 and 6.
71. E. Busch, pp. 322 and 326.
72. F.-W. Marquardt, *Theologie und Sozialismus*, pp. 50ff.
73. Karl Barth, *How I Changed My Mind*, Edinburgh 1969, p. 54.
74. Ibid. p. 46.
75. *Theological Existence Today*, tr. R. B. Hoyle, 1933, p. 84; cf. pp. 16f.: 'It can

open letter was too much even for most leaders of the Confessing Church, who now accused Barth of speaking, wrongly in their eyes, as a politician and not as a theologian.[76] And outside Germany those who had failed to observe Barth's continuing interest in politics also found his letter astonishing, even when they agreed with it politically. Reinhold Niebuhr asserted that it came 'from a man who has spent all his energies to prove that it is impossible to mix relative political judgements with the unconditioned demands of the gospel. Nothing discredits Barth's major theological emphasis more than his complete abandonment of his primary thesis in the hour of crisis.'[77] Barth defended himself both at the time and after the war. His stance was more subtle than his opponents allowed, and it clearly derived from the socialist debates of his earlier years. 'The Christian Community both can and should espouse the cause of this or that branch of social progress or even socialism in the form most helpful at a specific time and in a specific situation', he argued. 'But its decisive word cannot consist only in the proclamation of social progress or Socialism. It can consist only in the proclamation of the revolution of God against "all ungodliness and unrighteousness of man" (Romans 1.18).'[78] In 1939 Barth refused to agree that he had changed his mind; rather, he wrote, 'it seems possible to put the case in a formula: I have been occupied equally with the *deepening* and the *application* of that knowledge which, in its main channels, I had gained before.'[79]

After 1945 Barth upheld his position as a revisionist socialist, in the circumstances of the Cold War. As in the SPD of 1915, so now he preferred to give public support to socialists and to make his criticisms in private. He wrote an open letter to the Reformed Church in Hungary which helped to secure the election of the 'communist-dominated' Pastor Albert Berecsky as bishop. An American professor of theology complained that it was 'hardly fair' that Barth's later letter to Berecsky, criticizing his conduct as a bishop, was not also made public.[80] Barth,

always denote damage to a theologian's existence as such when he becomes a politician or a Church politician.' 'Brief an Professor Hromadka in Prag', in Karl Barth, *Eine Schweizer Stimme, 1938–1945*, Zürich 1945, pp. 58f.

76. J. R. C. Wright, '*Above Parties*'. *The Political Attitudes of the German Protestant Church Leadership 1918–1933*, 1974, p. 168.

77. 'Karl Barth and Democracy', *Radical Religion*, winter 1938, in R. Niebuhr, *Essays in Applied Christianity*, ed. D. B. Robertson, New York 1959, p. 164.

78. *Church Dogmatics*, III/iv (1951), ET 1961, p. 545. Cf. Karl Barth, *The Church and the Political Problems of our Day*, ET 1939, passim.

79. *How I Changed My Mind*, p. 42.

80. A. B. Come, *An Introduction to Barth's Dogmatics for Preachers*, 1963, p. 57.

however, insisted that Marx's critique of the capitalist system and the resultant organization of the proletariat had established 'more than one relatively effective barrier against the exploitation of the weak by the strong'.[81] Even if state socialism in Eastern Europe had not brought such exploitation to an end, it did not in his opinion fall to the churches of the West to point this out as their primary task. 'Christianity in the West', he insisted, 'has its main work cut out to comprehend the disorder in the decisive form still current in the West, to remember and assert the command of God in the face of this form, and keep to the "Left" in opposition to its champions'.[82]

Barth's statements about the political role of the churches of the West are paralleled by what he wrote about Christians living in Communist countries. In 1948 he suggested to the Christians of Hungary 'that a protest against the obvious danger and hurt to the church implicit in the Communist system was not exactly the first and most urgent duty'.[83] He himself had no desire to live under Communist rule. Indeed, he took care in these later years to distinguish Communism from his own kind of socialism. In 1950 he wrote, 'Anyone who does not want Communism—and none of us do—should take Socialism seriously.'[84] Nevertheless, he considered 'anti-Communism as a matter of principle an evil even greater than Communism itself'.[85] As Eduard Thurneysen expressed it, Barth refused to regard 'Communism as the devil or anti-Communism as the delivering angel, preferring instead to believe that God sets up the sign of his coming now in this camp and now in that'.[86] He never regarded Soviet Russia as in any way comparable to Nazi Germany, for he held that Soviet Communism had never set itself up as a new revelation alongside the New Testament. Indeed, he found it 'quite absurd to mention in the same breath the philosophy of Marxism and the "ideology" of the Third Reich, to mention a man of the stature of Joseph Stalin in the same breath as such charlatans as Hitler, Göring, Hess, Goebbels, Himmler, Ribbentrop, Rosenberg, Streicher, etc.' Barth went on to assert, 'What has been tackled in Soviet Russia—albeit with very dirty and bloody hands and in a way that rightly shocks us—is, after all, a constructive idea, the solution of

---

81. *Church Dogmatics*, IV/i, p. 543.
82. Ibid. p. 504.
83. *How I Changed My Mind*, p. 57.
84. E. Busch, p. 382.
85. *How I Changed My Mind*, p. 63.
86. Interview with W.-D. Zimmermann 'Politische Gemeinde,' in *Evangelische Kommentare*, Stuttgart, April 1972, p. 490.

a problem which is a serious and burning problem for us as well, and which we with our clean hands have not yet tackled anything like energetically enough: the social problem.'[87] Faced with the remarkable manner in which Barth passes over the many kulaks deported or exterminated during the period of Russian agricultural collectivization, as well as the liquidation of the Leninist old guard during Stalin's great purge, it is at least impossible to doubt that Barth had remained a man of the left.

Yet his naivety about Stalin ought not to obscure the fact that his commitment was to socialism rather than Communism. As young men neither he nor his friend Thurneysen troubled to study *Capital*. Their socialism was neither Leninist nor specifically Marxist, but essentially pragmatic.[88] Although on May Day 1919 Barth had marched behind the red flag alongside the workers of his parish, he defiantly told critics that far from glorifying the Bolsheviks or the Spartacists, he had warned the workers against them.[89] He was adamant that European socialists should not join the Third International and thus become subservient to Russia. And similarly, in the changed circumstances after 1945, 'his "No" to Soviet imperialism was synonymous with his "Yes" to a "more than Leninist" left-wing socialism.'[90]

This political and theological position enabled him always to make judgements against church and state of whatever complexion. In an open letter to a pastor in East Germany, Barth observed in 1958, 'I disapprove just as much the spirit and the word, the methods and the practices of the system under which you live as I do the powers and dominions that rule over us here in the West.' But, he contended, this did not mean that a pastor or a Christian should equate Communism with the 'roaring lion' of the Bible (I Peter 5.9). In the West, he said, the press, snobbish presumption, public opinion, and systems of private enterprise were all opposed to Christ. In order to understand how to live in a Communist land, men were, he said, to read some words of the prophet Jeremiah to the Hebrews exiled in Babylon:

'Build houses and live in them; plant gardens and eat their produce.
Take wives and have sons and daughters; take wives for your

---

87. 'Die Kirche zwischen Ost und West', in Karl Barth, *Against the Stream, Shorter Post-War Writings, 1948–1951*, 1954, p. 123.
88. As Thurneysen admitted, 'Politische Gemeinde', p. 489.
89. E. Busch, pp. 106f.
90. F.-W. Marquardt, 'Sozialismus bei Karl Barth,' p. 3.

sons and give your daughters in marriage, that they may bear
sons and daughters; multiply there, and do not decrease.

But seek the welfare of the city where I have sent you into exile,
and pray to the LORD on its behalf, for in its welfare you will
find your welfare.

For thus says the LORD of hosts, the God of Israel: Do not let
your prophets and your diviners who are among you deceive
you, and do not listen to the dreams which they dream, for it is a
lie which they are prophesying to you in my name; I did not send
them, says the LORD.' (Jeremiah 29.5-9)

More: they ought to remember that in the West too, their German
brethren had for years been engaged in a strenuous hand-to-hand battle
against the powers and principalities, the spirits and demons of the
land of the 'economic miracle', with its thoughtless participation in the
North Atlantic Treaty Organization, its re-militarization, its military
chaplaincy, its preparation for atomic re-armament, its panic-stricken
fear of Russia, its crusading moods, its old Nazis, and what Barth
called 'all the disagreeable connotations of Bonn and the CDU'.[91]

Barth undoubtedly was engaged in this fight in the West, and he
took care to remind his fellow Christians that he saw this as a spiritual
struggle, as their concern too. Thus, in 1966 he was asked to comment
on the 'confession' of the 'No Other Gospel Movement' issued by its
assembly at Dortmund. Instead of a comment, Barth put a series of
counter-questions to the participants. Were they ready to launch a
movement against attempts to equip West Germany with atomic
weapons? Were they prepared to campaign against the German alliance
with America in Vietnam? Were they ready to counter the increasingly
frequent outbreaks of anti-Semitism in West Germany? Were they
willing to urge a peace treaty between West and East Germany that
would recognize the frontiers of 1945?[92]

Barth's stance, toward both the West and the East, was hardly that
of most contemporary Christians, and he suffered the insults of 'many
small McCarthys'.[93] But it was consistent with his belief in the revo-

91. *Brief an einen Pfarrer in der DDR*, Zürich 1958, ET in Karl Barth and Johannes
Hamel, *How to Serve God in a Marxist Land*, New York 1959, pp. 52 and 78.

92. 'Antwort an die Bekenntnisbewegung "Kein anderes Evangelium"', 16 March
1966, in K. Kupisch *Quellen zur Geschichte des deutschen Protestantismus von 1945 bis
zur Gegenwart*, Siebenstern-Taschenbuch, Hamburg 1971, p. 32. Cf. H. Diem, 'Der
Sozialist in Karl Barth: Kontroverse um einen neuen Versuch, ihn zu verstehen', in
Evangelische Kommentare, May 1972, pp. 292-296.

93. *How I Changed My Mind*, p. 66.

lutionary God of his early days. He claimed to have learned of this God
from religious socialism. At the end of his life he asserted, 'From Kutter
I simply learned to speak the great word "God" seriously, responsibly,
and with a sense of its importance.'[94] Like Blumhardt, he professed an
unquestioning trust in this God. Commenting with Thurneysen on the
text 'I am the good shepherd' (John 10.14), he wrote, 'External pressure
shall not prevail against this "I". The might of men, be it ecclesiastical
or political force, shall not overcome it. But neither will our inner and
most inward problem, the disharmony between what we should be and
what we are, vitiate it.'[95] Barth's socialist commitment depended not
only on believing that this God was revolutionary but also on the
proposition that no earthly revolution could contain God's revolution.
So his *Römerbrief* of 1919 argued in favour of particular strikes, even of
general strikes and of street fighting where necessary; but it offered no
religious justification or glorification of them. And here Barth distanced
himself from Kutter and Ragaz. He was, he wrote, 'Social Democratic,
but not religious socialist'.[96]

On such distinctions Karl Barth based his theology of revolution.
The serious attempt to elaborate a theology of revolution is generally
taken to begin with the conference on 'Church and Society' organized
by the World Council of Churches in 1966. H. Etienne Du Bois,
however, has traced this line of ecumenical thinking as far back as
1948, when Karl Barth made a decisive intervention as the first-ever
meeting of the World Council was seeking to illuminate 'the plan of
God for a disordered world'. Barth contended that the city of God is
not built by human beings. It depends on God, not men. 'We must
remember', he announced, 'that all we can do is proclaim the kingdom
of God and his righteousness. We wait for a city without walls, so that
we exercise our mission as sentinelle in the domain of politics and
Good Samaritan in the social domain. We wait for that city which God
builds—and not for some future city of a liberal or authoritarian kind,
created with a "thank you" for Christ's help.'[97]

Throughout Barth's life he refused to identify the work of God with
the work of men. Barth's God remained the 'Wholly Other' (*der
Ganz-Andere*) who nonetheless 'changes everything' (*der Ganz-*

94. E. Busch, p. 76.
95. *God's Search for Man*, tr. G. W. Richards, Edinburgh 1935, p. 16.
96. *Der Römerbrief*, pp. 390f.
97. H. Etienne Du Bois, 'Karl Barth et la théologie de la révolution', in *Revue de Théologie et de Philosophie*, vol. 4, Lausanne 1970, p. 404.

Ändernde).[98] As his pupil Lochman later argued, to hold together both aspects of God remains essential; for the first without the second would enable men either to accept Christianity as merely a haven of pure spirituality or to reject it as the 'opiate of the people', whereas the second aspect without the first would enable others to clear the decks for revolutionary change undistracted by the demands of religion.[99] Barth preached not a God who gave his blessing to men's political or cultural or even religious achievements, but whose revolutionary demands brought all these achievements under judgement. The role of God's servants, as sentinelle or Samaritan, was consequently to recognize the injustice of the political order and to side with those who (however inadequately) were seeking to change it. So Barth told Thurneysen in 1915 that his socialism stemmed not from 'religion' but from his understanding of the future kingdom of God: to join the SPD was of a piece with what he preached in church. 'Just because I set such emphasis Sunday by Sunday on the last things, it was no longer possible for me personally to remain suspended in the clouds above the present evil world.'[100]

Barth acknowledged that he had learned from Christoph Blumhardt the belief that the future of Jesus Christ brought with it the prospect of an alteration on earth. As he observed in 1919, Blumhardt would remain alive among all those who could grasp what was 'the issue in his life—the victory of the future over the past'.[101] At that very moment the notion of 'the victory of the future over the past' was being explored by one of the most remarkable communists of the twentieth century, Ernst Bloch—a Jew, an atheist, and a man who was later recognized as 'probably the most original contributor to Marxist thought' after the Second World War.[102]

98. For the German pun and its sources in Barth's writings, see J. M. Lochman *Reconciliation and Liberation*, tr. D. Lewis, Belfast 1980, pp. 8 and 161n.1.

99. Ibid. p. 8.

100. E. Thurneysen, *Karl Barth. 'Theologie und Sozialismus' in den Briefen seiner Frühzeit*, pp. 27 and 29. Cf. *Revolutionary Theology in the Making*, p. 28.

101. J. M. Robinson, p. 45.

102. W. L. McBride, *The Philosophy of Marx*, 1977, p. 145.

5

Ernst Bloch:
the Christian Significance
of an Atheist

'Radical theology', wrote John Macquarrie, 'is a theology of revolution, and in that respect contrasts rather sharply with liberal theology,
which is much more a theology of evolution.' On that definition, Karl
Barth was the classically radical theologian. For the early Barth, as
Macquarrie observed, 'theology was identified with eschatology. Bitterly he blamed the theologians who had made God guardian of our
Western culture and our Christian religion. God is rather the judge
who accuses both culture and religion, and demands their radical
transformation in the face of the end.'[1] As we have seen, Barth derived
this aspect of his thinking from Christoph Blumhardt more than
anyone else. Some criticized it. Reinhold Niebuhr alleged that Barth's
theology was 'too "eschatological" and too transcendent to offer any
guidance for the discriminating choices that political responsibility
calls us to'.[2] Barth refused to repent. Indeed, he preferred to provoke
by the certainty of his convictions, and by the knowledge that his
theology cut across current orthodoxy. So, he provocatively wrote,
'One cannot refrain from bestowing on Blumhardt the heretical name
of a chiliast—if that is really a heresy.'[3]

In spite of his critics, Barth's eschatology represented an attempt to
grapple with that essential and immensely difficult element in Holy
Scripture identified by Weiss and Schweitzer and embarrassingly
ignored by many theologians. It illuminated Barth's politics. And it
brought him close, intellectually, to the Marxist theoretician Ernst
Bloch. Bloch's first book, *The Spirit of Utopia*, which appeared in

1. 'Liberal and Radical Theologies: An Historical Comparison', in *The Modern
Churchman*, N.S., vol. 15, no. 4, July 1972, pp. 215 and 219.
2. *Essays in Applied Christianity*, p. 184.
3. *Protestant Theology in the Nineteenth Century*, p. 652.

1918, concerned itself precisely with this biblical inheritance.[4] Bloch would later observe, with pardonable sarcasm, 'Even Christians, either with amazement or with a sleeping conscience, have spotted that all the Utopian aspirations of the great movements of human liberation derive from the Exodus and the messianic parts of the Bible.'[5]

What surprised many Christians was to find a Marxist acknowledging this fact. Yet such quasi-religious elements undoubtedly formed part of the communist tradition, as Kautsky's tireless historical researches demonstrated. Nor were they confined to the remote past. Bloch could be placed (by Jürgen Moltmann, for example), not only in the tradition of such left-wing Jewish messianists as Sabbortai Zwi, Moses Hess, Ernst Toller, and Leon Trotsky, but also alongside the chiliastic elements found in the Russian revolution.[6] Marxist phraseology reflected these elements to a remarkable degree. Karl Löwith, indeed, once described Marxism as 'the story of salvation in the language of economics'.[7] Sometimes the language of salvation took over. So the Hungarian communist Georg Lukács asked, after the death of Lenin, 'Must Russia too pass through the capitalist hell before finding salvation in socialism?' Lenin, said Lukács, had seen the final struggle between the bourgeoisie and the proletariat as *the onset ... of human salvation*.[8] The messianic and chiliastic tradition in Soviet Russia was virtually eliminated by Stalin; but such elements formed part of Bloch's environment in the early decades of the twentieth century. (Between 1912 and 1914 he and Lukács had worked together intensely as students at Heidelberg.)[9] Bloch re-instated the messianic, utopian elements in Marxism, making them central to his own philosophy. In so doing he was to play a major role in the Christian–Marxist dialogue of the twentieth century.

Bloch was born of Jewish middle-class parents in Ludwigshafen in

---

4. *Geist der Utopie*, Leipzig 1918, especially the concluding section: 'Gestalten der universalen Selbstbewegung oder Eschatologie,' pp. 436–445.

5. E Bloch, *Das Prinzip Hoffnung*, Frankfurt am Main 1959, I. 17.

6. J. Moltmann, *Im Gespräch mit Ernst Bloch. Eine theologische Wegbegleitung*, Munich 1976, pp. 15, 17n, and 30, citing E. Sarkisyanz, *Russland und der Messianismus des Orients*, Tübingen 1955, and *Russlands Chiliasmus. Seine Verbürglichung und Selbstauflösung*, Tübingen 1955.

7. Quoted, I, Fetscher 'Germany: Marxismus-Studien', in *Revisionism. Essays on the History of Marxist Ideas*, ed. L. Labedz, 1962, p. 349, n. 22.

8. G. Lukács, *Lenin, a Study on the Unity of His Thought* (1924), tr. N. Jacobs, 1972, pp. 15 and 1of.

9. E. Bloch, G. Lukács, B. Brecht, W. Benjamin, and T.-W. Adorno, *Aesthetics and Politics*, London 1977, p. 9.

1885. His father was a railway official. By the time he was twenty he had rejected enough of his class background and his faith to join first the German Social Democrats and then the Communist Party. He studied philosophy at Berlin under Georg Simmel, before joining Lukács and Karl Jaspers as a member of the circle around Max Weber in Heidelberg. As a pacifist, he spent the last year of the First World War in Switzerland, returning to Germany in 1920.[10]

He soon made a name for himself among those who were rethinking the nature of historical materialism in Germany at that time; but there was obviously no room for such a man in Hitler's Germany, and Bloch emigrated in 1933. By way of Zürich, Paris, Vienna, and Prague, he and his wife came to the United States, where he wrote—but did not publish—his life's major work, *Das Prinzip Hoffnung*. At the end of the Second World War he accepted the chair of philosophy at Leipzig in East Germany, where, however, his work met with increasing criticism.

In the 1950s, in a series of packed lectures at Leipzig, Bloch argued that Marxism, correctly understood, was a method of analysis requiring perpetual renewal. It could not be reconciled with the dictatorship of the proletariat, with neglect of democracy, freedom, and respect for the law. He consistently attacked the dogmatism and petrifaction of Marxist studies in East Germany in general. Such outspokenness was not acceptable to the regime headed by Walter Ulbricht. At the October 1957 Plenum of the Politbüro of the Communist Party Ulbricht engineered attacks on Kurt Hager (minister in charge of science and education), accusing him *inter alia* of being too lenient on Bloch.[11] Bloch's intellectual and political integrity was again proving costly. As he had written nearly thirty years earlier about the possibility of perversion in communism itself, 'In the citizen of the French revolution was hidden the bourgeois. God help us—we cannot tell what may be hidden in the comrade.'[12] His holiday in Bavaria in 1961 coincided with the building of the Berlin wall. Instead of returning to East Germany, Bloch accepted the chair of philosophy at Tübingen in the West. Thus began the period of his greatest influence, not least upon the Christian-Marxist dialogue. A decade later another Marxist exile from Eastern

10. Biographical details (unless otherwise stated) from E. Bloch, *Freiheit und Ordnung*, hrsg von E. Grassi, Munich 1969, p. 242, and E. Bloch, *Karl Marx*, tr. L. Tosti, Bologna 1972, pp. 25-29. See also 'Der greise Marxist und der Wanderprediger der Apo', in *Stern*, 18 October 1979, pp. 52-59.

11. J. Steele, *Socialism with a German Face*, pp. 109 and 111.

12. E. Bloch, *Spuren*, Frankfurt am Main 1959, p. 32.

Europe described him as certainly the most interesting among living Marxists. He added, 'Bloch's time has not yet come: his role in philosophy will go on growing.'[13]

The Latin American theologian Gustavo Guttiérez criticized some of the West German Christians who took up Bloch's principle of hope for being 'unable to penetrate the situation of dependence, injustice, and exploitation in which most of mankind finds itself', since their reflections had been developed 'far from the revolutionary ferment of the Third World'.[14] Bloch himself was immune to such a taunt. (Indeed, he himself greatly influenced and impressed Latin American Christians, including Guttiérez himself.[15]) His life was not that of a sheltered philosopher. *Das Prinzip Hoffnung*, written in exile, finished and edited in East Germany, finally published in West Germany, is not only (as Jürgen Habermas observed) 'a mirror in its outward history of Bloch's inner development—a spiritual odyssey in the spirit of the Exodus',[16] but also a response to the enormous insecurities of living in Europe in the twentieth century.

After his 'defection' to the West, Bloch remained allied to the spirit of Rosa Luxemburg's attack on undemocratic socialism: elitism, he maintained, cannot establish social justice.[17] But in the West too he remained a convinced Marxist, though amongst the varieties of twentieth-century Marxism this bald description is not adequate. After the First World War Bloch did not join the Communist Party in Germany, preferring to remain 'a heterodox sympathizer rather than an enlisted militant'.[18] Observers continued to question his Marxist credentials, and not only in East Germany: after his return to the West, he was repeatedly asked by those of the left and the right whether he was a Marxist, to which he would reply: 'I have built Marxism into my system.'[19] At other times he would speak of his thought as contri-

13. L. Kolakowski, in *The Listener*, 4 May 1972, p. 585. For Kolakowski's own place in Marxism at that time see H. Skolimowski 'Analytical-Linguistic Marxism in Poland', in *Journal of the History of Ideas*, vol. 26, 1965, pp. 242–245.

14. G. Guttiérez, *A Theology of Liberation*, 1974, p. 224.

15. Ibid. esp. pp. 216ff. Cf. J. M. Miranda *Marxism and the Bible*, esp. 'Faith and Dialectics', pp. 201–282.

16. J. Habermas, 'Ein marxistischer Schelling,' p. 1078.

17. E. Bloch, *Naturrecht und menschliche Würde*, Frankfurt am Main 1961, p. 13. See also 'Rosa Luxemburg, Lenin und die Lehren, oder Marxismus als Moral' (1974), in *Gespräche mit Ernst Bloch*, hrsg von. R. Traub and H. Wieser, Frankfurt am Main 1975, pp. 208–220.

18. *Aesthetics and Politics*, p. 10.

19. J. Moltmann, *Im Gespräch mit Ernst Bloch*, p. 66.

buting to 'a new philosophy, inaugurated by Marx'.[20] According to one Western admirer, he represented 'an independent and humanistic Marxism that had shaken off the chains of party dogma and exposed the vital parts of this tradition in a new way'.[21] Felix Flückiger, by contrast, dismissed him (along with Herbert Marcuse, Theodor W. Adorno, and Bertrand Russell) as representing the out-dated atheism considered *avant garde* in the years before the First World War.[22] Leaving aside the odd inclusion of Bertrand Russell, this assessment had the one merit of placing Bloch in the context of the Frankfurt Institute of Social Research. Although Bloch was never a formal member of the Institute, in re-assessing Marxist dynamics, he, Adorno and Marcuse all emphasized the prophetic elements in Marx's beliefs about the future. As Paul Tillich (one of the very few Christians involved in the Institute in the 1930s) was to observe, Marxism had apparently retained a doctrine of Providence: 'Providence', he wrote, 'still triumphs for both Hegel and Marx. For Hegel it triumphs in his own era; for Marx it will triumph in an indefinite future.'[23] Bloch's special contribution to this re-assessment of Marxism, said Flückiger,[24] was to look again at the prophetic and eschatological witness of the Bible.

Bloch's first major work was a study not of the Bible but of Thomas Münzer, the revolutionary Anabaptist opponent of Martin Luther. Münzer was regarded as a precursor of communism by both Engels[25] and Kautsky. The latter's book on More's *Utopia* begins, 'Two great figures loom large on the threshold of Socialism: Thomas More and Thomas Münzer.'[26] When Bloch came to take up the subject, Münzer (according to Kautsky) was still regarded by the German working classes as 'one of the most brilliant embodiments of rebellious heretical communism'. Kautsky, however, considered him greatly over-rated.[27]

20. Ibid. p. 7.

21. R. Ruether, *The Radical Kingdom*, New York 1970, p. 203.

22. F. Flückiger, *Theologie der Geschichte. Die biblische Rede von Gott und die neuere Geschichtstheologie*, Wuppertal 1970, p. 155.

23. P. Tillich, *Systematic Theology*, 1953, I.295.

24. Ibid. pp. 175f.

25. *Der deutsche Bauernkrieg*, which first appeared in *Die Neue Rheinische Zeitung*, nos. 5 and 6, Hamburg 1850. A translation of chapter 2, which contains Engels's assessment of Münzer, appears in Marx and Engels *On Religion*, pp. 96–117.

26. K. Kautsky, *Thomas More and His Utopia*, p. 1. On More's *Utopia* and its interpreters see the recent study F. E. and F. P. Manuel, *Utopian Thought in the Western World*, 1979, pp. 117–152.

27. *Die Geschichte des Sozialismus in Einzeldarstellungen*, by E. Bernstein and others; vol. 1, part I, K. Kautsky, *Die Vorläufer des Neueren Sozialismus*, Stuttgart 1895, p. 312. Chapter 4 is on the German Reformation and Münzer.

Nothing reveals the limitations of Kautsky's mind more than a comparison of his account of Münzer with Bloch's. Kautsky researched his subject with customary thoroughness.[28] But his central concern was to demonstrate the inadequacy of Münzer's egalitarian communism compared to the 'higher order' of communism of Kautsky himself. Bloch's attitude to Münzer was totally different. Karl Mannheim, who knew him well in the 1920s, wrote that the atheist philosopher possessed an 'inner affinity' with the sixteenth-century reformer.[29] In 1921 Bloch's *Thomas Münzer als Theologe der Revolution* described Münzer as 'the rebel in Christ' who preached the 'freedom of the kingdom of God' and the state as the devil.[30] He claimed that in Münzer the union of socio-economic revolution with religion indicated a way of deepening the crudely economic outlook of straight historical materialism[31]— an opinion hotly contested by Lukács, who found this too much of a deviation from Marxist orthodoxy.[32]

The book lifted the Christian–Marxist dialogue in Germany to a new plane. Forty years later Bloch wrote that it had been a 'coda' to the 'spirit of Utopia' that had appeared in Germany in 1919 and was to re-appear in 1923. He added: 'Its revolutionary romantic poetry found delineation and definition in my book *Das Prinzip Hoffnung*.'[33] The truth of this reminiscence is confirmed by a letter of 1919 in which

28. Kautsky's notebooks show that he went back to such sixteenth-century sources as *Protestation odder Empietung Tome Müntzers*, Altstedt 1524, and *Ordnung und Berechnung des Teutschenampts zu Alstadt*, Alddorf 1523. He also made folio and octavo notes on Sebastian Franck's *Chronica*, Strassburg 1531. He made thirty-five pages of notes on J. R. Leidmann *Thomas Münzer, seine Biographie*, Leipzig 1842, and thirty-eight on G. T. Strobel *Leben, Schriften und Lehren Thomas Münzer*, Alddorf 1795, as well as consulting an anonymous *Histoire des Anabaptistes*, Amsterdam 1702. Kautsky papers B–12 Dicke Kladde exzerpte; and I Kladde Postausgang 1915–1917.

29. *Ideology and Utopia* (1929), London 1936, p. 190. During the Weimar Republic Mannheim belonged to a discussion group that included Tillich, Adorno, and Max Horkheimer, though he was never a member of the Frankfurt Institute and in some ways decisively rejected its views.

30. *Thomas Münzer als Theologe der Revolution* (1921), Berlin 1960, p. 13.

31. Ibid. pp. 73ff.

32. G. Lukács, *History and Class Consciousness, Studies in Marxist Dialectics*, tr. R. Livingstone, 1971, p. 193. For Bloch's early dialogue with Lukács, see his 'Aktualität und Utopie zu Lukács Philosophie des Marxismus', in *Der neue Merkur*, vii, 1924, pp. 457–477, and 'Zur Rettung von Georg Lukács', in *Die weissen Blätter*, Zürich 1919, no. 12, p. 529.

33. Nachbemerkung to the 1960 edition of *Thomas Münzer als Theologe der Revolution*, p. 184; cf. Bloch's 'Politische Programme und Utopien', in *Archiv für Sozialwissenschaft und Sozialpolitik*, vol. 46, 1919, pp. 140–162. Bloch has continued to influence Münzer studies; see for example J. Werner, 'Thomas Münzers Regenbogenfahne', in *Theologische Zeitschrift*, Basle, Jan./Feb., 1975, p. 37.

Walter Benjamin observed that Bloch was already busy 'on his great work: a *system of theoretical messianism*'.[34] Undoubtedly, 1919 was a remarkable year in Germany, a year of unfulfilled hopes and fears of revolution. As a prelude to that *annus mirabilis*, Bloch's *Geist der Utopie* had appeared in 1918. When he began to write, 'utopia' was still a dirty word among Marxists and non-Marxists alike. Even in Thomas More's usage, the word, signifying both 'nowhere' and 'the ideal place', is ambiguous. By the end of the nineteenth century its usage was almost always pejorative. Engels's *Anti-Dühring* had attacked utopian socialists as unprincipled and dangerous. Robert von Pöhlmann's once famous *Geschichte des antiken Kommunismus und Sozialismus* (1893) had used massive learning to mock the utopian dreams of the early Christians (and many others). This pejorative tradition inhibited those who might have been more sympathetic to the utopian dreams of human history. Erich Fromm, for example, remained sensitive to and moved by the Jewish messianic traditions he had imbibed as a child and adolescent in Frankfurt. The promise of the 'end of days' in the Hebrew prophets fascinated him. 'The vision of universal peace and harmony between nations touched me deeply', he was to recall, 'when I was twelve and thirteen years old.'[35] Inevitably, he recognized this promise as it re-appeared among the first Christians. 'The content of the primitive Christian message was not an economic nor a social reform programme', he wrote, 'but the blessed promise of a not distant future in which poor would be rich, the hungry would be satisfied, and the oppressed would attain authority.'[36] But Fromm held that this promise was a fantasy, with no practical consequences in the real world. Kautsky's *Foundations of Christianity* entirely neglected the eschatology of the early church. But his encyclopaedic learning had brought him into contact with the utopian-chiliastic tradition in Christianity, quite apart from its manifestation in Thomas More. Extensive notes on the Bohemiam Brethren and on chiliasm in general appear in his private papers.[37] In 1911 his American comrade A. M. Simons wrote, 'In translating your "Weg zur Macht" I

---

34. Quoted, J. Moltmann, *Im Gespräch mit Ernst Bloch*, p. 12.

35. *Beyond the Chains of Illusion*, p. 5.

36. *The Dogma of Christ*, p. 28.

37. For instance, he made notes on an anonymous *Kritische Geschichte des Chiliasmus*, Frankfurt and Leipzig 1781-1783, as well as fourteen pages of notes on A. Gindely, *Geschichte der böhmischen Brüder*, Prag 1857: Kautsky papers B-1 Kladde Postausgang 1915-1917. Chapter 3 of *Die Vorläufer des Neueren Sozialismus* is about the Bohemian Brethren.

was struck with the statement to the effect that we needed something of the nature of a "new utopianism" and a fearlessness of prophecy.'[38] Kautsky went so far as to acknowledge the importance of messianic hopes in keeping alive the social teachings of the early Christians: 'Only through faith in the *Messiah* and in the *Resurrection* could the communistic organization maintain and extend itself in the Roman Empire as a secret body. But when united, these two factors—communism and faith in the Messiah—became irresistible.' But because Kautsky considered these hopes to be utopian and 'irrational', he never allowed the possibility that they could affect the real world.[39]

Bloch began the movement to rehabilitate utopia. In his judgement, utopian thought always acted as a counter to the prevailing ideology. And it refused to let men and women rest on their partial achievements. 'The function of utopia', Bloch wrote, 'is to rescue human culture from the idleness of mere contemplation on summits that have already been attained; it opens up a view of the true content of human hope, undissembled by ideology.'[40] Here again he and Lukács came into angry disagreement, crystallized in their dispute over Expressionism. Bloch argued that Lukács was in error to accuse Expressionism of failure because it did not objectively reflect the 'real'. Lukács, he believed, had reached the position of maintaining that 'there can be no such thing as an avant-garde within late-capitalist society; anticipatory movements within the superstructure are disqualified from possessing any truth.'[41] Such an analysis of 'reality' as Lukács favoured would have excluded utopian dreams and the messianic hopes in Christianity. In rejecting Lukács, Bloch was making room for a step forward in the Christian–Marxist dialogue.

Ten years after the appearance of Bloch's *Geist der Utopie*, Karl Mannheim described utopias (in a famous definition) as those 'orientations transcending reality' which, 'when they pass over into conduct, tend to shatter, either partially or wholly, the order prevailing at the time'.[42] Sociologists continued to debate whether such ideals had any practical effect on social or political life. Bloch entertained no such

38. Kautsky papers D 666, A. M. Simons to Kautsky, 6 March 1911.

39. *The Foundations of Christianity*, pp. 380f. Cf. his polemic against E. Belfort Bax: 'Utopischer und materialistischer Marxismus', in *Die Neue Zeit*, Jahrgang 15, 1897, pp. 713–727.

40. *Das Prinzip Hoffnung*, I.174.

41. *Aesthetics and Politics*, p. 20. Cf. T. Perlini, 'Metafisica e utopia in Bloch', in *Aut Aut*, vol. 125, Sept.–Oct. 1971, pp. 61–82.

42. *Ideology and Utopia*, p. 173.

doubts; historical novelties, he maintained, are always preceded by some dream or promise; our human dreams are not solely a longing for the past but are also a longing for the future, a curiosity about what is to come.[43] As a communist he was able to find some support for this view in the statement of the young Marx that the world is long possessed by the dream of a new state of affairs, which it needs only to take into its consciousness in order truly to possess it.[44]

'To be a human being', he claimed, 'means in effect to possess a utopia.'[45] Bloch's massive five-part study, *Das Prinzip Hoffnung*, is his attempt to expound the significance of virtually all the dreams of humanity. 'What arouses his interest', wrote Jürgen Habermas, 'is not the State but fiction about the State, not the norms of the law which are in force, but theories of justice.... Within the ideological shell Bloch discovers the Utopian core, within the yet false consciousness the true consciousness.'[46] The tragedies of Aeschylus, René Clair's films, Eden and Eldorado, Goethe, Jesus, Brecht, Augustine, Marx, Mozart, and Wagner contribute to the many human dreams Bloch examined with immense learning and sympathy. The conclusion of his work is, *'The real Genesis is not at the beginning but at the end.'*[47]

Such a massive work could not have been written without guiding principles. Dr Otto Morf has pointed out that a fulcrum, so to speak, of *Das Prinzip Hoffnung*, is Bloch's assertion that, 'Ever since Marx, the abstract character of utopias has been overcome.'[48] In consequence, the hidden future to which all utopias point is socialism, a *'socialism absconditus'*, as Remo Bodei put it, 'which has not yet revealed its true face'.[49] The history of utopias, Bloch averred, shows that socialism is as old as the occident. 'Zionism must issue into socialism', he asserted, 'or it issues into nothing at all.' 'Capitalist peace is a paradox, since it derives more from fear ...; socialist peace is a tautology.'[50] And so on.

43. *Das Prinzip Hoffnung*, I.87f. Cf. 'Utopische Funktion in Materialismus', in *Gespräche mit Ernst Bloch*, pp. 269–291.

44. This point is made by Walter Markov, 'Die Utopie des Citoyen', in *Ernst Bloch zum 70. Geburtstag*, hrsg von R. O. Grupp, Berlin 1955, p. 230.

45. *Philosophische Grundfragen*, Frankfurt am Main 1961, I.36.

46. J. Habermas, *Theory and Practice*, tr. J. Viertel, 1974, pp. 240 and 239.

47. *Das Prinzip Hoffnung*, III.1628.

48. O. Morf, 'Ernst Bloch und die Utopie', in *Ernst Bloch zum 70. Geburtstag*, p. 260, quoting *Das Prinzip Hoffnung*, II.680.

49. Introduction to E. Bloch, *Karl Marx*, tr. L. Tosti, p. 8.

50. *Das Prinzip Hoffnung*, II.680, 713, and 1053. N.B. Bloch gave up his public criticisms of the State of Israel after the Arab–Israeli war of 1967: A. Neher 'Job dans l'oeuvre d'Ernst Bloch,' in *Utopie-marxisme selon Ernst Bloch*, ed. G. Raulet, Paris 1976, p. 234.

Bloch's socialism, however, was by no means crudely materialistic and remained essentially democratic: 'There is no democracy without socialism, and no socialism without democracy.'[51] He argued that there could be no dignity or freedom in a world or a society 'structured from the top downwards'.[52]

Inevitably *Das Prinzip Hoffnung* included re-assessments of religious utopias. Jürgen Habermas wrote that Bloch was carrying out Marx's fourth thesis on Feuerbach. 'His work consists in resolving the religious world back into its worldly basis.'[53] Bloch's task encompassed an extraordinarily diverse religious world. Habermas described him as a Marxist Schelling, presumably because Schelling managed to bring into apparent coherence a pantheistic Christian theosophy that embraced Jacob Böhme, oriental mysticism, animal magnetism, Swabian pietism, and the visions of Oetinger. Such an ability and such interests might seem far removed from traditional Marxism and difficult to resolve back into a worldly base. But as Habermas observed, the young Marx himself, in a polemic against the mechanistic materialism of seventeenth-century England and eighteenth-century France, could quote with approval an apparently far-fetched expression of Böhme's about 'the *agony* of matter.'[54]

Hostile critics accused Bloch of providing an easy access for left-wing Christians who wanted a woolly encounter with Marxism. George Lichtheim described his work as 'a species of gnosticism or pantheism', appealing 'only to that section of the New Left which is eternally in search of a Weltanschauung to bolster its instinctive rejection of the modern world'.[55] (Lichtheim also lapsed into a disgraceful racist and political smear when he described this as 'a very Germanic trait ... at one time suggestive of fascist tendencies'.[56]) In truth, Bloch's creative work greatly suffered because of his uncompromising opposition to German fascism. Between 1938 and 1949 he lived in America, entirely supported by his wife, speaking no English, and unable to

---

51. *Naturrecht und menschliche Würde*, p. 15.

52. *Recht, Moral, Staat*, Frankfurt am Main 1971, p. 35.

53. *Theory and Practice*, p. 139.

54. 'Ein marxistischer Schelling', p. 1083, n.1., quoting 'The Holy Family', in *Die Frühschriften*, hrsg von S. Landshut and J. Mayer, Stuttgart 1932, p. 330.

55. G. Lichtheim, *From Marx to Hegel*, 1971, pp. 46 n.26 and 211.

56. Ibid. p. 211. Lichtheim had made the same smear, anonymously, a year before: 'Dialectical Methodology', in *Times Literary Supplement*, 12 March 1970, p. 271. Bloch's alleged gnosticism there appears as 'romantic mysticism'.

obtain a teaching post.[57] With half-a-dozen major books to his credit, he published nothing for eight years.

The fact is that Bloch contributed to a renewal of Christian theology quite apart from any Western desire for a dialogue with Marxism. Wolfhart Pannenberg (professor of systematic theology at Munich) wrote that Christianity would one day have to thank Bloch's philosophy of hope for giving it 'the courage to recover in the full sense its central category of eschatology'.[58] Bloch's chief influence on Christian theology was through the writings of his fellow professor at Tübingen, the theologian Jürgen Moltmann. Moltmann made his debt to Bloch absolutely clear: it is hard to imagine, he said, a more useful philosophy than that of *Das Prinzip Hoffnung* for enabling Christians to renew and elaborate their own philosophy of hope.[59] Bloch he characterized as 'a Marxist with a Bible in his hand, a Marxist who has hoped for greater things than socialism is able to fabricate'.[60] The very first definition of God advanced in Moltmann's influential *Theology of Hope* (in support of his Barthian contention that 'from first to last, and not merely in the epilogue, Christianity is eschatology, is hope') was taken from Bloch: God has 'future as his essential nature'.[61] Future became for Moltmann a new paradigm of divine transcendence.[62] The transcendent God, thus understood, could no longer be seen as cut off from earthly concerns; in Moltmann's thinking the future has power over men now because it will finally come; and although its completion is *God's* ultimate kingdom, this kingdom is represented in every relative human hope. Moltmann derived from Bloch the notion of 'creative expectation', defined (by Moltmann) as 'hope which sets about criticizing and transforming the present because it is open towards the universal future of the kingdom'. And he endorsed Bloch's observation that although the Jews were quite as much this-worldly as the Greeks, their life was incomparably more vigorously determined by future goals.[63]

57. F. Gillies, 'The Eschatological Structures of Marxism', p. 89. For some of Bloch's experiences as an exile see W. Mittenzwei, *Exil in der Schweiz*, Leipzig 1978, esp. pp. 144–147.

58. W. Pannenberg, *Basic Questions in Theology*, 1971, II.237f.

59. J. Moltmann, 'Die Kategorie *Novum* in der christlichen Theologie', in *Ernst Bloch zu ehren*, hrsg von S. Unseld, Frankfurt am Main 1965, p. 242.

60. J. Moltmann, *Religion, Revolution and the Future*, New York 1969, p. 15.

61. *Theology of Hope*, tr. J. W. Leitch, 1967, p. 16.

62. J. Moltmann, 'Die Zukunft als neues Paradigma der Transzendenz', in *Internationale Dialog Zeitschrift*, II/i, 1969, pp. 2–13.

63. *Theology of Hope*, pp. 335 and 208.

In *The Crucified God* Moltmann quoted Bloch's assertion that 'The drive towards immortality did not come from the old wish for a long life, for well being on earth now extended into the transcendent. It came rather from Job and the prophets, from the thirst after right-eousness.' (Moltmann envisaged this thirst as the expectation of *divine* righteousness.)[64] So, he wrote elsewhere, 'The social overthrowing of unjust relationships is the immanent reverse-side of the transcendent hope of resurrection. Only because the church limited itself to the happiness of souls in the heavenly beyond, and thus became docetic, did the active hope of a bodily resurrection emigrate out of the church and penetrate social utopias. In these utopias—as Ernst Bloch says, in striking and unmistakable harmony with the Bible—relationships were represented in which travail and burdens cease.'[65]

Yet Bloch's influence on contemporary theologians and his life-long interest in the manifestations of religion did not obscure his uncom-promising atheism. This essential ingredient of his stance as a Marxist remained even when he was pondering the notion of God.[66] As Haber-mas put it, in Bloch's thought, 'God is dead, but his locus has survived him. The place in which mankind has hitherto imagined God and the gods, after the decay of these hypotheses, remains a hollow space, whose "measurements in depth", i.e. atheism finally understood, reveal the blueprint of a future kingdom of freedom.'[67] 'God' finally becomes 'the kingdom of God'; and in this kingdom there is no room for God.[68] Bloch became especially sensitive to the atheistic elements in the Chris-tian tradition itself—its abhorrence of idol worship, its promise that men shall be as gods—and in 1968 he published an exhaustive study of atheism in Christianity (with the subtitle, 'studies in the religion of the Exodus and the kingdom'). One of the epigraphs in this book became famous: 'Only an atheist can be a good Christian; only a Christian can be a good atheist.'[69] Bloch, according to Adorno, had already presented in almost mystical fashion the paradoxical unity of theology and atheism.[70] Now he envisaged the possibility of a new dialogue between

64. *The Crucified God*, tr. R. A. Wilson and J. Bowden, 1974, pp. 198 n. 27 and 174. The quotation is from *Das Prinzip Hoffnung*, II.1324.

65. J. Moltmann, 'Existenzgeschichte und Weltgeschichte', in *Evangelische Kommen-tare*, vol. 1, January 1968, p. 19.

66. Cf. Theodor Heim, 'Blochs Atheismus', in *Ernst Bloch zu ehren*, pp. 157-179.

67. J. Habermas, p. 313.

68. *Das Prinzip Hoffnung*, III.1413.

69. *Atheismus im Christentum*, Frankfurt am Main 1968, p. 15.

70. T.-W. Adorno, *Noten zur Literatur*, Frankfurt am Main 1961, II.142.

'the believer freed from ideology and the unbeliever freed from taboo'.[71] Without doing exorbitant violence to the complexity of the Scriptures, Bloch saw the essential aim of the Bible as social revolution; in *Atheism in Christianity* he did the Bible more violence by his frequent assumptions that God appears there chiefly as either a redundant survival or a later interpolation.

The finest section of *Atheism in Christianity* is Bloch's exposition of the book of Job (a section that he had earlier shortened, made into a whole and broadcast).[72] *Das Prinzip Hoffnung* contained only a hand-ful of references to Job, though the correspondences between these and Bloch's later analysis show that in 1968 he was still exploring Job as part of the utopian dreams of humanity.[73] (And, since all utopias prefigure socialism, he carefully pointed out the anti-capitalist elements in Job!)[74]

Bloch expounded Job with characteristically wide-ranging learning: Alexander von Humboldt, Spinoza, Rudolf Otto, Oswald Spengler, Jean Paul, as as well as the Talmud and the Koran, are all enlisted. At a severely technical level he revealed some limitations as a biblical theologian, relying on Duhm's commentary and on Bertholet's *Theology of the Old Testament*, published in 1897 and 1911 respectively. (Bloch also referred once to von Rad's *Theology of the Old Testament*.[75]) The excitement of his analysis springs, however, not from his learning but from his personal response to the book of Job itself.[76]

Bloch decisively rejected the Christian tradition of Job as the man who suffers patiently because in the end he acknowledges the justice of God. The arguments of Job's three 'comforters' are dismissed as 'in-effective clichés'. Job not only doubts, he goes so far as to deny that God is just.[77] The injustice in the universe is indefensible if there is a good God. Job's stance therefore foreshadows that of the French enlightenment: the simplest solution to the problem of theodicy is *que*

71. *Atheismus im Christentum*, p. 12.

72. This version is in *Das dein Ohr auf Weisheit achte*, hrsg von K. H. Schröter, Berlin 1966, pp. 46-69.

73. *Das Prinzip Hoffnung*, I.245 and III.1456, and *Atheismus im Christentum*, pp. 153 and 157, quoted von Humboldt on Job 37 and Bertholet on Job 19.25-27.

74. *Atheismus im Christentum*, p. 150 (for the anti-capitalism of the prophets too).

75. Ibid. pp. 158, and 156, and 157. D. Gerbracht, 'Aufbruch zu sittlichen Atheismus-Die Hiob-Deutung Ernst Blochs', in *Evangelische Theologie*, vol. 3, 1975, pp. 223-227, examines Bloch's Job in the light of other biblical theologians.

76. According to A. Neher, pp. 233-238, Bloch's understanding of Job was much influenced by Margarete Susman.

77. *Atheismus im Christentum*, pp. 160, 150, and 148.

dieu n'éxiste pas. 'At the end of the day the whole theophany of the book of Job can be understood as moral atheism', Bloch wrote; 'if we add existential atheism, the whole problem of theodicy looks like a non-apologetic without a leg to stand on.'[78] Yet Job—and Bloch— recognize that this is not enough. With the disappearance of God, Job's problems are not settled. Death remains. A universe without feeling remains. Man is still oppressed rather than free. Atheism seems to make optimism about history more stupid than ever.[79] Because of this, the simplest solution to the problem of theodicy is not *que dieu n'éxiste pas*. 'The simplest solution is that in the world can always be found another Exodus leading out of the present situation, and a hope which involves rebellion.' Thus, said Bloch, into his criticism of the existing world Job put the presentiment of a better one.[80]

'With the book of Job begins above all the discovery of utopian possibilities in the religious sphere', Bloch wrote. Job exactly illustrates his contention that atheism neither negates religious insights nor destroys hope. Job, he concluded, remains a pious man who no longer believes in anything, 'save in the Exodus, and that the last word has not been spoken'. (Among further words Bloch here envisaged those of the Son of Man himself—whom he saw as the complete antithesis of an overweening Lord and Master.[81]) *Das Prinzip Hoffnung* made even clearer the importance of Job's religious background. There Bloch emphasized that Job's attack on Jahwe possessed a quite different edge from that of a rebellion against 'the tatterdemalion God of any other religion', for Job's God was the God of Moses, the God of the Promised Land. Had Moses never preached a God whose essential nature was to promise blessings, 'Job would have possessed light neither for his speech of indictment nor for his rebellious hope.'[82] The very God Job rejected was the source both of his hope and of his sense of justice. Hence, wrote Bloch, in a splendid paradox, 'the rebel assuredly trusts God without believing in God'.[83]

Bloch did not approve, however, of belief in *any* God. The Marxist tradition in which he stood accepted Feuerbach's discovery that man creates God in his own image, projecting onto God his highest ideals. But the process was not without social dangers. As Feuerbach ex-

78. Ibid. pp. 163f.
79. Ibid. p. 165.
80. Ibid. pp. 165 and 153f.
81. Ibid. pp. 150 and 166.
82. *Das Prinzip Hoffnung*, III.1456.
83. *Atheism in Christianity*, p. 165.

pressed it, 'Religion is the disuniting of man from himself; he sets God before him as the antithesis of himself.'[84] In Marxist terms, God alienates man from himself. Bloch's Job was remarkable for trusting only 'the specific Jahwe of the *Exodus from Egypt*, even though every mythological construction of God had been seen through and every reflection of Lordship into the heavens had come to an end'.[85] Nor did Bloch commend this as a stance for twentieth-century men, for in Job (as read by Bloch), 'the Exodus becomes radical: it is now a journey into an unknown Canaan and it is an Exodus from Jahwe himself.'[86]

Bloch could not have expected even the theologians most in accord with his politics to accept such an Exodus. Yet a number of Christians, even when they wished to maintain the political importance of belief, responded to the positive elements of his atheism. Moltmann conceded that whenever religion, in support of the ruling classes, uses God the Father to bless the *Landesvater* and the Lord God to bless the Lords of this world, then atheism becomes a weapon of freedom.[87]

Barth's disciple, Helmut Gollwitzer, saluted Bloch's atheism as being far more profound than that of Feuerbach. Bloch, wrote Gollwitzer, averred that 'the human is the whole point of religion, that religion means human possibilities, and that "God" must therefore be resolved into a "single human Holiest of all".'[88] This statement remarkably echoed a sentence attributed to Karl Marx himself, though not published until 1933 and of doubtful authenticity:[89] 'The religion of working men is religion without God because it seeks to restore the divinity of man.' But Gollwitzer disputed Bloch's contention (again derived from Feuerbach) that, 'Where the great Lord of the world is, there is no room for freedom, not even the freedom of the "children of God".'[90] Gollwitzer allowed that the task of reconciling the reality of God and the freedom of man was still unresolved; but Bloch, he argued, had not

84. L. Feuerbach, *The Essence of Christianity* (1841), tr. G. Eliot, New York 1957, p. 33.

85. *Atheism in Christianity*, p. 165.

86. *Das Prinzip Hoffnung*, III.1456. J. M. Lochman, *Reconciliation and Liberation*, pp. 131-134, pays generous tribute to Bloch's importance in 'discovering' the Exodus tradition, while adding some reservations about Bloch's cavalier treatment of the tradition.

87. J. Moltmann, *Im Gespräch mit Ernst Bloch*, pp. 7of.

88. H. Gollwitzer, *The Existence of God as Confessed by Faith*, tr. J. W. Leitch, 1965, p. 99, referring to *Das Prinzip Hoffnung*, III.1417.

89. According to O. Chadwick, *The Secularization of the European Mind in the Nineteenth Century*, p. 69.

90. *Das Prinzip Hoffnung*, III.1413.

solved the problem merely by liquidating one of its two poles. Against Bloch he asserted that man's exaltation cannot be separated from the kindness and love of God towards him (Titus 3.4). 'The approval of God and therewith the fact of being taken up into communion with God', he wrote, 'constitutes the dignity of man, a concrete dignity because one that rests on a concrete approach.'[91]

Not all Christians agreed with Gollwitzer. As we shall see, Dorothee Sölle disputed his contention that man's dignity rests on God's approval. But Bloch extended the dialogue with Christians still further by making the notion that man is his own God integral to his principle of hope. 'What man expressed in the hypostases of the gods', he said, 'was altogether nothing but *longed-for-future*.'[92] Moltmann (for once even more prolix than Bloch) expounded him thus: 'the Homo absconditus of the not-yet-discovered and the not-yet-successfully completed future is the "God" of the present man.'[93] Here, however, Bloch's ontological difficulties arose. The Czech theologian Jan Milic Lochman asked what was the ground of his hope once God was eliminated. Lochman insisted, against Bloch, that Christian hope is rooted neither in the potentialities of nature nor in the creativity of human history, but in the living God. '*Hope and God are inseparable*', Lochman asserted: 'to be "without God in the world" means to be "without hope".'[94]

The question of God thus remained central to the Christian–Marxist dialogue that was inspired and developed by Bloch. Jürgen Moltmann identified the concept of God as the supreme ground of hope after this life as the kernel of his differences with his friend. In consequence of their resolute atheism, death remained a problem for all Marxists. Marx himself defined death as the 'terrible revenge of the species upon the individual'.[95] In quoting this, Roger Garaudy (in dialogue with the Christian Giulio Girardi) went on to point out the positive aspects even of this terrible revenge. Death for the Marxist emphasizes the preciousness of this life, reminding him that the human project cannot be envisaged as simply an individual one. Death prevents the Marxist

91. H. Gollwitzer, pp. 101 and 106.

92. *Das Prinzip Hoffnung*, III.1402.

93. 'Hope and Confidence. A Conversation with Ernst Bloch', tr. J. W. Leitch, in *Religion, Revolution and the Future*, p. 151.

94. J. M. Lochman, 'Towards an Ecumenical Account of Hope', in *Ecumenical Review*, vol. 31, January 1979, p. 16, referring here to Ephesians 2.12.

95. Quoted, R. Garaudy in his postface to the French translation of G. Girardi, *Marxism and Christianity* (ET Dublin 1968): J. Girardi *Marxisme et chrétienisme*, Paris 1968, p. 313.

subordinating this life to another (in the way some Christians can live this life in terms of a possible reward or punishment in the hereafter). For communists, wrote Garaudy, hell disappeared along with torture and the pillory as a means of regulating this life. And, he added, this coincides with a Christian insight. 'We Marxists do not imagine eternal life in the form of a prolongation before and after our life, before and after our history, but we conceive it in terms of a certain quality of this life and not another life. Our life has this eternal dimension in so far as it is not limited to our own individuality, in so far as we are fully defined as human beings only in our relationship with another human being and with all human beings in the totality of their history.' Garaudy concluded: 'there again, I am not sure that we do not here take up a fundamental teaching of the authentic biblical tradition precisely when we profess the humanism of Marxism to the full.'[96]

Yet the problem remains. In the words of Girardi, 'Death is the supreme alienation, and the militant Marxist, having fought (at times victoriously) against partial alienations, finds that he must capitulate before the total alienation—he must lose the decisive battle.'[97] As T.-W. Adorno expressed it, with great bitterness, Grimms' fairy tales still come true: a man 'went out into the world to seek his fortune, got the better of numerous giants, but had to die all the same in New York'.[98]

As the references to Garaudy and Girardi show, discussion of the problem of death is by no means confined to German-speaking Christians and Marxists. But the question has particular relevance to the contribution of Ernst Bloch. Bloch's critics[99] pointed out that death is precisely what makes Christians look ambiguously on the temporal locus of the kingdom of God. Bloch himself was deeply conscious of the problem. 'Sheol, the underworld and the tomb for long remained man's lot', he wrote; and he judged man's dreams of the future life to be among his most poignant.[100] These hopes, however poignant, Bloch considered to be illusory. In his own words, 'The jawbone of

---

96. Ibid. p. 314.

97. *Marxism and Christianity*, p. 80.

98. T.-W. Adorno *Minima Moralia*, tr. E. F. W. Jephcott, London 1974, p. 88.

99. E.g. H. P. Bowman, 'Ernst Bloch et l'Eschatologie', in *Utopie-marxisme selon Ernst Bloch*, p. 203, Cf. E. Lévinas, 'Sur la Mort dans la Pensée d' Ernst Bloch', ibid. pp. 318-325.

100. *Das Prinzip Hoffnung*, III.1324. Cf. the whole section, 'Hoffnungsbilder gegen den Tod', pp. 1326ff.

death crunches everything, and the pharynx of decay devours every theology.'[101] Death mocks the Christian as well as the Marxist atheist. And yet the old hopes are not without strength and can sometimes support and sustain even in the face of death. 'Thanks to them, even without knowing it, modern man preserves security-in-himself', Bloch wrote, with scarcely a hint of irony. 'Thanks to them the impression is formed, not that man perishes, but that the world, one fine day, decides not to appear before him any longer.'[102]

Moltmann, however, did not allow Bloch to dismiss the problem thus, but instead drew attention to its relevance for Bloch's whole attempt to assimilate the biblical hope. Bloch admitted that his eschatology derived from the Bible, from the promise, 'Behold, I make all things new!' Moltmann argued that Bloch ultimately sought in vain for 'a *concept of history without a concept of transcendence*, an *eschatology of the world without the resurrection.*' Moltmann contended that 'without the occurrence of the resurrection of Jesus Christ and without the eschatological horizon opened up by this event, the full reality of "Behold, I make all things new!" is rendered incomplete in the historical passion depicted in *Das Prinzip Hoffnung*. An imminent *Weltanschauung* does not do justice to the eschatological openness of everything that exists.' In Bloch's schema, Moltmann observed, there was no place for the Pauline paradox, 'dying, and behold, we live'.[103]

Clearly Bloch and his critics were here arguing about different faiths: Bloch's faith in the future as against the Christian faith in the God of the future. As we have seen, Bloch wished to exclude this 'God', not as an atheist of the enlightenment, nor even because of the malign social consequences of belief that Marxists claimed to perceive and deplore. Bloch rejected God because he believed God diminished man. In traditional Marxist terms, he supported Promethean man against the Gods

101. Ibid. III.1301.

102. Ibid. III.1361.

103. J. Moltmann, *Im Gespräch mit Ernst Bloch*, pp. 26f., and 89, quoting II Corinthians 6.9. There was also a more personal reason for Bloch's attitude to death and resurrection. His first wife had been a remarkably devout Christian. In 1921 Bloch watched her slowly dying, kept a diary of that time and wrote a memoir of her, which he directed was not to be published until after his death. (They appear in E. Bloch, *Tendenz–Latenz–Utopie*, Frankfurt am Main 1978: 'Gedenkbuch für Else Bloch-von Stritski', pp. 1–50.) After that, according to Moltmann, Bloch put all thoughts of death out of his mind, arguing, 'When I am dead, I'm not alive. I'm alive now and not dead. Why think about it?' At the very end of his life, however, he began to speak differently. Shortly before his death he told Moltmann, 'I am curious about what will happen next.' (Information from J. Moltmann, personal conversation with the author, 27 October 1979.)

who would set limits to his achievements. Yet in considering the proper place of Prometheus as a model for humanity, Bloch once again decisively influenced the Christian–Marxist dialogue in German-speaking Europe.

6
Prometheus Versus Christ

For Ernst Bloch Job was a Promethean figure. His defiance of Yahveh corresponded to Prometheus's defiance of Zeus over the secret of fire; and his unmerited sufferings had their counterpart in the punishment of Prometheus, who was chained whilst an eagle tore at his liver, which continually renewed itself. While these correspondences between a biblical figure and Prometheus may seem obvious, it is nonetheless remarkable for a Marxist to find Promethean elements in the Christian tradition. To understand why, it is necessary to go back to Marx himself.

Greek mythology (like Greek art in general) raised serious intellectual difficulties for Karl Marx. First, it had flowered in a manner out of all proportion to what he regarded as its 'skeletal structure' or material foundation: the level of development of society at the time of its creation. Second, Marx felt that it ought to have disappeared from men's consciousness in nineteenth-century Europe, for it had been superseded. 'All mythology', he wrote in 1857, 'overcomes and dominates and shapes the forces of nature in the imagination and by the imagination; it therefore vanishes with the advent of real mastery over them. What becomes of Fama alongside Printing House Square? Indeed, what chance has Vulcan against Roberts & Co., Jupiter against the lightning-rod and Hermes against Crédit Mobilier?' Yet he knew that Vulcan, Jupiter, and Hermes were likely to be remembered when Roberts & Co., the lightning-rod and the Crédit Mobilier were forgotten. The problem of their continuing significance was greater than that of their origins in the social structure of ancient Greece. As Marx put it, 'the difficulty lies not in understanding that the Greek arts and epic are bound up with certain forms of social development. The difficulty is that they still afford us artistic pleasure and that in a certain respect they count as a norm and as an unattainable model.' His attempted answer to the problem was to assert that the Greeks should be regarded as part of the historic childhood of humanity, and that a man can legitimately find delight in a child's naivety provided he himself strives 'to reproduce its truth at a higher stage'.[1]

The question was all the more important for Marx because he drew personal inspiration from Greek mythology. When his daughter asked him who was his greatest prototype, he answered without hesitation: Prometheus. The foreword to his doctoral dissertation described Prometheus as 'the most eminent saint and martyr in the philosophical calendar'. His biographer Franz Mehring observed that in thus acknowledging the Titan who stole fire from the gods and gave it to men, Marx anticipated the struggles and sufferings of his own career. Contemporaries confirmed this judgement: when Marx's *Rheinische Zeitung* was closed down in 1843, a famous print showed him as Prometheus bound, chained to a printing press and attacked by the Prussian eagle.[2]

Each year Marx read the works of Aeschylus in Greek and thus allowed the myth of Prometheus to inspire him afresh. Professor Arend Th. van Leeuwen has explored how Marx might have identified himself with the myth in his description of the economic conditions of the urban proletariat, for the 'Economic and Philosophical Manuscripts' of 1844 describe the houses of this class as abodes of death, in complete contrast to the dwellings full of light which, since Prometheus, have helped to change savages into men. 'The implications are evident', declares van Leeuwen: 'what we need is a new Prometheus.'[3] Five years earlier, as Marx's notebooks on Epicurean philosophy reveal, the Promethean myth was illuminating his own philosophy of changing the world. In his own time, he wrote, philosophy was turning against the world as it found it, just as Prometheus, having stolen fire from heaven, had begun to settle the earth and build houses on it.[4] For Marx this Promethean stance was decidedly anti-Christian. He understood Christianity to 'preach cowardice, self-abasement, resignation, submission and humility—in short, all the characteristics of the *canaille*.'

1. Marx *Grundrisse*, tr. M. Nicolaus, London 1973, pp. 110f.

2. Marx and his daughter in J. M. Lochman, 'Platz für Prometheus', in *Evangelische Kommentare*, March 1972, p. 136. Doctoral dissertation in Karl Marx and Friedrich Engels, *Collected Works*, vol. 1, ET 1975, p. 31. Mehring in A. Th. van Leeuwen, *Critique of Heaven*, 1972, p. 82. The print appears as the frontispiece of K. Marx and F. Engels *Historisch-Kritische Gesamtausgabe*, ed. D. Rjazonov, vol. 1, Frankfurt am Main 1927.

3. A. Th. van Leeuwen, p. 84.

4. Marx and Engels, *Collected Works*, I.491.

In 1844 came his notorious assertion that religion was the opiate of the people and that to criticize religion was therefore to begin to criticize 'the valley of tears whose halo is religion'.[5] Prometheus seemed to Marx to exemplify this criticism, particularly when he said to Hermes, the servant of the Gods:

> Be sure of this, I would not change my state
> Of evil fortune for your servitude.
> Better to be a servant of this rock
> Than to be faithful boy to Father Zeus.[6]

Marx came to regard Christianity as one of the most immoral of all religions; a contemporary described him (along with J. Christiansen, Ludwig Feuerbach, and Bruno Bauer) as casting God, religion, and immortality from their thrones and proclaiming man himself as God.[7] Marx recognized that Christianity had narrowly failed to make this proclamation. 'The fantasy, the dream, and postulate of Christianity', he wrote, was 'the sovereignty of man—but of man as an alien being, separate from actual man.'[8] He believed, in consequence, that a satisfactory social policy must oppose Christianity. The myth of Prometheus, not of Christ, had set out the proper relationship between God and man. 'Philosophy makes no secret of it', declared his doctoral dissertation. 'The confession of Prometheus, "In simple words, I hate the pack of Gods", is its own confession, its own aphorism against all heavenly and earthly Gods who do not acknowledge human self-consciousness as the highest divinity.'[9]

In all this Marx was not highly original. His Prometheus had been the hero of the anti-religious Young Hegelians of the enlightenment.[10] Moreover, he wrote within a tradition that was almost certainly misreading Aeschylus. Professor Hugh Lloyd-Jones observed, 'To the Romantic poets of the revolutionary era, the Titan tortured by Zeus for his services to mankind appeared as a symbol of the human spirit in its struggle to throw off the chains which priests and kings had forged for it.' But, he added, whatever these Romantic poets might have thought, 'to the distinguished Hellenists who after the fall of

5. D. M. McLellan, *Karl Marx: His Life and Thought*, 1973, pp. 174 and 89.

6. Marx and Engels, *Collected Works*, I.31 and note d.

7. A. Ruge, *Briefwechsel und Tageblätter*, Berlin 1866, I.239. Bauer was Marx's closest friend at this time.

8. D. M. McLellan, p. 82.

9. Marx and Engels, *Collected Works*, I.30.

10. A. Th. van Leeuwen, p. 82.

Napoleon laid the foundations of German scholarship, no such naive and one-sided view of *Prometheus* seemed tolerable.' Aeschylus, in this view, is not 'for' or 'against' either Zeus or Prometheus. His immediate purpose is dramatic, not educational. 'Prometheus is indeed shown with much sympathy; but it does not follow that the audience is meant to regard Zeus with the indignation that we naturally feel.'[11] On this reading, Marxists have far too readily identified the Zeus of *Prometheus Bound* with the Jehovah whom Engels described as 'promising mercy on those who are converted and mercilessly smiting down the obdurate in accordance with the ancient *parcere subjectis ac debellare superbos*'.[12]

Classical scholarship, however, had little effect on the way Marxists[13] continued to interpret the myth of Prometheus. In the twentieth century Roger Garaudy defined Marxism itself as 'the Promethean enterprise of taking control of the process of development and of deliberately building up the future.'[14] And Ernst Bloch described Prometheus as 'the hero of antiquity' who 'is and remains the essential tragic hero'.[15]

Bloch portrayed Prometheus as 'the mythical primeval teacher of the way of rebellion to all nations' and *Prometheus Bound* as 'the central Greek tragedy from which every other is a decline'. The creed of Prometheus, he asserted, was *'the religion of Greek tragedy'*, which provided its temple, priesthood, and liturgy. Bloch therefore found it 'surprising' that the Greeks did not honour this friend of mankind more highly; that in Hesiod and Pindar (as well as in Virgil and Horace) he is presented as a wily insurgent, and the withdrawal of fire by Zeus is seen as a measure of prescient wisdom; that Plato's *Protagoras*

11. H. Lloyd-Jones, 'Zeus in Aeschylus', in *Journal of Hellenic Studies*, vol. 76, 1965, pp. 54 and 66. Cf. the discussion of the ideas of personal responsibility among the Greeks in H. Chadwick, *Some Reflections on Conscience: Greek, Jewish and Christian*, 1968, pp. 8ff., particularly Professor Chadwick's observation on p. 10 of 'the "good conscience" of Prometheus protesting, rather like Job, that he has done no wrong to deserve the disasters that have befallen him.'

12. Marx and Engels, *On Religion*, p. 340, from *Die Neue Zeit*, Jahrgang 13, 1895, pp. 36–43.

13. Or others in nineteenth-century Germany, for that matter: see, e.g. M. McHaffie, 'Prometheus and Viktor: Carl Spitteler's "Imago",' in *German Life and Letters*, N.S., vol. 31, no. 1, October 1977, pp. 67–77.

14. R. Garaudy, *Marxism in the Twentieth Century*, p. 6.

15. E. Bloch, *Naturrecht und menschliche Würde*, pp. 285 and 284. In a speech delivered at the Treviso conference to mark the 150th anniversary of Marx's birth, Bloch took the customary line of describing Marx himself as Prometheus: 'Marx: cominare eretti, utopia concreta', in E. Bloch, *Karl Marx*, tr. Luciano Tosti, p. 212.

maintained that Prometheus, in attempting to bring heaven down to earth, did not succeed in bringing the art of government, for law and custom, Plato held, came from Zeus, and 'Hermes, the messenger, not Prometheus, the rebel, brought them first to everyone.' By the end of antiquity, Bloch observed, the true Prometheus was so far forgotten as to be regarded no longer as the bringer of light, but as one who merely built in clay. Only the cynics still honoured him as the bringer of culture.

For some Gnostics (in what Bloch regarded as a demented reversal of the truth) Prometheus came to signify the devil. Bloch traced the subsequent transformation of Prometheus from devil to Marxist saint. Both Lactantius and Tertullian asserted that 'the true Prometheus is God'. In the Christian interpretation of Prometheus at this time, the demi-god of tragedy and its cults became a complete God, called to incinerate false idols. (Jesus, after all, declared, 'I came to cast fire upon the earth; and would that it were already kindled!' Luke 12.49[16]). Prometheus, opposed to the highest god of the heathen, could be seen as working against such idols, not against Yahveh himself. 'When, however, a social teaching arose in opposition to all authorities (and their heavenly counterparts)', Bloch wrote, 'Prometheus appeared in a new light, as the opponent *not only of Zeus but of the church's Yahveh*. Prometheus, who in antiquity had remained a demi-god, became the complete religious-atheistic symbol of the new era.' Bloch found the Prometheus of Marx foreshadowed in the thinking of Boccaccio, Scaliger, Shaftesbury (who called Prometheus an 'alter deus'), the essay *De sapientia veterum* (which he attributed to Francis Bacon), and then in Goethe, the French revolution, and Schelling. 'Prometheus is thus the God who expresses disbelief in God.'[17]

Bloch depicted the Zeus of Aeschylus not as a symbol of civilization but as a vengeful despot; Bloch's Prometheus shared with Goethe's a 'deep hatred, indeed contempt, for the ruler of the world'.[18] And this brought Bloch into both disagreement and dialogue with Christians. Bloch explicitly equated Zeus with the God of Christianity, and particularly with Karl Barth's 'God in transcendence'.[19]

Barth attacked religion as the most direct contradiction to faith, since it invested men with the form of God and God with the form of

16. This point was made to me by Mr Stephen Medcalf.
17. E. Bloch, *Das Prinzip Hoffnung*, III.1428 and 1430–32.
18. Ibid. III.1428.
19. E. Bloch, *Atheismus im Christentum*, p. 21.

man. *Homo religiosus*, he claimed, had natural and deplorable titanic presumptions, believing that because he could approach, intellectually, the evidence of God's self-disclosure in history, he could thereby grasp God himself.[20] Religion, Barth insisted, 'so far from dissolving men existentially, so far from rolling them out and pressing them against the wall, so far from overwhelming them and transforming them, acts upon them like a drug which has been extremely skilfully administered.' It confirms man's fatal tendency to rest upon his own competence and treat his own ambitions as adequate and satisfactory. The symbol of this 'assumption of independence in which God is forgotten' is Prometheus, who (according to Barth) drew down from heaven not the all-consuming fire of God but merely the fire of Zeus. Thus he kindled 'only a furnace from which a very peculiar kind of smoke pours forth'.[21] Heinz Zahrnt commented, 'Out of this furnace Barth sees arising and spreading over the plain of humanity the clouds of vapour and steam of every world-view, religion, and system', from the devotional exercises of the Benedictines to the vigorous and comprehensive programme of the Social Democrats.[22]

Bloch countered Barth by making a supremely Promethean figure out of Jesus Christ himself. Barth's transcendent heaven, Bloch declared, his 'secret closet and safe stronghold of transcendence', is something different from the heaven revealed by Jesus.[23] Jesus, 'the messiah because of his death on the cross, not in spite of it', died as a rebel against custom and domination of all kinds. He freed men from the rule of demiurges, of whom he said, 'Your father was a murderer from the beginning' (John 8.44), bringing instead the revelation of the true God, 'Your Father in heaven' (Matthew 7.11).[24]

In defence of Barth, F.-W. Marquardt[25] has maintained that Bloch did not perceive the essentially dialectical nature of Barth's theology. Barth's ethic envisaged man as always at work, ever active; but always, too, as 'the poor man', on whose side God ranges himself. God's own dialectic involves saying 'Yes' to the poor man and 'No' to the man who seeks to live as a hero. It is therefore an error to characterize the

20. H. M. Rumscheidt, *Revelation and Theology. An Analysis of the Barth-Harnack Correspondence of 1923*, 1972, p. 49.

21. Karl Barth, *The Epistle to the Romans*, pp. 168 and 236.

22. Heinz Zahrnt, *Die Sache mit Gott*, pp. 35f., alluding to Barth, p. 409.

23. *Atheismus im Christentum*, p. 80; cf. pp. 72ff.: 'Barths Geheimkabinett und feste Burg der Transzendenz'.

24. *Das Prinzip Hoffnung*, III.1489 and 1498.

25. Personal conversation with the author, 2 April 1978.

God preached by Barth as a 'stronghold', for a stronghold says 'Yes' to the great of this world, whereas God says 'No' to them. According to Marquardt, Bloch was led astray by reading only the second edition of Barth's *Römerbrief*, where admittedly Barth's anti-Promethean God is presented in his most extreme form.

Bloch's Jesus is the enemy of such a God. As Bloch put it, he inserted himself, so to speak, into Yahveh; he is '*Yahveh's usurper*', a saviour, but a '*subversive saviour*'.[26] Bloch was always ready to assert that his Jesus was by no means necessarily the Jesus preached by the church once it had been established. As he observed, ' "I am the resurrection and the life" and "Behold, I make all things new!" were not the slogans with which Christianity became the state religion at the time of Constantine.'[27] Bloch went still further in distancing himself from traditional Christianity by rejecting what he regarded as the false dialectic whereby Paul was enabled to assert that Yahveh himself willed Christ's sacrifice, to pay the price of sin. 'The real Jesus', he repeated, 'died as a rebel and martyr, not as a cashier.'[28]

This estimate of Jesus is far removed from that made by vulgar Marxism; but Bloch always insisted that 'vulgar Marxism is not Marxism'. He consistently refused to take up the crudely reductionist view of religion exemplified in Karl Kautsky's remark that the Reformation was nothing but the ideological expression of deep changes in the European wool market. Bloch described Kautsky's phrase 'nothing but' as a 'miserable conversion formula'.[29] The contrast between Bloch and Kautsky at this point reveals how far Marxist understanding had developed since Kautsky's *Foundations of Christianity*. Although Kautsky never lost his interest in Christianity,[30] his later analyses tend to confirm Marx's description of his mind as essentially Philistine. 'The materialist conception of history', he wrote, '... is not concerned to deny that every age has its particular ideas which condition it, and that these ideas form the dynamics of social development. It does not, however, stop at this point, but proceeds to investigate the forces which

26. *Atheismus im Christentum*, pp. 173f.: 'Einsatz Jesu in Jahwe'. *Das Prinzip Hoffnung*, III.1497 and 1496.

27. J. Moltmann, *Im Gespräch mit Ernst Bloch*, p. 57.

28. *Das Prinzip Hoffnung*, III.1490.

29. *Philosophische Aufsätze zur objektiven Phantasie*, Frankfurt am Main 1969, p. 280; cf. *Das Materialismusproblem, seine Geschichte und Substanz*, Frankfurt am Main 1972, pp. 129 and 387.

30. See, for example, 'Das neueste Leben Jesu', in *Die Neue Zeit*, Jahrgang 29, 1911, pp. 35–46.

set the machinery in motion, and these it finds in the material conditions.'[31] Kautsky was still applying this reductionist historical method
to Christianity in 1927. 'Among the ideas which determine the spiritual
life of our time it is still of great significance', he conceded. 'Yet', he
continued, 'it would be completely in vain to try to derive the ideas of
Christianity from existing economic conditions. If we want to understand it we must go back to the time in which it appeared in world
history as a new phenomenon. We must investigate its origins during
the first centuries of our era, when the democracy of antiquity broke
down and an all powerful Caesarism arose. The economic relations of
the time and their consequences, the impoverishment of the masses,
the concentration of wealth in a few hands, loss of population, constant
civil war between the holders of power, who thanks to their accumu-
lations of plunder could support large armies, the cessation of all
political activity among the people, for the impoverished masses became corrupted and could be bought while the rich sunk themselves in
debauchery: this was the real basis out of which Christianity arose and
makes it explicable.

'But by no means completely—only that which was distinctively
new to it—the longing for peace, scorn of the world, disgust with life,
lack of confidence in oneself and one's surroundings, etc.'[32]

Only rarely did Marx himself resort to such coarse reductionism.
His epigrams do contain some breath-taking judgements of a reductionist nature, such as, 'Religion, family, state, law, morality, science,
and art are only particular modes of production.' But it has been rightly
observed that 'neither his practice, not the full exposition of his mind,
can be confined within so strait an epigram.'[33] Not so with Kautsky.
And as the Christian-Marxist dialogue developed in the German-
speaking world, Marxists such as Ernst Bloch grew increasingly dissatisfied with his work. Thus Milan Machovec, noting Kautsky's contention that the Christian ideals of 'salvation' and 'deliverance' arose
out of the social and economic circumstances of the ancient world,
pointed out that Kautsky never managed to say precisely when those
circumstances were operative: was it, asked Machovec, 'in the epoch
between Gaius Gracchus and Marius until Nero and Trajan, or

31. *Thomas More and His Utopia*, p. 160.
32. *The Materialist Conception of History*, tr. in S. H. Hook, *Marx and the Marxists: The Ambiguous Legacy*, p. 164.
33. O. Chadwick, *The Secularization of the European Mind in the Nineteenth Century*, p. 60.

between the first and second conquests of Jerusalem by the Romans?'[34] Marxists still needed to ask such questions; ideas like 'salvation' did not descend from heaven; but, said Machovec, it was possible to ask the questions intelligently and not stupidly.[35]

Bloch's encounter with religion made further refinements of his Marxist inheritance. Unlike Marx, whose reaction to his own Jewish background took the form of anti-Semitism,[36] Bloch remained passionately responsive to the insights of Judaism and the Bible. And second, the Promethean and eschatological elements in his thought ensured that his own form of reductionism, over the notion of God, was far less crude than that of Feuerbach. In Moltmann's words, 'Whereas Feuerbach dissolved theology into anthropology, Bloch transposed theology into the atheist eschatology of Promethean self-revelation.'[37]

This enabled him to recognize that in Jesus 'the Bible once again sets out a titanism, a Promethean rebellion of which there are many traces in the Old Testament'.[38] Jürgen Habermas has observed that Bloch, in fact, 'understands Christ very much in the spirit of the Old Testament, a prophet of the kingdom of *this* world'.[39] The Old Testament figures he considered most important for this Promethean tradition are Moses, who insisted that God must remain true to the promise of Canaan or else he is not God, and his successor Job, the 'Hebrew Prometheus', 'the biblical Prometheus', 'the titanic challenger of the Godhead'.[40] Bloch traced Job's Promethean notion that men are better than God through Goethe's Promethean fragment (where it is mingled with ideas of the tragic understanding and the *Sturm und Drang* movement) as far as Shelley's *Prometheus Unbound*.[41]

Emphasizing Bloch's originality in all this, Jürgen Moltmann wrote that 'since the time of German idealism it seems that men have had to

34. *Jesus für Atheisten*, p. 8.

35. Ibid. p. 9.

36. W. H. Chaloner and W. O. Henderson, 'Marx/Engels and Racism', in *Encounter*, July 1975, pp. 18-23. Isaiah Berlin, 'Benjamin Disraeli, Karl Marx and the Search for Identity, in *Against the Current*, 1979, pp. 276-286, attempts to explain this as a form of 'Jewish self-hatred'.

37. J. Moltmann *Im Gespräch mit Ernst Bloch*, pp. 29f.

38. *Das Prinzip Hoffnung*, III.1498.

39. 'Ein marxistischer Schelling', pp. 1083f.

40. *Das Prinzip Hoffnung*, III.1456. *Atheismus im Christentum*, pp. 103, 155, 166, and 324.

41. *Das Prinzip Hoffnung*, III.1432.

choose between Christ and the "holy" Prometheus, acknowledging no correspondence between Christian and revolutionary hope'.[42] In truth, others besides Bloch have seen the connections. They were noticed, for example, by Arnold Toynbee, whose learning surpassed Bloch's, and by Erich Fromm, who shared with Bloch a Jewish background and the same intellectual environment in Frankfurt before Hitler came to power. Toynbee drew the connection between Prometheus, Christ, and the Suffering Servant of Deutero-Isaiah; and Fromm made the observation, 'Both the Hebrews and the Greeks taught that human endeavour and human history began with an act of disobedience.'[43] Where Bloch differed from these two men was first in exploring the correspondences in much greater depth and then in going further to ask how these Promethean figures differ from one another. Astonishingly for a Marxist atheist, he regarded Jesus Christ as more Promethean than Prometheus himself.

The reasons for this judgement lay in Bloch's philosophy of hope and in his social principles. According to Kierkegaard, the hope that Prometheus brought was a dubious gift, since it made men refuse to accept their own limitations.[44] Bloch, in contrast, saw the hope that springs from human longings as the precursor of new life.[45] In the words of Harvey Cox, whereas Freud studied the *Nicht-mehr-bewusst*, that which has come to consciousness but has now passed into unconsciousness, 'Bloch has discovered the *"Noch-nicht-bewusst"*, that which scampers teasingly on the threshold of consciousness, sensed only in anticipation, not yet fully realized.'[46] Therefore he finds Prometheus wanting precisely because he remained locked in his own limitations. True, he was not destroyed (unlike Bellerophon or Icarus); Zeus failed to overcome his will; and he grimly waited for the end of his own era. But the rebellion of Prometheus remained a purely mental affair, partly because (unlike those of Moses and Jesus) it was established not by real persons but only as a myth. 'For the most important invasion of the beyond that took place before the time of Jesus, the Greeks possessed only the two personae of a poet who was not a

42. J. Moltmann, in *Ernst Bloch zu ehren*, p. 261.

43. A. Toynbee *A Study of History*, vol. 12: *Reconsiderations*, 1961, p. 617. E. Fromm, *The Dogma of Christ*, p. 114.

44. S. Kierkegaard, *Either/Or*, tr. D. F. Swenson and L. M. Swenson, 1944, I.240.

45. 'Die Formel *incipit vita nova*', in *Tübinger Einleitung in die Philosophie*, Frankfurt am Main, 1970, pp. 357-369.

46. H. Cox, 'Ernst Bloch and "The Pull of the Future"', in *New Theology No. 5*, ed. M. E. Marty and D. G. Peerman, New York 1968, p. 195.

prophet and a demigod who was not a human being.'[47] So the tragedy of Prometheus lay locked in its religious sphere, in the cult of Dionysus. Its creative possibilities never came to fruition. Its hope remained unfulfilled.

In addition, it was hope devoid of any social or political content comparable to that found in Moses and Jesus. The hope found in Jesus, Bloch argued, contains new possibilities for man in society. 'Jesus as the son of man projects himself into the above', he wrote, '... not as man in his present state, but as the utopia of a possible humanity whose essence and eschatological brotherhood he has already exemplified.' As an instance of the social effects of this utopia, Bloch, as might be expected, seized upon the early Christian community of Acts 2.32, built, he said, on communism and love, where no one called anything that he possessed his own and they had all things in common.[48]

At this point the discussion was taken up from the other side, by the Czech theologian Jan Milic Lochman. Lochman, as a member of a minority church in his own country, accepted its decision (under the leadership of Josef Hromadka) to make its work and witness an integral part of a Communist state. Czech Protestants, he believed, had a special mission to bring peace and reconciliation not only to divided Christians but also to politically divided nations.[49] In the light of St Paul's doctrine that Christ 'died for the ungodly' (Romans 5.6), and convinced of the profound relevance of Christianity for atheists as well as for believers,[50] Lochman helped to lead those Christians who co-operated with the political reformers in Czechoslovakia in the late 1960s, attempting, as he put it, both 'to face the reality of a new socialist society' and 'to be open for its experiments and ready to support it whenever it was acceptable from a Christian point of view'.[51]

47. *Das Prinzip Hoffnung*, III.1427-29; cf. 'Auch Prometheus ist ein Mythos', in *Atheismus im Christentum*, pp. 55-86. Bloch's concern to assert the historicity of Moses may be contrasted with the view of his distinguished contemporary G. von Rad, *Theologie des Alten Testaments*, Munich 1957, I.23f., and 288f.

48. *Das Prinzip Hoffnung*, III.1417.

49. J. M. Lochman, 'Theology in the Age of the Cold War', in *Die Not der Versöhnung*, Hamburg 1963. Cf. J. F. Hromadka, *Thoughts of a Czech Pastor*, ET 1970, and C. C. West, *Communism and the Theologians*, 1958, esp. pp. 64-73.

50. J. M. Lochman *Church in a Marxist Society*, p. 161. 'Gottesbeweis und Atheismus', in F. Buri, J. M. Lochman and H. Ott, *Dogmatik in Dialog*, Gütersloh 1974, II. 185-189, esp. p. 188. J. M. Lochman, *Christus oder Prometheus? Die Kernfrage des christlich-marxistischen Dialogs und die Christologie*, Hamburg, 1972, esp. the preface, 'Jesus für Atheisten', pp. 9-16.

51. *Church in a Marxist Society*, p. 180.

In 1968, when the Russian invasion of Czechoslovakia shattered this endeavour, Lochman had just relinquished his chair of systematic theology and philosophy at the Comenius faculty in Prague and (with the approval of Dubcek's government)[52] had taken up Barth's old chair in the University of Basle.

Lochman did not abandon political theology. In 1965 he had taken part in the colloquy between Marxists and Christians held at Salzburg, where (as a Roman Catholic participant observed) the stress on the 'creative' character of Christian hope and the talk of 'creative eschatology' offered clear affinities with impetuous Prometheus and the young Marx.[53] In 1972, largely under the inspiration of Ernst Bloch, Lochman took up this theme again.

Bloch's approach to Christian millenarian ideals and hopes was especially congenial to someone from Lochman's confessional background. Whereas, Lochman observed, 'orthodox Protestantism loathes chiliasm', he himself could quote with approval the words of the Czech theologian and teacher Jan Amos Comenius, written shortly before his death in 1670: '*Audeo pronunciare verum chiliasmum christianismum, antichiliasmum vero esse antichristianismum.*'[54]

Lochman believed that in discovering anew the creative power of biblical thought and especially of biblical christology, Bloch had pointed to 'a new epoch and a higher plane' of the Christian-Marxist dialogue; both sides were beginning to recognize that their quarrel was about how to interpret a common legacy. This was made supremely clear by Bloch's interpretation of Prometheus. 'The question *whether Prometheus has a place in the Christian calendar* is fundamental and controversial', wrote Lochman. 'Are the biblical-Christian and Promethean-Marxist views of humanity mutually exclusive? Is Christ the opposite of Prometheus? That is the question at the heart of every Christian–Marxist dialogue.'[55]

Just as Bloch set Christ in the Promethean tradition, so Lochman concluded that Christians should find a place for Prometheus in their calendar. He argued that Prometheus is paradoxically more at home

52. Information to the author from J. M. Lochman, 28 March 1978.

53. J. B. Metz, ' "Politische Theologie" in der Diskussion', in *Diskussion zur 'Politischen Theologie'*, hrsg von H. Peukert, Munich/Mainz 1961, p. 295.

54. F. Buri, J. M. Lochman, and H. Ott, *Dogmatik in Dialog*, Gütersloh 1973, I.288, in the section 'Das Problem des Chiliasmus'. For Comenius and his significance for communists and non-communists alike in the Slavic world, see Manuel and Manuel, pp. 309–331, esp. p. 318.

55. J. M. Lochman, 'Platz für Prometheus. Das gemeinsame Erbe von Christentum und Marxismus', in *Evangelische Kommentare*, March 1972, p. 136.

there than in Greek mythology, because of the way the biblical understanding of God and man differs from that of ancient Greece. The God
of the Bible (unlike Zeus) does not impose eternal limitations upon
man as a potential rival. And the Bible envisages man as a free, creative,
'eschatological' being who aims at transcendence, provokes the status
quo, changes the world, and seeks for the greater justice of the coming
kingdom.[56]

This understanding of biblical man, however, complicated Lochman's relationship to Marxism. He ranged himself alongside Marx's
hopes for mankind while refusing to grant that these are thwarted by
the Christian religion, that (as Marx expressed it in 1843) after the
Greeks, man's self-respect disappeared from the world into the blue
haze of the Christian heaven.[57] Marx's demand for 'the decisive and
positive abolition of religion' was not acceptable to Lochman. In a
famous sentence, Marx had declared, 'The criticism of religion ends
with the doctrine that man is the highest being for man, that is, with
the categorical imperative to overthrow all circumstances in which
man is humiliated, enslaved, abandoned, and despised.'[58] Omitting the
criticism of religion from this sentence, Lochman quoted only the
categorical imperative. This obligation, he declared, is 'the true Promethean mission—for Christians and for Marxists'.[59]

Yet he insisted that Christian theology could not simply note the
place of Prometheus and leave it at that. 'In the mirror the Marxist
holds in front of us, we see repeatedly that the Promethean elements—
better, the dynamic aspects of our own radical inheritance—have been
continually pushed aside and rejected.' Even though the great theological pioneers of our century (Barth, Bonhoeffer, Niebuhr, and Hromadka, as listed by Lochman) had brought to light neglected parts of
this legacy, Prometheus remained a challenge to Christians. Lochman
cited three such challenges. First, Prometheus challenged authoritarian
notions of God, the idea that God is 'an inhuman structure imposed
upon mankind', rather than the God of Abraham, Isaac, and Jacob,
who is also Father of Jesus Christ. In the sight of the true God,
Lochman argued, there is a place for Prometheus, for this God is not

56. 'Platz für Prometheus', p. 137. Lochman's discussion of the differences between
Greek and Christian insights is elaborated in *Dogmatik in Dialog*, I.210f., 'Das Wesen
der christlichen Hoffnung'.

57. Marx/Engels, *Historisch-Kritische Gesamtausgabe*, I.i.561.

58. 'Critique of the Hegelian Philosophy of Law, tr. in Marx, *Early Texts*, ed. D. M.
McLellan, 1971, p. 123.

59. 'Platz für Prometheus', p. 141.

affronted by man's emancipation; it is part of his own revealed concern. Second, Prometheus challenged the doctrine that sees sin simply as an act of *hubris*. 'In the light of Christ', Lochman wrote, 'sin is revealed not only in the "eritis sicut deus" ... but also in the opposite temptation, the denial of the liberating engagement of God in history and the refusal to co-operate in the liberation. Inactivity is as basic a form of sin as *hubris*.' Third, Prometheus challenged an inadequate understanding of grace and justification. The doctrine of grace is suspect in Marxism, since it readily degenerates into an ideology of quietism, leading to the notion that one's own work and actions are not important. Lochman argued that in the biblical understanding of grace, human activity is neither excluded nor devalued, for the effect of grace is to open new and unexpected possibilities of action in human history; grace mobilizes man's creative powers; it may even be said to stimulate human beings to 'Promethean existence'.[60]

In the course of this dialogue Lochman rightly observed, 'God's transcendence becomes an issue of new moment.'[61] For a Marxist, Roger Garaudy asserted, 'Transcendence is a dangerous expression, ... heavy with confusions and mystifications.' Traditionally, he stated, it has meant 'belief in a world beyond, in the supernatural, with the irrationality, the miracles, the mystery, and finally the deception that these notions carry with them.' Nonetheless, Garaudy proceeded to ask where in human experience this faith in transcendence can be located. 'The claim to transcendence', he concluded, 'is the actual human experience that man, though belonging to nature, is different from things and animals and that man, forever able to progress, is never complete.'[62] Lochman, who had long been in dialogue with Garaudy, would no doubt have gone along with much of this. But for him the notion of transcendence also indicated a major difference between a Christian and a secular utopia. Christian utopianism, he maintained, is essentially transcendent. 'The kingdom of God is no earthly utopia, but literally *God's* kingdom. The new heaven and the new earth do not emerge as a result of the process of the world's history; they "come down from above". It is strictly a matter of the transcendent, not of "transcending" or the "transcendental".'[63]

Care not to confuse Christian with socialist hope appeared in the

60. 'Platz für Prometheus', pp. 137-139.

61. Ibid. p. 141.

62. R. Garaudy, 'Communists and Christians in Dialogue', in *New Theology No. 5*, p. 216.

63. J. M. Lochman, *Dogmatik in Dialog*, I.300.

Christian–Marxist dialogue in the 1920s and 1930s in German-speaking Europe. In 1926 Paul Tillich, elaborating the distinction between atheistic utopianism and the eschatological hope of religious socialism, insisted as did Lochman nearly half a century later: 'The eternal is that which invades.'[64] 'The eschatological movements of the socialist and revolutionary sort', he wrote, 'are directly positive and optimistic. Insofar as they have not been weakened by fatigue or the tactics of reform, that is by the spirit of capitalist society, they are supported by the spirit of Utopianism. But Utopianism is direction to the eternal conceived as the goal of this-worldly activity. In all Utopianism there is an element of faith, a transcending of the finite. But insofar as it is Utopianism it also contains unbelief and bondage to the finite. As a result of this unbelief, this inability to break through to the Unconditioned beyond time, the religious enthusiasm of Utopianism is lost and—regarded in retrospect as the product of disappointment—is replaced by progress or reaction.'[65]

Georg Wünsch, the Marburg professor who edited the *Zeitschrift für Religion und Sozialismus*, was even less willing to grant similarities between Christianity and Marxism at that time. In 1932 he accused some fellow religious socialists (Karl Thieme in particular) of equating Marxist and Christian eschatology as one might equate a horse and a cow on the general grounds that both possess legs, head, and tail. He represented Marxist as totally different from Christian eschatology, though not opposed to it. The day of the Lord, he said, is not simply the same as the classless society; nor (he pointed out) did Marx equate the classless society with the end, but with the beginning of true—albeit thoroughly profane—history.[66]

By the time Lochman came to engage in dialogue with Bloch, such judgements had been greatly refined by the progress of the Christian-Marxist dialogue. Yet Lochman did not attempt to minimize the differences between the Marxist and the Christian understanding of Prometheus. Classical Marxism tended to see Prometheus not simply as a pioneer, but also as one who brought (in Bloch's phrase) 'rebellious-human salvation'.[67] His kingdom not only fulfilled but also *replaced* the expectation of the kingdom of God. Lochman held that

64. P. Tillich, *The Religious Situation*, New York 1956, p. 176.
65. Ibid. p. 175.
66. G. Wünsch, 'Christliche und marxistische Eschatologie', in *Zeitschrift für Religion und Sozialismus*, Band iv, Heft 4, 1932, pp. 231f.
67. E. Bloch, *Das Prinzip Hoffnung*, III.1432.

this cannot be reconciled with Christianity, since it excluded the essential transcendent element of the Christian hope. He wished to maintain that in Christianity 'the hope of redemption is inseparably connected with the name of Jesus Christ and with what this stands for', namely the liberating engagement of God in history.

Once again dialogue between Christians and Ernst Bloch indicated the central importance of the question of God. Christian insistence that the future kingdom belongs to God was seen to have two important political consequences by those engaged in dialogue with Marxists. First, it did not allow those desiring to change society (or those wishing to preserve it, for that matter) to confuse the kingdom of God with any earthly order. This applied to some of those theologians who, partly under Bloch's influence, had come to accept the necessity of revolution to overthrow unjust political regimes. Gustavo Gutiérrez, for example, has been accused of coming 'close to providing carte blanche legitimation for joining almost any allegedly revolutionary struggle to replace almost any allegedly repressive regime. The absence of conceptual clarity in the statement of the goal is matched by a deep obscurity about the means by which the goal is to be achieved.'[68] This seems to me untrue of Gutiérrez specifically, precisely because of his doctrine of God. The Christian hope, he wrote, 'keeps us from any confusion of the Kingdom with any one historical stage, from any idolatry towards unavoidably ambiguous human achievement, from any absolutizing of revolution'.[69]

Redemption inseparably connected with God, as distinguished from the rebellious-human salvation of Prometheus, has a second important social consequence. It means, as Lochman pointed out, that for the Christian 'the secular dimension is not the only and final one.' It means that a man is not ultimately defined by his talents, that his salvation is not dependent on the success or failure of his own exertions.

Prometheus himself, Lochman claimed, needs demythologizing, for to include the notion of self-salvation in the Promethean model of authentic human existence is to saddle man with an impossible soteriological function.[70] To demythologize Prometheus, on the other hand, is to protect a legitimate political concern. Once man is not expected

---

68. R. J. Neuhaus, 'Liberation Theology and the Captivities of Jesus', in *Worldview*, New York, June 1973, p. 6.

69. G. Gutiérrez, *A Theology of Liberation*, p. 238.

70. J. M. Lochman, *Christus oder Prometheus?*, pp. 65-72: 'Die Entmythologisierung des Prometheischen'.

to redeem himself, his proper work becomes clear. Politics under the heading 'eritis sicut deus' is hopeless hubris; under the heading 'eritis sicut homines' it is an obligation. In Lochman's words, 'We have to build not the New Jerusalem but—in the light of the New Jerusalem—our own secular cities.'[71]

71. 'Platz für Prometheus', p. 141.

7
Dorothee Solle: Political Theology

'In Bloch's thought the hope for the new thing of the future is linked with what men can do', wrote Jürgen Moltmann. 'But do we not need also a hope which is connected with what we must suffer in sacrifice, in pain and in dying? We naturally have hope when we are young. But do we not need hope also when we are old and incapable, when we can no longer help ourselves and when finally death robs us of all hope? Do we not need hope also for those who are gone, for the dead in order to remain in love? Here the militant optimism of *Das Prinzip Hoffnung* is silent. There is for Bloch a hell on earth, and even worse, a hell in which there is no Easter.'[1] Whatever Bloch may have felt about Moltmann's diagnosis, he had no time whatsoever for his remedies. The cross and the resurrection were for him both absurd, and he said so publicly. In 1965 he took issue both with Moltmann's theology of the cross and with his theory of its political consequences. Moltmann contended that once the cross is understood 'as an expression of real human affliction, then the resurrection acquires the significance of the true "protest" against human affliction. In consequence, the missionary proclamation of the cross of the risen one is not opium of the people, which intoxicates and incapacitates them, but the ferment of a new freedom. It leads to the awakening of that revolt which "in the power of the resurrection", as Paul expresses it, follows the categorical imperative to overthrow all conditions in which man is a being who labours and is heavy-laden.'[2]

In public debate with Moltmann, Bloch refused to accept this blend of Christian theology and Marxist politics. He asked what was so

1. *Religion, Revolution and the Future*, p. 17
2. 'Existenzgeschichte und Weltgeschichte', p. 17. This is the most concise of Moltmann's statements about the political significance of the cross; but see *The Crucified God*.

special about the crucifixion of Jesus. 'One can find numberless crosses', he observed, 'without going to Golgotha.' Pauline theology, he added, was scarcely relevant to the eight thousand slaves crucified on the Appian Way, after the war over Spartacus. As a Marxist wishing men to change the world, Bloch took particular exception to those who used the cross to inculcate patience. Luther, he observed, had preached, 'Cross, cross, suffering, suffering' to the German peasants. How then could Moltmann contend that the crucifixion was a 'protest' against affliction?[3]

Moltmann's response during this particular dialogue was to deny that either Pauline theology in general or the theology of the cross in particular necessarily implied patience in the face of unjustified suffering. Far from urging docility on slaves, Paul had laid the basis of their emancipation. Nor was Moltmann on the side of Luther against Münzer and the German peasants. What he did accept from Luther was the exposition of the crucifixion of Jesus as integrally bound up with the notion of his descent into hell: with hope for the hopeless; with the possibility of resurrection for those who must die. Thus, Moltmann argued, the theology of the cross enabled Christians to stand alongside the utterly oppressed in this world.[4] Moltmann at this time and later was directing his theology of the crucifixion partly against the kind of theologian who urges Christians to say: 'where is God active in the world? Let us join him.' This, Moltmann argued, leads to callousness: this year, as it might be, the action is on a University campus; last year, it was in Vietnam. Moltmann wished Christians to say: 'Where are people suffering? There God is identified with them, and we must be identified with them.'[5] Later, in an open letter to Bloch (on the latter's ninetieth birthday), Moltmann identified more specifically some of the suffering and some of the weak with whom Christians ought to identify: those 'children of Abraham' imprisoned in South Korea, the unemployed in Tokyo, the 'strangers in their own land' in the United States, those scarred with persecution in South Africa.[6] The implications of the Christian–Marxist dialogue in German-speaking Europe were becoming increasingly worldwide.

These themes in the dialogue between Bloch and Moltmann were also being explored in greater detail by Dorothee Sölle, one of the few

3. J. Moltmann, *Im Gespräch mit Ernst Bloch*, p. 56.
4. Ibid., pp. 60f.
5. Personal conversation with the author, 30 October 1973.
6. *Im Gespräch mit Ernst Bloch*, p. 93.

contemporary Christian theologians whose writing had made an impact on the general public in Germany as well as on the academic world. Born in 1929, Sölle studied philosophy and classical philology at the University of Cologne, before going on to read theology at the universities of Göttingen and Freiburg. She gained considerable notoriety in 1965 at the *Kirchentag* in Cologne, when she said that after Auschwitz Germans could no longer sing 'Praise to the Lord, who o'er all things so wonderously reigneth.' After Auschwitz, she believed, the concept of God as a father who never does wrong had become intolerable. In the 1960s and 1970s the radicalism of her views led her into dialogue and disagreement not only with right-wing elements in German theology, but also with fellow theologians of the left, and in particular with Barth's disciple Helmut Gollwitzer. As a theologian who had come to accept many of the premises of the 'Death of God' school of American theologians,[7] she (unlike Gollwitzer) felt no need to take issue with Bloch's atheism. As we shall see, this aspect of her theology was a major cause of her disagreement with Gollwitzer and the Barthians, for in her understanding their 'inadequate' theology threatened to produce an inadequate Christian politics.

She was entirely at one with Bloch's contention that Christianity, far from helping men and women to deal with unnecessary human suffering, actually contributes to it. Before co-operating with others in trying to abolish 'the conditions under which people are exposed to senseless, patently unnecessary suffering', Christians, she insisted, must first abolish their own traditional masochism.[8]

Christianity, she asserted, mistakenly tried to picture God as simultaneously the ruling omnipotent Father and the God of the poor, the peasants, and the slaves. As a result, theologians attempted to develop a 'theology of the cross' from the impossible perspective of a God who is supposed not only to originate suffering but also to suffer with its victims. The cross itself was thus used to make acceptable what ought to have been recognized as intolerable. The result was Christian masochism. At a personal level Christians had, for example, required unconditional submission to the unhappiness of a totally unsatisfactory

7. *Atheistisch an Gott glauben*, Stuttgart 1968, esp. pp. 77–96, 'Atheistisch an Gott glauben'; pp. 52–76; 'Theologie nach dem Tode Gottes'; and pp. 97–102, 'Auferstehung nach dem "Tode Gottes"'. Cf., for the American sources of this theology, T. J. J. Altizer, *The Gospel of Christian Atheism*, 1967, and T. J. J. Altizer and W. Hamilton, *Radical Theology and the Death of God*, 1968.

8. *Suffering*, tr. E. R. Kalin, 1975, chapter 1, 'A Critique of Christian Masochism'. The quotation, derived from Karl Marx, occurs on p. 2.

marriage. At a social level they had felt able to classify war, pestilence, and famine as belonging to the punishments, trials, and afflictions sent by God himself. In consequence, Sölle argued, instead of working for the abolition of this kind of suffering, Christians tried to deal with it through the inadequate means of 'illusion, minimization, suppression, apathy'.[9] Yet, she pointed out, this way of looking at suffering is far from biblical. The sufferings of the children of Israel at the time of the Exodus are ascribed in Scripture not to God but to blindness, tyranny, and absurdity. They are not to be endured.

Sölle found the same attitude to suffering in the Old Testament figure of Job, the Job as interpreted by Ernst Bloch, the Job who refused to allow a degenerate God to renege on the promises of the Exodus. Job did *not* suffer patiently. The God of the Exodus spoke with Moses 'as a man speaks with his friend' (Exodus 33.11). Job insisted on the same right (though it was denied him). In the end he looked elsewhere for salvation. Sölle concluded, 'Job's call for the advocate, the redeemer, the blood-avenger, and blood-satisfier is to be understood only as the unanswered cry of the pre-Christian world, which finds its answer in Christ. Job is stronger than the old God. Only the one who suffers can answer Job, not the one who causes suffering. Not the hunter but the quarry.'[10]

After the Exodus and after Job's attack on a God who bends justice and rules with naked force, who treats the blameless and the wicked alike (Job 19.6f., and 9.22), how could there have survived in the Christian tradition the notion that suffering, however unmerited, is somehow acceptable? Dorothee Sölle attempted an answer by taking up Simone Weil's suggestion that everyone despises the afflicted to some extent, that by nature people respond to affliction as hens who converge on a wounded bird and slash it with their beaks. 'The idea of suffering as punishment', she commented, 'is only the theological expression of this contempt.'[11] It ought not to be found in Christian theology. The proper Christian response to suffering is identical to the response advocated by Karl Marx: to work for its abolition, politically if necessary as well as personally. Once having abandoned their traditional masochism, she argued, Christians need to develop an adequate

9. *Suffering*, p. 4.
10. Ibid., pp. 109 and 119. For Bloch, p. 118, notes 34–37; cf. the way Sölle follows Bloch in separating the older folk-tale from later elements in the Book of Job, and like him refers to Abu Iyyub as the nickname of the camel.
11. *Suffering*, p. 114.

political theology. In so doing she urged them to look not only at European Marxism, but also at the experience of Christians and Marxists in other parts of the world.

By the time she came to write about suffering, Sölle had already set down her thoughts on the relationship between politics and Christian theology. In spite of the strong influence on her work of both Bloch and such politically committed Christians as Tillich and Bonhoeffer,[12] she did not attempt to maintain that Jesus sketched out political objectives for present-day Christians to follow, or even that a precise political programme can be deduced from his teachings. She distinguished discipleship (*Nachfolge*) from mere imitation (*Nachahmung*) of the historically ascertainable words and deeds of Jesus. Discipleship, she wrote, 'is not a question of describing his actual conduct and imitating it, but of recognizing the tendency of his conduct and then bringing about his goals anew in our world. Thus it is meaningless to ask whether he was a revolutionary or what his attitude was to violence or private property. Rather we must try, as his friends, responding to the tendency of the crisis he brought about, to say where we stand today with regard to revolution, private property, or violence.'[13] In this respect Sölle's Christian Marxism was closer to that of Albert Kalthoff than, for example, to that of the young Barth, who had 'no doubt' that 'Jesus rejected the concept of private property'.[14]

Dorothee Sölle was, however, perfectly clear where she thought the crisis Jesus brought about was leading. His thought and behaviour indirectly broke and altered the social structures in which he lived. He asked, 'Who is my mother? Who are my brothers?' (Mark 3.32). He destroyed conventional pieties: 'Let the dead bury their dead' (Mark 8.22). To the blind and the lame, who had no place in the Temple, he restored religious rights. He went about with outcasts, with women, who were also socially and religiously depressed. He challenged social rank, a new assessment explicitly carried into the church: 'Do not be called Rabbi, for you have one leader, the Christ, and you are all

---

12. See D. Sölle, 'Liebe Deinen Nächsten wie Dich', *Merkur*, April 1977, pp. 333–339, for Marx and Ignazio Silone. For Tillich and Bonhoeffer, see D. Sölle, *Politische Theologie. Auseinandersetzung mit Rudolf Bultmann*, Stuttgart 1971, pp. 7 and 9. Cf. her criticism of Bonhoeffer in chapter 14 of *Christ the Representative. An Essay in Theology after the 'Death of God'*, tr. D. Lewis, 1967, as well as her approval elsewhere in the book, pp. 148ff. Bonhoeffer meditated on the role of the bourgeosie at the end of his life; see his *Fragmente aus Tegel*, Munich 1978.

13. *Politische Theologie*, p. 82.

14. *Karl Barth and Radical Politics*, p. 31.

brothers. And do not call anyone on earth your father, for you have one father, who is in heaven. And do not be called leaders, for you have one leader, the Christ. But the greatest among you shall be your servant' (Matthew 23.8–11). His proclamation began what Sölle called 'an Exodus' from traditional and familiar structures of authority (cf. Matthew 20.25f.).[15]

In the light of this political, potentially revolutionary dimension at the heart of the gospel, Sölle took particular issue with Rudolf Bultmann's existential interpretation of Christianity. According to Bultmann, 'Jesus sees man as standing here and now under the necessity of decision, with the possibility of decision through his own free act. Only what a man does now gives him his value. And this crisis of decision arises for the man because he is face to face with the coming of the Kingdom of God.'[16] Bultmann, however, envisaged this crisis as an almost entirely personal affair, limiting it, *de facto*, exclusively to matters that affected the individual as an individual. The consequent lack of any political content in his presentation of Christianity had already been criticized by Ernst Bloch.[17] Sölle took up the attack in detail. Bultmann, she alleged, though aware that man is a social animal, distorted the gospel by making it solely a private concern. His presentation of Christianity thus contained no impetus toward political change or constructive criticism of society, let alone development through revolution.[18] He played into the hands of the Lutheran attitude to the powers-that-be, with its strong attachment to the principle of non-resistance and its horror of rebellion.[19]

The political content of the gospel was further effaced by Bultmann's insistence that the great images of Christianity (such as that of the kingdom of God) must be applied invariably to the present if they are to become meaningful. Sölle took his statement that, 'The meaning of history always lies in the present',[20] and set against it questions originally raised by Karl Marx. In whose interest is it always to perceive the meaning of history in the present? To what class do people belong who talk in this way? Such questions forced her to look beyond the confines

15. *Politische Theologie*, pp. 84f.

16. R. Bultmann, *Jesus and the Word*, tr. L. P. Smith and E. H. Lantero, Fontana edition, 1958, p. 46.

17. E. Bloch, *Atheismus im Christentum*, pp. 69–72.

18. *Politische Theologie*, pp. 57f. and 60.

19. On this see W. D. J. Cargill Thompson, 'Martin Luther and the "Two Kingdoms"', chapter 3 of *Political Ideas*, ed. D. Thomson, 1966.

20. R. Bultmann, *History and Eschatology: The Presence of Eternity*, New York 1962, p. 155.

of her own part of the world. Would the inhabitants of Brazilian ghettos agree that the meaning of history lies in the present? Could Bultmann's statement be endorsed by the two-thirds of humanity that belongs to the wretched of the earth? In Sölle's view, 'a future is precisely what those who happen to be the under-dogs and the also-rans at any given time need more than everything else.'[21] Bultmann, as Bloch argued, confused the eschatological moment with the present.[22] In so doing he extirpated the promise of the gospel for the future.

The inadequacy of Bultmann and his followers with regard to the political implications of Christianity was aggravated, Sölle maintained, by their quest for what they termed the *kerygma*: the essential, changeless kernel of Christian proclamation, divorced from the historical details and daily events of the life of Jesus. Dorothee Sölle was not one of those Marxist Christians indifferent to the historical Jesus; on the contrary, she was as insistent as Ernst Bloch on his importance. 'The renunciation of the historical Jesus', she wrote, 'would also be the renunciation of the political Jesus.'[23] She argued that Bultmann's attempt to substitute kerygmatic formulas for Jesus's own words and actions prompted the 'depoliticizing' of the gospel. Inevitably, a *kerygma* must be expressed in abstract terms, such as sin, salvation, grace, resurrection. Sölle pointed out that the more theology uses such abstract terms, 'the more kerygmatically pure and unworldly it thinks itself, the further will it distance itself from the words and works of Jesus, from his worldliness.'[24] The result is that reality is ordered in two parts: above is belief, below comes politics. It is nonetheless a mistake to assume that this kind of theology has no political consequences. The purer and less worldly theology imagines itself to be, the better it functions as a means of social adaptability. Sölle quoted contemporary theologians to demonstrate how notions of obedience and trust in God could be used to inculcate fatalism and a refusal to seek freedom. Similarly, concepts like love and justice, apparently free from political bias, can in reality be adapted to sanction existing authorities. As an example, she quoted the argument of a school religious textbook: 'The message of the Bible does not abrogate social differences but takes away their poison. Their solution is not equality, but justice and love.'

21. D. Sölle, *Christ the Representative*, p. 110.
22. F. P. Bowman, 'Ernst Bloch et l'Eschatologie', in *Utopie – marxisme selon Ernst Bloch*, ed. G. Raulet, p. 201.
23. *Politische Theologie*, p. 52.
24. Ibid., p. 46.

Sölle commented that 'the political content of such statements is class domination', however pure and unworldly they may claim to be.[25] By contrast, she affirmed Jesus's words in favour of the poor and against the rich (Matthew 19.24, Luke 6.20, etc.) to have been decidely impure.

Yet even when she disagreed with Rudolf Bultmann, Sölle consistently praised him for attempting to make the Bible intelligible to the modern world. She had no wish to abandon his achievements, and especially not his demythologizing. Bultmann identified the mythological elements in the Bible as the principal difficulty for twentieth-century readers. How can we give meaning, for example, to the statement that Jesus descended into hell, or that he ascended into heaven? Can we look for the return of the Son of Man on the clouds of heaven or hope that the faithful will meet him in the air (I Thessalonians 4.17)?

Bultmann's answer was to eliminate nothing from the New Testament, but to interpret everything, and by interpreting to demythologize it. For him, for example, the resurrection was not essentially about the empty tomb or the physical risen body of Jesus, but was to be understood 'simply as an attempt to convey the meaning of the cross'.[26] Belief in the resurrection, Bultmann stated, is nothing more than belief that the crucifixion of Jesus was a saving event for all humanity, which, of course, was stating a great deal. It pointed to our present ability to understand ourselves as crucified and risen with Christ. Bultmann strove to find the deeper meaning within the obsolete mythical language of the Bible, so that men and women of his time could still encounter the essential Jesus, and through him, God. In existential philosophy Bultmann believed he had found 'the right concepts for speaking of God non-mythologically'.[27] Though not everyone agreed,[28] Sölle held that by and large he had succeeded in his aims.

She wished to go further, advancing from existential to political theology, from believing and understanding to perceiving and acting.[29] In her view, both political and existential theology were required to rebut the Marxist criticism of religion. 'The reproach of the enlightenment and Marxism against religion amounts to this: that the Christians, and especially the theologians, are "deceived deceivers"—de-

25. Ibid., p. 49; cf. the whole chapter: 'The de-politicizing of the Gospel', pp. 46–53.
26. R. Bultmann, *Kerygma and Myth*, tr. R. H. Fuller, 1953, I.38.
27. Ibid., p. 104.
28. For a clear exposition of (and disagreement with) Bultmann, see S. Neill, *The Interpretation of the New Testament 1861–1961*, edition of 1966, pp. 222–235.
29. *Politische Theologie*, p. 11; 'believing and understanding' is a reference to Bultmann's famous *Glauben und Verstehen*, Tübingen 1933.

ceived by the mythological dogmatic speculation imposed on them by the institution; deceivers because they make use of this unperceived (or half-perceived) deception to sanction existing peace and order.' The demythologizers had been able to remove the sting of the first reproach, she argued; only if they went further and came to a political interpretation of the gospel would they escape the second.[30]

Dorothee Sölle maintained not that 'the question of individual existence must be silenced or classed as inessential, but that this question (like all others) can be answered only in social terms and in the context of social hopes'. She supported this contention with the example of the man Jesus encountered at the Pool of Bethesda (John 5.2ff.), whose problem was not so much that he was a cripple as that he could find no one to help him. Sölle asserted: 'To say baldly to a man, "God loves you!" achieves nothing. Because all reality comes to us in the world and in society, this sentence too must be mediated politically: it makes sense when it signifies the beginning of a change in the status quo.' The love of God is mediated to us through and in our relationships with other men and women.

Political theology, then, as expounded by Sölle, was not a theoretical underpinning of a political programme or a new form of the social gospel. It was certainly not 'the naive moralizing of a village priest on the wicked world'. It was rather a theological hermeneutic, a means of understanding and interpreting the Scriptures. 'Its leading hermeneutical principle', Sölle stated, 'is the question of an authentic human life for all mankind.' In consequence, her political theology remained resolutely international, concerned, for example, with the activities of American soldiers in Vietnam or the connections between the international oil interests and the attempted secession of Biafra from Nigeria between 1967 and 1970. She aimed at illuminating theologically what she described as 'the hypothetical isolation of men brought about by the social structures of late capitalism', and she wished to break this isolation down. God's promise, 'You shall be my people' (Exodus 6.7), she observed, will become true only when it affects those who produce and sell napalm, 'When as a result it opens men's eyes to the concomitant destruction of life to whom the same promise was made.'[31]

Political theology thus impelled Sölle to look beyond German-speaking Europe. The Christian–Marxist dialogue was once again concerned

30. *Politische Theologie*, p. 66.
31. Ibid., pp. 74, 86, 98, and 102.

with men and women suffering oppression, whose lives might be immeasurably improved by social revolution. Sölle was particularly concerned to make a critique of the international activities of the United States, partly because America constituted the dominant capitalist power in the world, and partly simply because of her own nationality. Germany had established closer military and economic links with America than any other European country, and this affected German political attitudes. As a leading American statesman (Averell Harriman) acknowledged, 'the Germans gave more help to the American intervention in Vietnam and showed greater understanding of it than any other European country.'[32] By contrast, Sölle unremittingly criticized the effects of American imperialism not only in Vietnam but in Latin America too. (She also condemned 'the exploitation of Chile through British imperialism'.[33]) She did not exclude herself from condemnation: 'With every banana I eat, I cheat out of a greater part of their wages those who cultivate bananas, and I support the United Fruit Company in its exploitation of Latin America.'[34]

Her assessment of the effects of economic imperialism on the Third World was shared by observers whose political stance was quite different. 'The problem of the poor countries', wrote the American sociologist Peter Berger, '... is not that they lack resources, technical know-how, modern institutions, or cultural traits conducive to development, but that they are being exploited by a world-wide capitalist system and its particular imperialist agents, both foreign and domestic.' Berger agreed with the proposition that, he observed, dominated the thinking of most politicians and intellectuals of the Third World: 'there is little hope for the Third World countries to emerge from poverty unless they free themselves from their present state of dependency on the rich countries.'[35] Meeting at Medellín in 1968, the Roman Catholic bishops of Latin America attributed to this state of dependency 'hunger, poverty, massive disease and infant mortality, illiteracy and marginalism, profound inequalities of income and tensions between the social classes, outbreaks of violence and scanty participation of the people in the management of the common good'. These conditions, the

32. Quoted H. Gollwitzer, *The Rich Christians and Poor Lazarus*, tr. D. Cairns, Edinburgh 1970, p. 58.

33. *Suffering*, pp. 33ff., 45ff., and 121ff.

34. *Politische Theologie*, p. 106.

35. P. L. Berger, *Pyramids of Sacrifice. Political Ethics and Social Change*, 1974 edition, pp. 29 and 274f. Cf. H. Gollwitzer, *The Rich Christians and Poor Lazarus*, pp. 48f.

bishops commented, made it impossible for men and women properly to fulfil themselves.[36] In varying degrees all the developing, mostly poor countries of Africa, Asia, and Latin America that had experienced a colonial past shared these conditions. To Sölle, the United States more than any other country seemed willing to perpetuate this state of affairs. Increasingly she began to side with the political enemies of America. During the early 1970s she claimed to have discerned in North Vietnam 'the socialism of which we dreamt' and (especially as revealed in the North Vietnamese treatment of former cabinet ministers and prostitutes) 'the capital of human dignity'.[37]

But not all participants in the Christian–Marxist dialogue were convinced that a socialist revolution was the immediate solution to the problems of the Third World. Helmut Gollwitzer warned Latin American countries wishing to use such a means to escape from dependency that they faced the dangers of terrorism and dictatorship, 'because only central leadership, with a long renunciation of individual freedom and utilization of the hitherto untapped sources of labour, can make possible the initial accumulation of resources which are the precondition of further economic prosperity'.[38] Many leading Latin American Christians, on the other hand, were now willing to take that risk.[39] Some of these Christians had been influenced by European Marxists like Ernst Bloch and Vitezlav Gardavsky;[40] but it was becoming clear that they were now ready to contemplate political praxis of a far more radical kind than that envisaged by their European comrades. Jan Milic Lochman noted how strikingly this was revealed at the World Council of Churches conference on Church and Society, held in Geneva in 1966. At that conference, whereas almost all the delegates from the developing countries (especially in Africa and Latin America) approved of the use of revolutionary force to alter unjust social conditions, nearly every other delegate wished to rule it out.[41] It is hard not to conclude that this cleavage derived at least as much from

36. Quoted H. Küng, *On Being a Christian*, tr. E. Quinn, 1977, pp. 562f. J. Miranda, *Marx and the Bible*, pp. 4f., pointed out that in 1957 Mexico contained 223,411 families with an average monthly income of 185 pesos and 134,998 families with an average monthly income of 11,592 pesos.

37. *Junge Kirche*, January 1973, pp. 6–10.

38. *Rich Christians and Poor Lazarus*, p. 53.

39. J. M. Bonino, *Christians and Marxists. The Mutual Challenge to Revolution*, 1976, esp. p. 8.

40. Ibid., pp. 54–6 and 148 n. 29.

41. J. M. Lochman, 'Ecumenical Theology of Revolution', in *New Theology No. 6*, ed. M. E. Marty and D. G. Peerman, New York 1969, pp. 111f.

the different social and economic backgrounds of the delegates as from their purely theological differences.

One year after this conference, Sölle made her most concentrated attempt to bring the thinking of Christians in the Third World to the attention of German-speaking Europe, by broadcasting and writing about the Nicaraguan revolutionary and Christian poet Ernesto Cardenal.[42] To Sölle, Latin America seemed precisely a place where people were exposed to 'senseless, patently unnecessary suffering'. It was, she said, 'torn by social contrasts to an extent that we can hardly imagine (for the bourgeois revolution has produced a completely different development in Europe). Because landed property and modern capitalism played into each other's hands, the members of the feudal upper class, owners of plantations and mines, have brought the small farmers and Indians into a misery that demands political change.'[43]

For most of his life Ernesto Cardenal had worked for such change, seeking to overthrow the Somoza dictatorship in Nicaragua by violence, and suffering imprisonment and torture for this. Then in 1957 he became a Christian. He renounced violence, but not communism, and entered the Trappist monastery of Gethsemani, in Kentucky in the United States. The novice-master there was the renowned Thomas Merton, who had himself been a communist in the 1930s. Though his politics had changed, the man who introduced Cardenal to the contemplative life never forgot the proper demands of the world.[44] Nor did Cardenal. For a time he lived with Benedictines in Mexico and Colombia, before his ordination as a priest in 1965. A year later he returned to Nicaragua to found the tiny Trappist community of Our Lady of Solentiname. Sölle described this community as 'a piece of utopia, the attempt to find a way of life between capitalism and communism, as one man's life develops through revolution, poetry, and Christian spirituality'.[45] Each Sunday Cardenal would conduct a discussion with those who came to worship. He summed up his whole aim as to preach 'the spirit of community and unity, the spirit of service to others, the

42. D. Sölle, 'Gott und die Revolution', in *Almanach für Literatur und Theologie I*, ed. D. Sölle *et al.*, Wuppertal 1967, pp. 126–136; broadcast on West German Radio, 26 March 1967.

43. Ibid., p. 127.

44. See T. Merton, *Elected Silence*, 1949, pp. 82, 116–119, and 289–294; *Contemplative Prayer*, 1973, p. 114; *The Secular Journal*, 1977, pp. ix–xv; and M. Furlong, *Merton. A Biography*, 1980, p. 263, for his letter to Cardenal, dated 17 November 1962.

45. 'Gott und die Revolution,' p. 131.

spirit of the society of the future, the spirit of proletarian struggle, the spirit of equality, the spirit of love'.[46]

Though his community was small, Cardenal's prestige as the leading poet of Latin America[47] made it impossible for the Nicaraguan authorities to ignore him; and though he preached non-violence, the content of his theology inevitably disturbed them. Every Sunday at Solentiname the discussion of the gospel was plainly communist. (In view of the abilities of the participants, it was also far more naive than anything Sölle would have permitted herself.) Jesus was called a liberator of the subversive kind needed in Nicaragua, and the Virgin Mary described as a proletarian, a 'revolutionary *campesina*'. If King Herod had heard her Magnificat (Luke 1.46-55), it was said he would have dubbed her a communist. Private property was deemed theft. 'It's up to us to fix the world, to establish justice on earth, to make the Revolution', declared one participant. 'There cannot be true peace', said another, 'while capitalism and imperialism exist.' The Exodus was seen as a journey 'from colonialism to liberty'. Granted, life in Nicaragua had momentarily improved, but 'only with total change, with a Revolution, could things be put right once and for all'.[48] All this was read out from (or read into) the pages of Scripture.

Cardenal, it was said, possessed a double vocation, 'as a revolutionary Catholic priest and as a socially committed poet'.[49] He appealed both to the literary critic and to the political theologian in Dorothee Sölle. Her literary skills helped her to achieve some notoriety in Germany by creating acts of public worship that emphasized the political aspects of the gospel, by means of meditation on, for example, works by Max Frisch and Bertolt Brecht.[50] Cardenal used his own gifts to give fresh relevance to Holy Scripture. In 1964 he published versions of twenty-five of the Old Testament psalms. In them, as Sölle observed, Cardenal was not 'transporting something from the past into

46. E. Cardenal, *Love in Practice. The Gospel in Solentiname*, tr. G. D. Walsh, 1975, pp. ixf.

47. See, for example, *Marilyn Monroe and other Poems*, ed. R. Pring-Mill, 1975, and *Latin American Revolutionary Poetry*, ed. R. Marquéz, New York 1974.

48. *Love in Practice*, pp. 1of., 15, 27f., 3of., 40, and 92f.

49. Robert Pring-Mill in *Marilyn Monroe*, p. 9.

50. *Atheistisch an Gott glauben*, chapter 2 'Zur Dialektik der Liebe', two literary texts interpreted theologically, pp. 26-36. Cf. 'Meditation über ein Wort', in *Herausforderung durch die Zeit*, Stuttgart 1970, pp. 80-82. *Politisches Nachtgebet in Köln* (written with F. Steffensky), 2 vols, Stuttgart 1969-1971; 'Zum Dialog zwischen Theologie und Literaturwissenschaft', in *Internationale Dialogzeitschrift*, vol. IV, 1969, pp. 299ff.; and F. Habsmeier 'Das Experiment als Gottesdienst. Liturgie der Revolution', in *Verkündigung und Forschung*, vol. 1, Munich 1970.

the present before it can be understood and enjoyed. The movement of the poetry is the other way round: Cardenal is trying to articulate the present, and for this task scriptural pictures and language offer themselves.'[51]

In commending Cardenal's psalms to Christians and Marxists in Germany, Sölle responded to their doctrine of God. The two great themes of this poetry she defined as 'God and the revolution'. God's absence is palpably experienced in the helplessness of men. In these psalms the question repeatedly arises, When will God finally intervene?

> How long, Lord, will you remain neutral? How long will you watch indifferently? Deliver me from the torture chamber, rescue me from the concentration camp. Far from serving peace, their propaganda provokes war. You hear their radios and see their television stations. Do not keep silence! Up Lord! Arise, my God, to stand at my side in my defence! (Psalm 34)

Cardenal's psalms call upon the God of hope. 'But what the atheists lack—and this', Sölle maintained, 'is above all decisive for anything like faith in God—is a hope to hold out to those who have no rights.'[52]

In Sölle's accusation, one reason Christians have felt obliged to tolerate suffering is that they have often worshipped an apathetic God. Against such a God she quoted the Prague Manifesto of 1521, written by Thomas Münzer: 'Thomas Münzer will pray to no mute God but only to a God who speaks.'[53] Cardenal's psalms likewise demand that God should act. 'You shall be with me, my refuge on the day of the Bomb.' 'Arise, Lord! Do not forget the oppressed. Let not the rulers rest in the belief that they can escape.' (Psalms 5 and 9) And Cardenal's God, like Sölle's, is not impartial. He remains the enemy of the dictator and the oppressor. Here, recognizably, is the God preached by the young Barth: a partisan of the poor, a God who exists 'in solidarity with society', who has revealed through Jesus Christ that one 'has to be a comrade to be a man at all'.[54] Sölle and Cardenal shared a conviction of

51. 'Gott und die Revolution', p. 131. I discuss Cardenal's poems and other writings at greater length in 'Dorothee Sölle: Political Theology and the Experience of Latin America', in *Papers in Religion and Politics*, University of Manchester Department of Government and Faculty of Theology, No. 6, Michaelmas 1978, pp. 1–25.

52. Ibid., p. 134. Here as elsewhere Cardenal's psalms are translated from *Zerschneide den Stacheldraht*, Wuppertal 1967, as quoted (sometimes slightly shortened) by Sölle.

53. *Suffering*, p. 75; cf. pp. 41–45: 'The Christians' Apathetic God'.

54. Quoted, E. Busch, p. 71.

their own solidarity, and God's, with all who suffer and have no rights. And this one form of suffering Sölle specifically distinguished from Christian masochism. At this point men and women suffering in the world represent the crucified God. 'Representation permits a form of suffering which does not make us blind, impotent, and sterile', she asserted, 'which does not succumb to the self-destruction which the sufferers bring upon themselves and the world.' Here Sölle specifically endorsed Bonhoeffer's interpretation of the crucifixion of Jesus: 'Man is challenged to participate in the sufferings of God at the hands of a godless world.'[55]

Cardenal similarly derived from the crucifixion his notion of God's solidarity with those who suffer. He expressed it above all in his version of the psalm that Jesus prayed on the cross:

> My God, my God, why have you forsaken me? I have become a caricature. The people despise me and in every newspaper I am held up to ridicule.
> Tanks surround me. Machine guns threaten me. Electrified barbed-wire fences imprison me. I am contaminated by radio-activity, and people avoid me for fear of infection.
> But I will tell my brothers about you, my God. In our assemblies I will praise you.
> The poor shall feast. The people shall celebrate a great feast.
> (Psalm 22)

As a Christian, identified with Christ, Cardenal believed he shared in this solidarity. 'It is not presumption', wrote Sölle, 'when Cardenal dares to speak of those murdered in Auschwitz as "we", when he speaks of "our" skin and "our" fat.'[56]

He and Sölle were here very close to Moltmann's understanding of the cross as symbolizing hope for the hopeless and as bringing Christians to stand alongside the oppressed of the world. Cardenal's gesture was not that of a condescending or generous patrician to the lower orders, but rather the identification of one who had been politically oppressed with those who were socially oppressed. As such

---

55. *Christ the Representative*, p. 148. D. Bonhoeffer, 18 July 1944, in *Letters and Papers from Prison, The Enlarged Edition*, p. 361 (where the sentence is retranslated from earlier editions, 'Man is summoned to share in God's sufferings at the hands of a godless world.').

56. 'Gott und die Revolution', p. 134.

it was authentically socialist as well as Christian. As Bertolt Brecht wrote:

> the compassion of the oppressed for the
> oppressed is indispensable.
> It is the world's one hope.[57]

At this point, however, both Cardenal and Sölle went on to locate God in a manner that few theologians (and certainly not Barth and Moltmann) would have found acceptable. For them, God was virtually identified with the creative proletariat and the revolutionary peasantry. God liberates men, Cardenal told the worshippers at Solentiname, not directly but through the Messiah; 'now the Messiah isn't only Jesus but all of us', he added, 'and that's why he's also called Emmanuel, which means "God with us". Liberation is accomplished through God working through us.'[58] Sölle similarly located God: 'God is not above human parties and classes. He is involved. He is partisan. He is always on the side of the oppressed, and he exists only at the point where the oppressed take action.'[59]

As a theologian of the 'death of God', Sölle abandoned traditional theism. In her day, she observed, society had taken over very many of the functions reserved in the past for God. She went further than most such theologians in declaring that in some respects ('for example, in providing an explanation of the world, in healing the sick, in affording protection against disasters') society can perform these functions better than the God of former ages, so often appealed to in vain. She therefore welcomed the growing consciousness of men and women over the previous two hundred years that 'God is dead.' In our technological age, she asserted, 'Naive theism, a direct childlike relationship to the father above the starry sky, has become impossible.'[60] We can surrender ourselves to God, she argued, only when we surrender ourselves to men. Sölle's theology refused to allow that men could be forgiven directly by God, behind the backs, so to speak, of those they had wronged. Forgiveness needed to be mediated politically, through the one historical reality in which men lived. So an individual Pole, whose

57. Tr. M. Hamburger, in B. Brecht *Poems, part iii, 1938–1958*, ed. J. Willett and T. Manheim, 1976, p. 328.

58. *Love in Practice*, p. 35.

59. Quoted from a paper given at Melun, France, in 1972, B. L. Cordingley, 'An Essay in Faith and Radical Politics', in *Theology and Politics*, Industrial Mission Association, Manchester 1978, p. 6.

60. *Christ the Representative*, pp. 131f. Cf. 'Ist Gott von gestern?' pp. 13–18 of D. Sölle, *Die Wahrheit ist konkret*, Olten 1967.

family was murdered by the Germans, could forgive Dorothee Sölle, an individual German, only if Germany accepted the boundaries of a new peace, only when fear was calmed by political action. Sölle offered as a model of such political forgiveness 'the group indictments and defence, self-criticism and exclusion from the party, expiation, punishment and readmission to the group which take place in socialist countries in the collectives and among people who work together. There', she claimed, 'society has created instruments similar to those of the old monasteries, whereby wanderers, those in error and the guilty can make a new start.'[61]

Yet, Sölle acknowledged, society still failed to provide men and women with an adequate meaning and purpose to life. And although she found biblical support for locating God among the oppressed in Matthew 25.40 ('Inasmuch as you did it to one of these, my brethren, you did it to me'), it remains important to ask whether she offered God any other status than this, or whether the 'world's one hope', the compassion of the oppressed for the oppressed, had in her theology, as in Bloch's, really eliminated God altogether.

This theology certainly brought her closer than any other Christian theologian to Bloch's critique of the God expounded by the Barthians. Sölle set out her own criticisms of Barth's notion of God in a disagreement with Helmut Gollwitzer over Prometheus and Christianity. In 1969 Gollwitzer had urged that, 'To make the relative utopia the image of our activity signifies no Promethean tower of Babel, but is the consequence of the proclamation of the kingdom of God, mobilizing us to action in the present. That is what Marxism has reminded Christians, and we should be grateful for the reminder, instead of rejecting it through a false antithesis between Christ and Prometheus.'[62] The following year he repeated that in his view no antithesis between the two existed.[63] This statement, remarkable in coming from Barth's chief disciple and heir, occurred in a major work in which Gollwitzer sought the meaning of life, under the influence of Bloch as well as his theological master. Gollwitzer described his book as a journey from Kant, who characterized man as a bent piece of wood, to Bloch's vision of a human utopia in which men should walk upright. The lineaments

61. *Politische Theologie*, pp. 124ff. The last chapter of the book is called 'Forgiveness, Politically Interpreted'.

62. 'Die Revolution des Reiches Gott und die Gesellschaft', in *Diskussion zur Theologie der Revolution*, hrsg von E. Feil and R. Weth, Munich 1969, p. 56.

63. *Krummes Holz – aufrechter Gang. Zur Frage nach dem Sinn des Lebens*, Munich 1970, p. 13.

of this utopia included Barth's notion that Christian groups inevitably developed into socialist groups.[64]

This particular assertion Gollwitzer made on flimsy enough evidence, in part still under the heady influence of the radical students of Berlin, who had been at the peak of their political activity in 1968. (He had then made the unwarranted assumption that the majority of children of pastors became socialists under the stimulus of the gospel.[65]) Nonetheless, such a work seemed so much in line with the thinking of Sölle that her attack was startling. The precise point at issue arose over Gollwitzer's contention that man derives meaning ultimately not from himself but solely from God. The 'central point' of the disagreement she defined thus:

'So long as Gollwitzer, like all Barthians, holds fast to the self-sufficiency of God, for so long must they be attacked as "Theists". They erect as the measure of greatness and perfection something that in fact serves to bring it into contempt. They are not ashamed to praise independence and self-sufficiency as in some sense "godly", although it is precisely here that the projection of the capitalist, whose highest goal is autonomy, has taken hold. They remain bourgeois in that they cannot radically conceive of God as solidarity. Instead they demand, in power and certainty of victory, more than the strength of the weak (whose sole strength is that they belong to God).'[66] As visual evidence of this Feuerbachian projection of a bourgeois God, the master who has no need of his subjects, who gives as they passively receive, she instanced the Protestant liturgies in which the people do nothing but meekly accept the word of God, handed down from on high.

Although Sölle shared with Gollwitzer a concern for Marxist politics and for the Third World, their diverse theological heritage (his from Barth, hers from Gogarten and Bultmann) made theological disagreement likely if not inevitable. Yet it is not clear that her assessment of the political consequences of Barthianism was either fair or correct. To describe Barth as projecting a God of the bourgeoisie was almost entirely unjust. In the first of his commentaries on Romans he wrote:

64. Cf. his article 'Muss ein Christ sozialist sein?' in *Jenseits vom Null-punkt*, hrsg von R. Weckerling *et al.*, Augsburg 1972, pp. 151-169. For Barth's socialist church, see F.-W. Marquardt, 'Sozialismus bei Karl Barth', p. 3.

65. *Die Reichen Christen und der Arme Lazarus*, Munich 1968, p. 31 (mistranslated on p. 17 of *The Rich Christians and Poor Lazarus*). K. L. Baker, 'The Acquisition of Partisanship', in *American Journal of Political Science*, vol. 28, no. 3, August 1974, pp. 576 and 580f., does not bear out Gollwitzer's contention.

66. 'Christus oder Prometheus', in *Merkur*, vol. 43, 1972, p. 708.

'Certainly God is a God of the Jews *and* of the heathen, but he is not a God of the exalted *and* the lowly. He is one-sidedly a God of the lowly.'[67] It is similarly difficult to accept her picture of Gollwitzer's God as a bourgeois father who allows his children to suffer because of his desire to remain aloof. Gollwitzer's understanding of God, as well as his political alignments, drove him to expound guilt as the acceptance of 'each avoidable suffering—and that truly is the fault of all. Guilt', he concluded, 'ceases to be something private, which a person can commit essentially alone and for himself. The truth of the concept of sin expands in the political dimension. ... Sin is the refusal of help, and especially involves the willing acceptance of the status quo. Sin is collaboration.'[68] Ironically, Sölle too regarded the privatization of sin as one of the major problems to be overcome in contemporary theology. 'Theology is dominated by a depoliticized understanding of sin', she judged. 'The collectives in which we live—nations, races, classes, communities, groups—are not glimpsed.' This she held, erroneously, to be a special fault of the Barthians.[69]

Gollwitzer's teaching by no means urged men and women to remain passive in face of trouble. 'The Bible', he wrote, 'forces us, demands that we do not give up.'[70] He had learned from Blumhardt the need to persist. Blumhardt believed in 'the ceaseless prayer for the spirit of persistence',[71] and Gollwitzer took up this theme. In *The Rich Christians and Poor Lazarus* he wrote: ' "One must be an active man day and night", says Christoph Blumhardt, who simply took it for granted that no hard and fast lines could be drawn between care for a man's salvation and care for his welfare. With his father, Blumhardt profoundly abhorred the traditional Christian spirituality which sat so comfortably on the self-satisfied possessors of wealth. He was concerned, day and night, here and there, to repel injustice, in order that here and there a man might rejoice in his God-given rights.'[72] The socialist element in the Barthian tradition was too strong for Sölle's criticism to stand. Her own theological inheritance obscured the fact that she and Gollwitzer were essentially on the same side.

67. *Römerbrief*, p. 366.
68. *Das Recht ein anderer zu werden*, Neuwied and Berlin 1971, p. 146.
69. *Politische Theologie*, p. 107. See also p. 105: 'Word of God theology separates itself from a political understanding of the gospel in nothing so much as its underlying understanding of sin.'
70. *Krummes Holz – aufrechter Gang*, p. 326; cf. pp. 66 and 343.
71. Quoted J. Moltmann, *The Crucified God*, ET 1974, p. 16.
72. *The Rich Christians and Poor Lazarus*, p. 23. Elsewhere in this book (p. 95 n. 7) Gollwitzer refers to Blumhardt on the political consequences of the Eucharist.

Yet in one important respect a difference had arisen between them, one that aligned her closer to the Marxist camp than he was. Although Gollwitzer asserted that there was no antithesis between Christ and Prometheus, he refused to modify his contention that the meaning of a man's existence derives not from his own performance but from the grace of God. Gollwitzer believed that in the kingdom of God, supreme value is to be found not in people's achievements but in personal relationships of love—which led Helga Krüger Day to the conclusion that he had become a Marxist in action and social analysis but had remained a Lutheran in regard to the meaning of life.[73] This sharp contrast between grace and human achievement is what Sölle defined as the debate between Christ and Prometheus. She advanced two reasons for disagreeing with Gollwitzer. First (against Horkheimer and Wittgenstein as well as Gollwitzer), she refused to allow that the question of the meaning of life is inseparable from the question of God, and that in consequence whoever is seeking the meaning of life is seeking God. Second, she took up the Marxist contention that a man dependent on others is alienated from himself, and that therefore the concept of a totally superior God is a major cause of such alienation. 'A God with whom we stand in an asymmetrical relationship', she wrote, 'has become humanly intolerable.'[74] In her view Gollwitzer's insistence on the importance of grace retained humanity in a state of dependency, even infancy, seeking a security that brought back the God of omnipotence instead of solidarity, the God of superiority instead of love.

Gollwitzer's response was that 'If you think a little, all is grace. If I can speak with you and don't have a breakdown in my mind, that is not my achievement. If I define this as dependence on God, why are you against such dependency? Man is a dependent animal; and why not? Freedom is also a gift. The consequence of all this is not to become a fatalist. Grace doesn't paralyse my activity.' Gollwitzer described Sölle as thinking with her heart and feelings more than with her head. When he insisted that it was still possible to say, 'God the Lord', she no doubt would describe him (in the jargon of the women's liberation movement of the 1970s) as a 'male chauvinist'. But because Christianity must live inside a tradition, it is impossible to eliminate the past and the language of the past. 'The task is not to eliminate words', he argued, 'but to purify them.'[75]

73. H. K. Day, 'Christlicher Glaube und Gesellschaftliches Handeln', p. 472.
74. 'Christus oder Prometheus', p. 708.
75. Personal conversation with the author, 30 October 1979.

Sölle did not take her Marxist critique of traditional Christianity as far as insisting (to quote Gollwitzer's summary of traditional Marxist thinking) that 'God cannot exist because his existence would exclude self-redemption'.[76] Rather, she urged Christians to abandon the alternative of either achieving or receiving meaning in life. The proper relationship with God, she said, involved simply co-operating with him. So giving and receiving become one. Thus Isaiah, preaching God's comfort to Israel (Isaiah 40.1f.), both gave and received comfort. Jesus, breaking into the cry of dereliction on Golgotha, was given meaning and also gave meaning to the crucifixion. And, she asserted, all this corresponds to the reality of everyday life. 'The theological alternative of *either* achievement *or* grace, of God as the one who acts or man as creative, of taking action or being dealt with, disappears in the reality of living. The schema "achievement or grace" does not correspond to the reality of eating together, sleeping together, working together, where we learn the meaning of life.' To express this, Sölle typically sought a new liturgy in place of the familiar Protestant gathering, in which one leads and the rest docilely receive. 'In singing hymns', she observed, 'I both give and receive. When we work together, we take from each other and we hand on.'[77]

Sölle was perfectly willing to allow that co-operation with God involved people serving God as well as God serving people. The conclusion of her *Christ the Representative*, published in 1965, was that in Christ God 'put himself at risk, made himself dependent upon us, identified himself with the non-identical'. God had worked for us long enough. 'From now on', she wrote, 'it is high time for us to do something for him.'[78]

Dorothee Sölle urged that co-operation with God was possible even at the moment of death. As we have seen, Ernst Bloch saw death as an unsolved problem in his dialogue with Christians. 'If the martyr's name has an altar in the heart of the working class', he wrote, 'this does not restore to his name either his eyes or his bodily presence.'[79] Marxism, as Paul Tillich observed, 'sees no fulfilment of human destiny except in the collective fulfilment'.[80] This, however, was not quite true to Marx himself, who lamented, 'Men have defended themselves until now against death in various ways, but they have still not undertaken the

76. *The Christian Faith and the Marxist Criticism of Religion*, p. 102.
77. 'Christus oder Prometheus', p. 709.
78. *Christ the Representative*, p. 152.
79. *Das Prinzip Hoffnung*, II.1300.
80. *Systematic Theology*, I.295.

struggle against it.'[81] In contrast, Sölle wished neither to defend herself against death, nor resignedly to put up with it, but instead, in co-operation with God, to embrace it. 'We shall not die well', she wrote, 'if we merely accept (*hinnehmen*) death; we need to learn to welcome (*empfangen*) it.'[82] In the theology of Dorothee Sölle, hope for the dying, which Moltmann had failed to discover in the writings of Bloch, did not finally force people into total dependence on God. Hope in death still involved what people could do for themselves.

81. Quoted J. M. Miranda, *Marx and the Bible*, p. 281.
82. 'Christus oder Prometheus', p. 709.

8

'Jesus for Atheists'

In 1968 the frontiers of the dialogue appeared to be changing. Jürgen Moltmann observed that on the one hand Marx was becoming the property of Christian revolutionaries and on the other hand Christianity was ceasing to be the exclusive property of the churches. Outsiders were reading the Bible in new ways. Brecht declared it to be his favourite book. The process begun and continued by Ernst Bloch could now be seen in the writings of the Polish philosopher Leszek Kolakowski, and above all in a book of essays by the Czech atheist Viteslav Gardavsky, recently published in Germany under the title, *God Is Not Yet Dead*.[1]

The peculiar position of Czechoslovakia in the Christian–Marxist dialogue has already been indicated by the importance of the theologian Jan Milic Lochman in the debate over Prometheus. An accidental reason for this position was the inclusion of a German-speaking population in Czechoslovakia in 1918. As a result, Christians and Marxists in that country remained closely in touch with their counterparts in Germany (sometimes suffering together at the hands of the Nazis). The Communist coup d'etat in Czechoslovakia in February 1948 did not bring this contact to an end. And, contrary to the intentions of those who engineered it, the Communist seizure of power helped to bring about a remarkable flowering of the Christian–Marxist dialogue in Czechoslovakia over the next thirty years.

The coup undoubtedly surprised many Czechs. (A few weeks earlier Visser t'Hooft, soon to be the first general secretary of the World

---

1. *Im Gespräch mit Ernst Bloch*, p. 49. This section, 'Hat die Schlange doch recht?' pp. 49–54, first appeared in *Der Spiegel*, no. 40, 1968, under the title 'Und die Bibel ist doch links'. For Kolakowski at this time see, e.g., his article 'Jesus Christus–Prophet und Reformator', in *Almanach I für Literatur und Theologie*, pp. 141–157. In 1968 he was to be dismissed from his chair of philosophy in Warsaw and had in fact been expelled from the Polish United Workers' Party in 1966.

Council of Churches, visited Prague and was taken by Josef Hromadka to meet President Eduard Beneš. Beneš requested him to 'tell everyone that the Russians have never interfered with us.'[2]) A good many Christians were distressed as well as surprised by the coup.[3] Hromadka, however, who was now a Christian leader of international stature, was convinced that he and his fellow Christians could and should co-operate with the new regime. His own first experience of co-operating with Communists had been in the 1930s, in an attempt to strengthen democracy in Spain. He had been very much influenced by T. G. Masaryk's understanding of the 'spiritual drama' of Russia.[4] He perceived communism as in part a judgement on the churches' failure properly to develop a social conscience. And such judgements had been reinforced by his long friendship with Karl Barth. (Hromadka too had spent the war years in exile in Switzerland.) As a Barthian, he held that anti-communism was not an acceptable stance for Western Christians, a position re-affirmed (under Barth's influence) by the last public statement issued by the Confessing Church after the collapse of the Third Reich, the so-called 'Darmstadt Word' in August 1947.[5]

Thus Hromadka's experience of the Christian–Marxist dialogue governed his response to the events of 1948 in Czechoslovakia. In October of that year he preached on 'The Present Problems of the Church':

'The Church of Christ belongs to no era, and cannot be identified with anything in this world. Today we are involved in a radical change in the very structure of society. Rougher classes are taking over the direction of our society, and the problem for us Protestants is that these people have always lived on the fringe of national life, and have never been schooled by religion and by the Church. The middle classes, whose faith was never conspicuous for its vigour, have nonetheless received a certain religious culture: Socialists have no such tradition. From the human point of view, the present situation is much more painful for the Church. All outside support has been withdrawn. And yet, from the point of view of the Church of Christ, we are on the threshold of a finer and more blessed age. In future, we shall not be

2. Visser t'Hooft: personal conversation with the author, 24 October 1979.

3. Sir Robert Birley, who was in Prague at the time: personal conversation with the author, 5 October 1979.

4. J. R. Hromadka, 'The Situation in Czechoslovakia', in *The World Year Book of Religion: The Religious Situation*, ed. D. R. Luther, 1970, II.48.

5. H. Ludwig, *Die Entstehung des Darmstädter Wortes*, Bremen 1977; the text of the 'Darmstadt Word' is printed on p. 1.

able to depend upon anything at all—neither upon wealth, nor upon the homage paid to us by society, nor upon any human aid, but solely upon the grace and love of God.'[6]

Hromadka did not find it easy to persuade his fellow Christians to remain open to Marxism and together with the new rulers of Czechoslovakia to attempt to build a more humane society. The Communist takeover in 1948 involved the nationalization of church lands, in return for public economic support for religion (chiefly, from 1949 onwards, in the form of paying the clergy's stipends). At the same time, the church ceased to be established, suffering many pinpricks from the state as well as active hostility toward leading laymen—doctors, artists, scientists, and civil servants—who wished to remain church members.[7] In March 1948 British Foreign Secretary Bevin told the Cabinet that in Czechoslovakia 'a purge of the whole country is in progress and all Western influences will shortly be suppressed.'[8] Yet insofar as Christianity was regarded as an undesirable Western influence, it proved impossible to suppress. In 1966 Erika Kadlecova, the sociologist in charge of religious affairs in Czechoslovakia, estimated that religious belief still survived among forty per cent of the population.[9] After 1956, when Nikita Khrushchev, as first secretary of the Central Committee of the Soviet Communist Party, denounced certain aspects of Stalinism at the Twentieth Congress of the party,[10] the Czechs began to develop a freedom of discussion that was not destroyed until, on the orders of Leonid Brezhnev, the country was invaded by armed forces of the Soviet Union, East Germany, Poland, Hungary, and Bulgaria twelve years later. During those years Czechoslovakia proved fertile soil for a remarkable growth in the Christian–Marxist dialogue.

Hromadka's influence ensured that the dialogue included his German and Swiss friends and teachers. Together with Hans-Joachim Iwand (a staunch ally of the Confessing Church in the struggle against Hitler and a collaborator with Barth in preparing the 'Darmstadt

6. Quoted from Ecumenical Press Service, 22 October 1948, in J. B. Barra and H. M. Waddams, *Communism and the Churches, A Documentation*, 1950, p. 50.

7. J. M. Lochman, *Church in a Marxist Society*, pp. 86–104.

8. 'Czech Coup Shook Britain', in *Daily Telegraph*, 3 January 1979, quoting newly released Cabinet documents in the Public Record Office.

9. P. A. Toma and M. J. Reban, 'Church-State Schism in Czechoslovakia', in *Religion and Atheism in the USSR and Eastern Europe*, ed. B. R. Bociurkiw and J. W. Strong, 1967, pp. 288 and 291 n.27.

10. For the general importance of this in the Christian–Marxist dialogue, see R. R. Ruether, *The Radical Kingdom*, p. 188.

Word'),[11] Hromadka called together a Christian Peace Conference at Prague in 1959.[12] Both Barth and Martin Niemöller gave their support.[13] One of the chief speakers was Helmut Gollwitzer, who argued that every earthly good comes from the repentance of those who are willing to acknowledge their own guilt. The attitude of the church, especially in its attacks on the East and on communism in general, frequently makes credible, he said, many of the criticisms directed by Marx against Christianity.[14]

This was the tradition of dialogue in which Jan Milic Lochman came to maturity. Born in Nové Mešto in 1922, he had studied under Hromadka in Prague and under Barth in Basle. Strongly identified with the social ideals of Jan Hus and T. G. Masaryk, he taught at the Comenius theological faculty in Prague between 1948 and 1968, where he succeeded Hromadka as professor of systematic theology. Acknowledging Hromadka's pioneering role,[15] Lochman developed and promulgated the themes of his teachers both inside and outside Czechoslovakia. In the growing ecumenical movement, he developed Barth's doctrine of the revolutionary God in the light of his own Hussite background as well as Barthianism. Lochman agreed with Helmut Gollwitzer's contention that it is far more difficult to justify the traditional Christian defence of a just war (which aims always at preserving the status quo) than to defend the traditional Christian rejection of revolutionary violence (even when aimed at liberating the oppressed). Yet, under the influence of Jan Hus, Lochman refused to go so far as to give unqualified support to such revolutionary violence. 'The revolutionary Hussites', he wrote, 'endeavoured to change the way of life of the entire society and were therefore concerned with the problem of the responsible use of violence. The Bohemian Brethren endeavoured to apply the full binding force of the authority of Jesus Christ through

11. See H. Ludwig, pp. 2f.

12. The third organizer of this conference was Bohuslav Pospisil. For Hromadka's ecumenical and political aims in calling the Conference, see Ruth Puffert, 'Kirchliches Leben in der CSSR', in *Evangelische Kommentare*, June 1969, p. 348. See also C. Ordnung, *Christen im Ringen um eine bessere Welt. Zum Selbstverständnis der christlichen Friedenskonferenz*, Prague 1969.

13. K. Gust, 'East German Protestantism under Communist Rule,' p. 193.

14. H. Gollwitzer, 'Zehn Thesen über "Krieg und Christentum"'. Vortrag von Helmut Gollwitzer auf der christlichen Friedenskonferenz 1959', in *Junge Kirche*, vol. 20, 1959, pp. 228ff. For Gollwitzer's praise of Hromadka, see his essay 'Von der Religion zum Menschen', in *"Antwort". Festschrift zum Karl Barths 70. Geburtstag*, Zürich 1956, pp. 596-709.

15. J. M. Lochman, 'Zur Frage der "Geschichtsphilosophie" J. L. Hromadkas', in *Evangelische Theologie*, Munich 1965, pp. 413-428.

non-violent means to the Christian minority.' It was essential, Lochman concluded, to consider both points of view in the ecumenical study of the question of violence. His own view was that, since violence could not be justified theologically by the cross of Christ, the 'proprium Christianum in the sphere of ethics will always be to endeavour to stress the non-violent possibilities and strategies.'[16]

Lochman's contacts in German-speaking Europe were not confined to Christians. He developed a deep friendship with the Swiss Marxist Konrad Farner, whom he first met when Farner visited Prague in the 1950s as secretary of the Swiss Communist Party. In 1956 Farner had been (in Lochman's words [17]) 'a kind of communist martyr' in Switzerland, where he was physically attacked and molested after the Russian invasion of Hungary. Farner argued that both the moral revolution required by Christians and the social, political, and economic revolution demanded by Marxists were necessary and complementary,[18] and he welcomed Lochman's analysis of the place of Prometheus in the Christian calender.[19]

Inside Czechoslovakia Lochman for his part welcomed both the 'ruins of the Constantinian structures' of Christianity and what he described as *'the end of the quarantine for theologians'*.[20] Christians were now cut off neither from the outside world nor from Marxists in their own country. Lochman was committed both to the political experiments of the 1960s in Czechoslovakia and to the complete rejection of Stalinism. ('How often an "orthodox idea" was recklessly imposed upon facts and social reality!' he wrote. 'How often any deviation from the official image was severely reprimanded!'[21]) Along with Stalinism, Lochman sought to destroy outmoded critiques of Christianity. Just as he insisted that the Prometheus of traditional Marxism needed demythologizing, so he sharply criticized such Marxists

---

16. 'The Just Revolution', in *Christianity and Crisis*, no. 32, New York 1972, pp. 163f. I am grateful to Mr Martin Howarth for drawing my attention to this article.

17. In conversation with the author, 26 October 1979.

18. *Marxistiches Salz für christliche Erde-Christliches Salz für marxistische Erde*, Zürich 1972. Cf. his volume of essays *Für die Erde: geeint-Für den Himmel entzweit*, Zürich 1973, which is dedicated to Lochman.

19. Farner reviewed Lochman's *Christus oder Prometheus* in *Junge Kirche*, October 1972, pp. 491-493. Cf. his article ' "Christus oder Prometheus?" ' in *Neue Zeit. Zeitkritische Montatsblätter*, Zürich, November 1978, pp. 321-323. The same issue, pp. 318-320, contains Lochman's appreciation of his friend, 'Konrad Farners aufrechter Gang'.

20. *Church in a Marxist Society*, pp. 134 and 10.

21. 'Marxism, Liberalism and Religion, an East European Perspective', in *Marxism and Radical Religion*, ed. J. C. Raines and T. Dean, Philadelphia 1970, p. 17.

as refused to acknowledge that Christianity too could be demythologized. Marxist criticism of religion, which saw it as mythology, as an out-of-date view of the world, derived to a large extent, he insisted, 'from the thought forms of the nineteenth-century attack on religion' and ought to be abandoned.[22] Although recognizing clear points of divergence between Marxists and Christians (in particular, over the question of God and the doctrine of grace), Lochman in the 1960s was especially concerned to emphasize where the two sides converged. Both agreed, he maintained, that man is a being who must take history seriously; both asserted that man's thinking should be directed towards the future in the hope of changing the world.[23]

In 1966 the dialogue in Czechoslovakia began to gather momentum with the publication in the highly influential Prague journal *Líternárni noviny* of Gardavsky's series of articles under the provocative title 'God is not yet dead'. Brought together as a book, they became a philosophical best-seller both in Czechoslovakia and in Germany. Gardavsky, who was born in 1923, was professor of philosophy at the military academy in Brno. Well acquainted with Christian thinking both in his own country and in contemporary Germany,[24] he was responsive—while remaining an atheist—to the work of Rudolf Bultmann, Dorothee Sölle, Sigmund Freud,[25] and Erich Fromm.[26] He accepted Roger Garaudy's analysis of the creative power of mythology, and especially of Hebrew mythology. Whereas (as the story of Icarus demonstrates) Greek mythology set limits to what men can achieve, in Hebrew mythology, Gardavsky observed, man was set no unalterable norms: the cosmos contained no taboos.[27]

Since, as Gardavsky wrote, 'Jesus causes the theologians a lot of trouble',[28] he decided to ask what the religious concept of Christ might

22. 'The Gospel for Atheists', in *Concurrence*, no. 3, Basle, Autumn 1969, p. 240.

23. *Church in a Marxist Society*, pp. 173-177. Cf. 'Solidarität und politische Verantwortung der Christen', in *Das radikale Erbe. Versuche einer theologischen Orientierung im Ost und West*, Zürich 1973, pp. 97-112, and ibid., pp. 173-186, where he argued that Comenius preached a hope that altered this world.

24. His *Habilitationsschrift* was on 'Das Phänomenon Deutschlands', before which he had specially studied German Catholicism.

25. The recognition of Freud by Czech Marxists dates from a conference on Kafka organized by Eduard Goldstücker in Prague in 1963. The addresses, including one by Roger Garaudy, were published in *Franz Kafka in Prager Sicht*, ed. E. Goldstücker, *et al.*, Prague 1963.

26. *Hoffnung aus der Skepsis*, tr. D. Neumärker, Munich 1970, pp. 38 n.17, 57, n.24, and 65 n.27.

27. Ibid. pp. 38 n.19, 42 and 49.

28. *God Is Not Yet Dead*, p. 31.

mean for Marxist atheists. Lochman summed up Gardavsky's answer
to the perennial question of what sort of man Jesus was: Gardavsky
gave 'first of all a very simple answer. *Jesus is a Jew*. Is that too little?
For Gardavsky it is very much. For the Jewish notion of humanity
perceives man as revolutionary potentiality.'[29] Gardavsky described
this revolutionary man at the very beginning of Hebrew history, in the
patriarch Jacob. He saw Jacob wrestling with God (in Genesis 32) as
Promethean in the classicly Marxist sense. Transcending all accepted
boundaries, Jacob took charge of his own fate. His action was 'the first
authentic human action'.[30] As Lochman later observed, in the thinking
of Gardavsky at this time, 'Jacob of the Old Testament virtually takes
the place of Prometheus as the historical model of authentic existence.'[31] Gardavsky then proceeded to argue that Jesus went even
further than Jacob in Promethean daring. Jesus showed that man can
perform miracles, transcending everything that is trivial, banal, ordinary, natural, normal. 'Why be afraid of this type of miracle?' asked
Gardavsky. 'Why not wish for one instead?'[32]

All this Gardavsky attempted to relate to orthodox Marxism.
Because Karl Marx was a Jew, Gardavsky asserted that he carried 'in
his innermost heart' all the individual experiences gleaned over thousands of years by the Jewish people. But, Gardavsky admitted, this
rendered Marx's materialism questionable in the extreme.[33]

Such thinking made Gardavsky a specially valued participant in the
Christian–Marxist dialogue. His rediscovery (along with Ernst Bloch)
of the creative power of biblical thought was acknowledged by Christians to have raised the dialogue to a new and higher plane.[34] Though
an atheist, Gardavsky was proud of his country's religious inheritance.
'The Reformation has a special significance for Czechs and Slovaks',
he wrote, 'for our ancestors were the first to herald its arrival.'[35] And
he also found in Comenius the insights of Pascal about the reality of
the God of Abraham, Isaac, and Jacob compared with the God of the
philosophers.[36] Yet Gardavsky remained critical of Christianity for
frequently failing to measure up to its own potential, for holding aloof

29. *Christus oder Prometheus*, pp. 19f.

30. His story 'tells how man becomes a subject, a person': *God Is Not Yet Dead*, pp.
29 and 31.

31. 'Platz für Prometheus', p. 136.

32. *God Is Not Yet Dead*, p. 49.

33. Ibid. p. 33.

34. J. M. Lochman, 'Platz für Prometheus', p. 136.

35. *God Is Not Yet Dead*, p. 13.

36. *Hoffnung aus der Skepsis*, p. 32 n.14.

from politics and the class war, for caring about its own prestige, and for 'not being capable of digging down to its own roots'.[37] These roots, for Gardavsky, included the Old Testament insight that possessions delude and imprison instead of freeing human beings, as well as Jesus's attack on 'the sterilityof the official dogmatic religion'.[38]

So Gardavsky remained an atheist, but (as Lochman put it), 'an atheist of a "higher order", or better: an atheist *de profundis*'. His atheism had nothing in common with the self-confident propagandistic atheism of the Enlightenment.[39] In an adaptation of Tertullian's famous *Credo quia absurdum*, Gardavsky recognized that it is equally as absurd for communists not to believe as it is for Christians to believe.[40] Gardavsky, moreover, turned Marx on his head by asserting that because man is not yet quite alive, God could not be quite dead. He asked what were the functions that belief in God apparently still fulfilled (however inadequately) and Marxism, properly understood, ought better to fulfil. The question could be answered, he said, only when Marxism had soaked up Christianity. 'The Marxist', he wrote, 'is convinced that Christianity as a religious movement can be altered to fit in with socialism.' And he considered it 'patently obvious that until we are capable of making a fair assessment of the epoch-making phenomenon that is Christianity, we shall not be able to establish how far it has failed to live up to its own potential'.[41]

One year after Gardavsky's articles appeared in print, the dialogue in Czechoslovakia became a public as well as a literary affair. In 1965 and 1966 the *Paulusgesellschaft*, 'a group of German-speaking theologians and scientists whose aim was to find a contemporary language for faith',[42] had organized two open meetings with Marxists in Salzburg and Chiemsee. Although these meetings did not break new ground in the debate, they demonstrated its mounting public importance. They involved a number of leading Roman Catholic theologians along with the Protestant participants of the dialogue. They also caught the attention of Milan Machovec, who was professor of philosophy at the University of Prague. In 1967 Machovec was responsible for organizing a similar meeting in the city of Marienbad, the first ever public

37. *God Is Not Yet Dead*, p. 13.
38. *Hoffnung aus der Skepsis*, pp. 48 and 61.
39. 'Gardavskys Wandlung von Jakob zu Jeremia', in *Orientierung. Katholische Blätter für Weltanschauliche Information*, Zürich, no.10, 1978, pp. 110f.
40. *God Is Not Yet Dead*, pp. 7 and 218.
41. Ibid. p. 15
42. P. Hebblethwaite, *The Christian–Marxist Dialogue and Beyond*, 1977, p. 17.

meeting of Marxists and Christians in Eastern Europe. Again, the meeting was important not so much for advancing the dialogue as for showing how far it had already progressed. As Jürgen Moltmann observed, 'It was expected that the theologians would be assigned the care of transcendence, while the Marxists would assume responsibility for the formation of this world in a revolutionary way. However, paradoxically enough, we found it to be exactly the reverse.'[43] At the Marienbad gathering Moltmann described the seizure of privileges by Christians or Marxists as 'the perversion of freedom'. The French Communist theoretician Roger Garaudy spoke of the 'latent atheism' in Christianity, which prevented it from serving false Gods. Amongst the Roman Catholics brought into the debate by the *Paulusgesellschaft* was Giulio Girardi, a professor at the Salesian university in Rome. (During Vatican II, Girardi had worked as a consultant on atheism and unbelievers, and he had spoken in the Christian–Marxist conference in both Salzburg and Chiemsee.) Another Roman Catholic, Johannes Metz, declared at Marienbad that Christian love could command even revolutionary violence.[44]

As part of the Czechoslovak contribution to the Marienbad debate, Gardavsky asserted that Christians and Marxists should be able to trust each other to bear responsibility for the future of mankind, or, as Christians would put it, 'to work for the coming of God's kingdom'. Professor Milan Pruha of the University of Prague pleaded for a pluralism in Marxism. Out of intellectual honesty alone, he said, Marxists should read Wittgenstein, Husserl, Heidegger, Merleau-Ponty, and Teilhard de Chardin. 'For a long time', he observed, 'we Marxists have tried to criticize and retard the Christian striving for transcendence. Should it not, rather, be our task to encourage the Christians to be even more radical in their striving for transcendence?' Pruha admitted that Christians had even awakened in some Marxists an 'appetite for transcendence'. The concept raised problems; but, he suggested, these might be solved if philosophers would refuse to fix the concept of being in a premature fashion—neither as deriving solely from matter nor as deriving solely from God.[45]

43. 'Christians and Marxists Struggle for Freedom' (January 1968), in *Religion, Revolution and the Future*, pp. 63f.

44. J. M. Lochman, *Church in a Marxist Society*, pp. 187f. J. Moltmann, *Religion, Revolution and the Future*, p. 64. The two final chapters of G. Girardi, *Marxism and Christianity*. For J. B. Metz cf. his *Zur Theologie der Welt*, Mainz/Munich 1968.

45. *Religion, Revolution and the Future*, p. 64. *Church in a Marxist Society*, p. 189. 'Marienbade Protokolle', in *Neues Forum/Dialog*, 1967, pp. 162–163.

Important though these speeches were, the Czech Marxist who spoke with most authority at Marienbad in 1967 was Milan Machovec. Of all the atheist participants he had made the most profound study of Christianity. In preparation for the conference, he had the previous year privately brought together a number of Marxists and Christians to discuss a wide variety of human concerns. But his interest in Christianity and its relationship with Marxism had arisen much earlier. He had collaborated with and learned from Helmut Gollwitzer.[46] And in 1962 he had published in Czechoslovakia an appraisal of three Christians—Barth, Bonhoeffer and Hromadka—from an atheist communist viewpoint. The book appeared in a German translation in 1965. Here, as one born into a Roman Catholic family,[47] Machovec displayed great sensitivity to the insights and achievements of Protestantism. He acknowledged the traditions of Jan Hus and the genius of Martin Luther. (The epigraph to chapter two is from Karl Marx: 'By restoring the authority of belief, Luther broke up belief in authority.') Machovec's book contains a warm appraisal of Hromadka (which casts some doubt on Lochman's statement that until the late 1960s Machovec regarded Hromadka as a good citizen *in spite of* his Christian beliefs).[48]

The book's central achievement is its estimate of the legacy of Karl Barth. Machovec accepted as valid the critique of Liberal Protestantism set out most clearly in Barth's *Protestant Theology in the Nineteenth Century*. The history of Liberal Protestant Christianity, Machovec observed, was 'properly speaking a battle to find the kernel of religion. Most frequently—from the English Deists of the eighteenth century through Kant to Ritschl, Harnack, and his many disciples—men found the kernel of Christianity in its *morality*: an exalted, godly, superhuman morality.'[49] In opposition to this tradition Machovec noted the importance of Blumhardt and the religious socialists Kutter and Ragaz. Of all three he made the perceptive remark: 'We can today read the ideas of this movement in the books of its representatives; but we must not forget that to speak truly their appearance was not in

---

46. 'Aufgaben des Dialogs. Gespräch zwischen Helmut Gollwitzer und Milan Machovec', in *Partner von Morgen. Das Gespräch zwischen Christen und Marxisten*, Stuttgart 1968, pp. 61-78.

47. Information from Jürgen Moltmann, in conversation with the author, 30 October 1973.

48. Milan Machovec, *Marxismus und dialektische Theologie. Barth, Bonhoeffer und Hromadka in atheistisch-kommunistischer Sicht*, tr. D. Neumärker, Zürich 1965, pp. 144f., 17, and 124-144. J. M. Lochman, *Church in a Marxist Society*, pp. 181f.

49. *Marxismus und dialektische Theologie*, pp. 57f.

book form, but in preaching and speaking, in the often exalted, dramatic, effective presentation which in a given moment can sweep people along.' The last sentence of the book was a prescription for the relationship of Barthian theology and Marxism: 'Barth's disciples should read anew the Apocalypse and today throughly comprehend its words, "Behold, I make all things new!".'[50]

Having thus aligned himself with the central tradition of the Christian–Marxist dialogue in German-speaking Europe, Machovec proceeded to write and publish a study of the significance of Jesus for atheists. This too was translated into German, and was published in Germany with an introduction by Helmut Gollwitzer. Machovec's book constituted a remarkable attempt to pass beyond the old controversies. Marx, he said, formulated his atheism as a critique of the way God was presented in his own day. Insofar as presentations of God had changed, the Marxist must reformulate his critique. 'In the twentieth century', Machovec conceded, 'modern theologians have worked out such new and dynamic presentations of God that Marxists today no longer know (so far as these theories are concerned) whether we are still atheists or why the whole question should be radically rejected.' Machovec here was referring to Karl Rahner's notion of 'God as the absolute future', Herbert Braun's God as the question of the ultimate whence and whither of my existence, Josef Hromadka's God as the final reason why man must not capitulate, and Martin Buber's God as the counterpart of the human 'I'.[51]

Machovec therefore recognized that earlier Marxist attempts to grapple with Christianity were seriously outdated. He included in this judgement the most impressive of these attempts, Kautsky's *Foundations of Christianity*. To present Jesus as a social revolutionary and primitive Christianity as a kind of early communism was, Machovec wrote, 'certainly not absolutely stupid'; but such characterizations, he added, completely fail to comprehend the eschatology of the New Testament, 'which did include certain socio-political aspects, but cannot be reduced to these'.[52] In Machovec's opinion, Kautsky's desire to demonstrate that Christianity began with a dreamer and ended with well-fed clergy led him to explain away much that was valuable in the

50. Ibid. pp. 63; cf. the whole section, pp. 63–71; and p. 214.

51. *Jesus für Atheisten*, 2nd edn, Stuttgart 1973, p. 6. Cf. K. Rahner, *Theological Investigations*, vol. 6, ET 1966, pp. 58–68; H. Braun, 'Die Problematik einer Theologie des Neuen Testaments', in *Zeitschrift für Theologie und Kirche*, vol. 58, 1961, supplement 2; M. Buber, *I and Thou* (1923), tr. W. Kaufmann, Edinburgh 1970.

52. *Jesus für Atheisten*, pp. 288f.

life of Jesus, in whom he had little genuine interest.[53] In order not to fall into the same trap, Machovec embodied his own account of Jesus in a very careful analysis of the historical problems involved, grappling with the difficulties caused by the lateness of the sources, their language (Greek, whereas Jesus spoke Aramaic), their apparent contradictions, and the effect on their composition of the Easter experience. He followed Harnack in distinguishing preaching *about* Jesus from the preaching *of* Jesus and he naturally enough distinguished between what he called 'the dogmatized image of Jesus Christ' and 'the man, Jesus of Nazareth'. The inhumanity and horror of the two thousand years in which the message of Jesus had been preached could inspire despair.[54] As for modern man, Machovec, adapting Marxist analysis, described him as 'so much estranged from his own humanity, hired out, lost in fetishized things, rites, stereotypes, and the institutionalized relationships of an over-organized society' as to have no notion of the spiritual and moral power of a truly mature personality such as Jesus.[55]

Machovec's speculations, which go beyond the biblical evidence, are sometimes extremely moving. He refused to dub Judas Iscariot a traitor, and speculated on a re-encounter between him and Jesus after death. He presented the Lukan Christmas story as a projection of Easter joy into the minds of children. And he most movingly allowed himself to hope that the agony of the crucifixion was brief.[56] For Machovec, the 'dialectic of the cross' constituted 'the fundamental paradox of early Christianity. It involved hope for the overturning of relationships, not a flight from the world as many have wrongly and one-sidedly understood it.'[57] For the followers of Jesus drew no line between this world and the next, between their longings for an earthly future and their longings for a heavenly one; and what Jesus preached were the present demands of the kingdom of God.[58] This preaching became the touchstone of Machovec's hermeneutic. It enabled him to ally even the concern Jesus showed for children with the Marxist critique of capitalism. Jesus's words 'Let the children come to me' (Mark 10.14) implied the demand that 'every truly mature person rise up against the way egoistical class interests and fetishized civilization tend to destroy humanity' and the need for 'truly revolutionary effort

53. *Jesus für Atheisten*, pp. 20 and 26.
54. Ibid. p. 249.
55. Ibid. p. 93.
56. Ibid. pp. 193, 235f., and 198.
57. Ibid. p. 95.
58. Ibid. p. 99.

that does not give up after two or three failures'[59]—a great deal to hang upon one text.

In Machovec's view the dynamic basis of nineteenth- and twentieth-century Marxism was the future kingdom mapped out by the Old Testament prophets and freed by Jesus from its alienated, apocalyptic, and fantastic elements.[60] Yet in asserting all this he was no convert to Christianity. He acknowledged that Christian theologians would want to put many questions to him. He translated Jesus's call in Matthew 4.17, 'Repent for the kingdom of heaven is at hand', as 'Live responsibly, because perfect humanity is possible.'[61] 'The kingdom of God is near' meant for him that one can be more moral, purer, more a man, and that this is one's own doing; but at the same time he recognized that the message of Jesus could not be reduced to human activity alone.[62] At times Machovec exemplified the accusation that 'the Marxist–Christian dialogue, for all its seriousness, involves tendentious translations of the classic texts on both sides of the divide', that 'Marxists, straining to make sense of Christianity and be open to it, easily distort both their own traditions and the religious tradition.'[63]

Nonetheless, in seeking Jesus Machovec was acknowledging what he said at Marienbad in 1967: that Marxism had not found the solution to every human problem. Indeed, he went on to suggest that after the solution of economic problems, the 'search for the meaning of life' would become the crucial question of the future.[64] As he observed in Jesus for Atheists, the first generation of Marxists, like the first Christians, expected the future paradise immediately. But, again like the Christians who had expected the immediate return of their Lord, these Marxists had to readjust and come to a more realistic relationship with the surrounding world.[65] Machovec suggested that the insights of the Bible might help them to do so. Marxists, he wrote, initially hated such New Testament stories as that of the Good Samaritan, since they had learned (from George Bernard Shaw, among others) that individual charity leads to Pharisaism. From now on, it was argued, the state

59. Ibid. p. 120.
60. Ibid. p. 103.
61. Ibid. p. 102.
62. Ibid. p. 108.
63. David Martin, 'Revs and Revolutions: Church Trends and Fashionable Theologians', in *Encounter*, January 1969, p. 16. Professor Martin added, 'The same happens to Christians who wish to incorporate Marxist perspectives.'
64. J. Moltmann, *Religion, Revolution and the Future*, p. 64.
65. *Jesus für Atheisten*, p. 14.

alone should care for the sick, the old, and the handicapped. As a result, said Machovec, in a Marxist state few care for the suffering next door, for that too is the business of the state.[66] In a fascinating passage, Machovec hinted at the persecutions that had disfigured Communist societies in the twentieth century. During the past one hundred and fifty years, he wrote, when a Marxist read in the Bible of 'heaven, animals, paradise, sin, and naked Eve', he looked upon it all as boring mythology, fairy stories and old wives' tales. 'Today, after his experience of the established socialist society, when he reads the same pages of the Bible, although there are no reasons for becoming a Christian immediately, at the question, "Where is your brother Abel?" he tends to say quietly to himself, "How fascinating and up-to-date!".'[67] Marx undoubtedly enjoined revolutionary violence, wrote Machovec, and here the gap between his teachings and those of Jesus seems virtually unbridgeable. But, he added, in the twentieth century Marxists have themselves suffered so much from ill-directed and unjust violence that many now think far more in terms of the 'violence' of the Sermon on the Mount and of Gandhi.[68]

Machovec described his book as 'certainly only a beginning of a possible positive encounter of a modern atheist with Jesus'.[69] It was to prove the literary high-point of the Christian–Marxist dialogue in Czechoslovakia in the sixties. The hopes of those who participated in it were soon to be dashed.

These hopes depended in part on the political transformation that was taking place in the country, and the Christian–Marxist dialogue itself was enormously helped (and was indeed part of) the reform movement within the Czechoslovak Communist Party, a movement that began after Khrushchev's denunciation of Stalinism in 1956 and gathered momentum from 1963 onwards. Between January and August 1968, the party leadership, headed by Alexander Dubček, who had replaced Antonín Novotný as head of state at the beginning of the year, responded to this movement by pluralizing the political system, abolishing censorship, and attempting to find a way towards what was termed 'socialism with a human face'. As a result, as Lochman put it at the time, practical co-operation between Marxists and Christians reached a 'unique intensity . . . in the memorable year of 1968 as a

66. Ibid. pp. 17f.
67. Ibid. p. 19.
68. Ibid. pp. 22 and 132.
69. Ibid. p. 29.

result of the attempts at a far-reaching democratization of our socialist society. . . . New relations of growing mutual respect and solidarity developed in the common search for the humanization of our society. Thus Czechoslovak Christians started to play a new role in their cultural and social environment.'[70]

In August 1968 the Russian government sent half a million Warsaw Pact troops into Czechoslovakia, with the aim of arresting the proposed political changes expected to be set in motion by the fourteenth congress of the Czechoslovak Communist Party, due to be held the following month. (In fact, none of the proposed changes would have altered the system of public ownership or the collectivization of agriculture.[71])

The fourteenth congress was held nonetheless, secretly in a Prague factory. Of 1,543 elected delegates, 1,192 were present and overwhelmingly voted for a reforming Central Committee.[72] In response the Russians brought the Czechoslovak political leaders to Moscow and forced them to sign a protocol annulling the secret party congress. (One member, Dr Frantisek Kriegel, refused to sign.) The events outraged both Christians and Marxists. As the Warsaw Pact troops invaded, church bells and factory sirens together announced their support for democratic socialism.[73] '*The socialist house was built*', wrote Hromadka. '*But . . . we were not able to inhabit it with socialist man.*' True communism, he argued, desired to free men politically, personally, and socially. The dialogue had shown that this ideal was not totally dead, but the events of August 1968 now raised the question 'whether socialism is able to develop creatively'.[74] Lochman was equally outraged. 'The quarantine of the fifties was challenged in the sixties, with the Christian–Marxist dialogue clearing the way', he wrote. Yet he recognized that only in 1968 had Christians been fully accepted as qualified

70. *Church in a Marxist Society*, p. 12.

71. On this point see Ota Šik, *The Third Way*, 1976. Šik had argued for political reform at the thirteenth party congress in 1966. Cf. Jiri Pelikan, *The Secret Visocany Congress*, 1971, which showed that the draft party plan of 1968 was still thoroughly Marxist. Pelikan, like Šik, was a leading figure of the Czechoslovak reform movement during the first eight months of 1968. Both went into exile. H. G. Skilling, *Czechoslovakia's Interrupted Revolution*, Princeton University Press 1976, is a comprehensive account of the whole movement.

72. *Times* report, 18 August 1978, ten years after the events.

73. J. M. Lochman, *Church in a Marxist Society*, p. 110.

74. 'The Situation in Czechoslovakia', pp. 49 and 46. Cf. his article 'Gemeinsames Unglück' in *Neues Forum/Dialog*, August-September 1968, p. 517.

members of society, with a unique contribution of their own. In April of that year, at the first public dialogue outside the universities, 3,000 people had joined in a passionate five-hour debate on the importance of religion. The invasion had brought all this to an end. Yet Lochman refused to share Hromadka's complete despondency. He insisted that in spite of what had happened, the Czechoslovak experience remained 'a model of hope and of the future—for many of our Marxists and for Christians in a Marxist society'.[75] Now, however, the question of the relationship between the Marxist, liberal, and bourgeois traditions had broken forth with a new unexpected urgency.[76] Günther Nenning in Vienna attacked the aggression. Machovec described what had happened as *Panzersozialismus*. Ernst Fischer wrote of the dishonour of the Soviet Union. Roger Garaudy urged Brezhnev to retreat. Ernst Bloch quoted the words of Friedrich Wilhelm IV of Prussia in 1848: 'Gegen Demokraten helfen nur Soldaten.'[77] Ernst Bloch shared the confidence as well as the outrage of Lochman. He told Eduard Goldstücker, who had served in Dubček's government, that the Soviet invasion of Czechoslovakia had trampled the red flag in the mud. At the same time, he warned the countries of the West that anyone who remained silent on the American forces in Vietnam had no right to pass judgement on what had happened in Czechoslovakia (a stance also adopted by Dorothee Sölle).[78] Bloch agreed with Eduard Goldstücker that the Prague experiment would retain its significance for the whole of the left even if an earthquake should swallow it. 'Now the earthquake had come', he said; but he added that 'this desecration of socialism, this invasion, has awakened the socialist conscience.'[79]

Yet in spite of this optimisn, the invasion was an immense blow to the dialogue. Dubček was not dismissed until April the following year. (He spent a brief time as ambassador to Turkey, before being relegated to working in the garage of the Slovak forestry commission.) But the reforms were halted. After April 1969, tens of thousands who refused

75. J. M. Lochman, *Church in a Marxist Society*, pp. 11, 106–110, and 198.

76. J. M. Lochman, 'Marxism, Liberalism and Religion: an East European Perspective', p. 11.

77. Their articles all appeared in *Neues Forum/Dialog*, August-September 1968: G. Nenning, 'Konsequenzen aus der Aggression', pp. 513-515; E. Bloch, 'Enkel der Ochrana', p. 517; R. Garaudy 'Breschnjew, abtreten!', p. 519; M. Machovec, 'Panzersozialismus', pp. 520f.; E. Fischer, 'Schändung der Sowjetunion', pp. 522f.

78. D. Sölle, 'CssR–Santo Domingo–Vietnam', in *Politisches Nachtgebet in Köln*, I.15-27.

79. 'Wer zu Vietnam schweigt, hat kein Recht über die CssR zu urteilen', in *Gespräche mit Ernst Bloch*, p. 126.

to accept the Soviet form of socialism were dismissed from their jobs. Religious repression began again.[80]

Inevitably, those who had stood in the forefront of the dialogue suffered, and particularly the Marxists. What happened to Vitzslav Gardavsky, personally and intellectually, will serve as an example. At the time of the invasion of Czechoslovakia he had been lecturing in the West,[81] but he chose to return to his own country. The professor of philosophy was forced to find work as a labourer in a Moravian village, living apart from his family and returning to them only on week-ends. He now chose a new model from the Old Testament: Jeremiah took the place of Jacob. Lochman has described this journey from Jacob to Jeremiah as the rejection of 'blind hope' in favour of 'creative hopelessness'. Gardavsky's model was no longer the man who crosses every boundary and challenges God, but the 'prophet of grief'. Jeremiah is the hero of the central part of a trilogy on which Gardavsky was working at the time of his death. (Its provisional title was *The Angel on the Point of the Sword*.) It is easy to see how this theme related to his own experiences and those of his fellow Czechoslovaks. He conceived of Jeremiah as a man attempting to deprive the powerful of their certainties and the weak of their foolish hopes. Both parties find the prophet intolerable and seek his destruction.[82]

Traces of such thinking can be found in Gardavsky's earlier writing. In *Hope Out of Scepticism* he was still responding to the notion that man should acknowledge no unalterable norms, no taboos in the cosmos. But even then he called for a pause in the headlong rush towards the millennium. He drew back from Feuerbach's dictum that the point is to *change* and not simply *interpret* the world. True, he wrote, the world still needs to be changed. 'But if this topsy-turvy world is not to perish, we must once again try to interpret it.'[83]

In spite of his attempts to avoid political entanglement or provocation after his dismissal,[84] Gardavsky was continually harassed by the political police. On the day before his death in 1978 at the age of fifty-five, they interrogated him for the whole day. He returned home

80. P. A. Toma and M. J. Reban, 'Church-State Schism in Czechoslovakia', pp. 284–289.

81. *Times Literary Supplement*, 26 October 1973, p. 1319.

82. J. M. Lochman, 'Gardavskys Wandlung von Jakob zu Jeremia', in *Orientierung. Katholische Blätter für Weltanschauliche Information*, no. 10, Zürich 1978, pp. 110f.

83. *Hoffnung aus der Skepsis*, p. 15.

84. J. Bentley, 'Vitzslav Gardavsky, Atheist and Martyr', in *The Expository Times*, vol. 91, no. 9, June 1980, p. 276.

peacefully, opened a book, and died. His body was found four days later.[85] In *God Is Not Yet Dead* he had written, 'In the very moment of victory we are exposed to an even more terrible threat—that we might die earlier than we really do die, before death has become a natural necessity. The real horror lies in just such a *premature* death, a death after which we go on living for many years.'[86] The Czechoslovak authorities tried to consign Gardavsky to a premature death. But, Lochman insisted, 'the dialogue that he so admirably stimulated and enduringly enriched will not be silenced in his grave.'[87]

Yet even Lochman was forced to abandon some of his optimism. 'Too many attempts at reform and renewal had been suppressed', he conceded. 'Too many hopes had been disappointed. In most parts of our world, the images of the future have become rather sombre in tone.'[88] Even in Switzerland, Marxist participants in the dialogue were not immune from persecution. Lochman's friend Konrad Farner strongly condemned the invasion of Czechoslovakia in 1968. The Swiss Communist Party expelled him.[89]

Others were far more pessimistic. 'It is now winter in Prague', said Jürgen Moltmann in 1973, 'and will be for twenty more years.'[90] Günther Nenning, the Austrian Catholic Marxist, declared that after 1968 the dialogue died. Helmut Gollwitzer too suggested that the era of dialogue was over for a time.[91] Machovec, however, refused to believe that the dialogue had come to an end. Instead, he argued, it had profoundly changed.

After the invasion of 1968 he too was, of course, dismissed. He earned his living teaching Latin privately (and also by playing the organ of a Roman Catholic church in a Prague suburb, until the authorities put pressure on the parish priest to dismiss him). He conceded that the great charismatic 'prophets of dialogue' in the 1960s—Karl Barth, John XXIII,[92] and Josef Hromadka—had died and

85. J. M. Lochman, personal conversation with the author, 26 October 1979.

86. *God Is Not Yet Dead*, p. 214.

87. 'Gardavskys Wandlung von Jakob zu Jeremia', p. 111.

88. 'Towards an Ecumenical Account of Hope', in *Ecumenical Review*, June 1979, p. 14.

89. J. M. Lochman, personal conversation with the author, 26 October 1979.

90. Jürgen Moltmann, personal conversation with the author, 30 October 1973.

91. M. Machovec, 'Zum Anfang der Zweiten Phase des Dialogs', in *Junge Kirche*, May 1973, p. 275, citing Günther Nenning, 'Warum der Dialog starb', in *Neues Forum/Dialog*, March 1972, and the preface to Helmut Gollwitzer, *Krummes Holz–aufrechter Gang*.

92. For an account of John XXIII's 'opening to the left' and its aftermath, see Robert A. Graham, 'The Vatican's East-West Policy Since Pope John XXIII', in *The Vatican and World Peace*, ed. F. Sweeney, 1970, pp. 151–178.

not been replaced. ('Of this prophetic generation of the dialogue', he wrote in 1972, 'only Ernst Bloch is still alive.' [93]) Others of the next generation, such as Roger Garaudy, Konrad Farner, Albert J. Rasker, Georges Casalis, and Heinz Kloppenburg, seemed to Machovec to have withdrawn from the struggle.[94] It was equally clear to him that the most powerful in this world had clamped down on the dialogue, that they 'could no longer watch the practice of dialogue spread, fascinating more and more people, in their thousands, reaching out into new social dimensions and consequences, relativizing every power.' Yet, Machovec insisted, it was necessary to look clearly at what had and what had not died. Some things that had died might have deserved this fate. Machovec was glad, he said, that the great 'show dialogue' had died, for he had begun to fear that some of the 'stars' of the dialogues were becoming 'professionals', performing in Bremen and Rome, New York and Prague. Each year, he wrote, these professionals, who had been quite useful in the beginning, displayed an increasing mixture of exhibitionism and routine. 'No great harm was done by saving these top debaters from the fate of *prima ballerinas*, ever needing to display their muscular skills to new beginners.'[95]

Second, the dangerous, beautiful illusion had died that those who were (in Hromadka's phrase) 'on the threshold of dialogue' could, without too much trouble, slip over it and find themselves at home. Now Marxists and Christians had been once again reminded of their essential homelessness. Other members of the dialogue reached the same conclusion. Analysing the homelessness of the Christian left, Dorothee Sölle quoted Ernst Bloch's paradox: 'Home is something that shines for everyone in childhood and where no one has ever been.'[96] Machovec pointed out that neither Christians nor Marxists should find anything new or odd in this homelessness, since it represented an ancient fact of history—the history of alienation and self-alienation, of sin and guilt—as well as the ancient protest against all this.[97]

93. 'Zum Anfang der zweiten Phase des Dialogs', p. 275.

94. A. J. Rasker and M. Machovec, *Theologie und Revolution. Ein west-östlicher Dialog*, Hamburg 1969. G. Casalis, 'Anmerkungen zur Christologie auf dem Hintergrund lateinamerikanischer Erfahrungen', in *Junge Kirche*, May 1973, pp. 250-255. In the same issue Farner published 'Konfrontation mit dem Christentum—warum ich Marxist bleibe', pp. 258-264, and Kloppenburg was congratulated on his 70th birthday, pp. 245-249. Lombardo Radice was an Italian Marxist who had recognized that 'there is an authentic revolutionary impulse in religious faith', quoted J. M. Bonnino, p. 55.

95. 'Zum Anfang der zweiten Phase des Dialogs', p. 276.

96. 'How Homeless is the Christian Left?', in *Jenseits vom Null-punkt*, ed. R. Weckerling *et al.*, Augsburg 1972, p. 249.

97. 'Zum Anfang der zweiten Phase des Dialogs', p. 276.

Machovec admitted his regret at the ending of 'institutional' dialogue in universities, public debates, and congresses. But here too he detected some gains. The notion of an institution in dialogue is in a sense contradictory, he said; persons, not institutions, engage in dialogue. The ending of institutional dialogue had not killed the principle of dialogue. And in any case, he argued, congresses and great assemblies, though they have a part in history, have never brought anything sublime into being. 'Anything really significant in history almost always arises from insignificant beginnings and only seldom from that which in a given epoch believes itself to be powerful', he observed. 'In the eyes of the politicians and historians of the time, St Paul and his strivings were not worth a mention in the contemporary annals. Similarly, there was no room for Marx in the huge philosophical compendia of the nineteenth century.'[98]

So, Machovec pleaded, the only legitimate response to the 1960s, the classic decade of dialogue, was to recognize that the first phase of dialogue had ended and to ask what the necessary tasks were for beginning the second phase. He suggested three. First, a transition was required from the 'prophetic' generation to a more mundane, less sensational working out of limited themes. Some had argued that the dialogue was bound to come to a standstill simply because each side had now absorbed and assimilated the positive suggestions, impulses, and values of the other. Machovec disagreed. There were, he maintained, hundreds of traditional 'Christian' themes that Marxists ought to work on from their perspectives and presuppositions; and vice versa. Only through this work could a third phase emerge, envisaged by Machovec as the comprehensive synthesis of all the treasures of men's meaningful quests, 'beginning with Abraham's restlessness and leading to the programme for building the classless society'.

Second, Machovec called for the de-professionalizing (*Entprofessionalisierung*) and de-academizing (*Entakademisierung*) of the dialogue. Here there can be heard a pardonable hint of bitterness in the ex-professor: 'I will be forgiven for ventilating my secret fear of what German professors with the traditional abilities and inclinations of the German intellect and their often dangerously lop-sided thoroughness could make of this second phase of the dialogue.' Real truths, he insisted, such as those of the Sermon on the Mount, able to inspire millions of people, do not appear as multi-volumed compendia but in relatively simple forms. Deliberately utilizing Christian language,

98. Ibid., p. 277.

Machovec declared, 'If the dialogue is to be something that "re-deems" (and not merely the hundredth illusion of the intellectuals), from now on it urgently needs not complicated serpentine constructions but simple, though *charismatic and effective primitive truths.*'⁹⁹

Lastly, Machovec argued, the Western world could no longer con-tain the dialogue. Indeed, in spite of all the failures and difficulties involved in dialogue between Marxists and Christians, he had come to believe that in the last resort this was a dialogue between opponents who were children of the same intellectual tradition. In such a dialogue the greatest 'victory' could constitute nothing more than a narcissistic stunning of oneself. The future dialogue must draw in other traditions as well. Machovec was not the only participant in the dialogue to have come to such a conclusion. Dorothee Sölle had perceived the need to enrich the German experience by means of the Latin American. Jürgen Moltmann agreed. Indeed, he came to believe that the Christian–Marx-ist dialogue had 'emigrated' to Latin America. The Frankfurt School of Marxism had lost ground in German universities in the 1970s (symbolized in Habermas's move to the Max Planck Institute, where he virtually ceased to publish his thinking). And in Eastern Europe (partly because of Russian behaviour in 1968) Marxism itself was out of favour with many of the people. There the churches were reluctant to engage with what they increasingly regarded as an obsolete ideol-ogy.¹⁰⁰ The dialogue was leaving German-speaking Europe. In 1973 a Czech Protestant theologian declared, 'The theology of liberation has a framework that is yet too European.' It needed not only to take into account the 'political theology' of men like Jürgen Moltmann but also to study the lives of Che Guevara, Camillo Torres, and Nestor Paz, as well as the socialist revolutions of Russia, Cuba, and China.¹⁰¹

But Machovec was demanding more. In the 1960s the American sociologist Talcott Parsons had observed that 'for the first time in history something approaching a world society is in the process of emerging. For the first time in its history, Christianity is now involved in a deep confrontation with the major religions of the Orient, as well as with the modern political religion of Communism.'¹⁰² Machovec insisted that this was the third major task in the new phase of the

99. 'Zum Anfang der zweiten Phase des Dialogs', pp. 278f.
100. Personal conversation with the author, 27 October 1979.
101. A. Ham, 'Introduction to the Theology of Liberation', in *Communio Viatorum*, 16, no. 3, summer 1973, pp. 119f.
102. 'Christianity and Modern Industrial Society', in *Religion, Culture and Society*, ed. Louis Schneider, New York 1964, p. 298.

dialogue. 'If Western man (whether Christian or Marxist, teacher or politician) really wishes to preserve the beloved treasures of the West—from Aristotle to Hegel, from the Song of Songs to Thomas Mann—if he really wishes to "continue in dialogue"..., then he must, with both passionate zeal and humble patience, finally begin the attempt not only to understand the treasures of the East as well (above all those from the realms of India and China), but also to assimilate their perspectives.' For Machovec this task involved profound political consequences. As he put it, 'The only real alternative to colonialism and imperialism (which in the history of Western self-confusion and error has so far found its most terrible and absurd expression, though probably not its last, in the long-protracted annihilation-bombing of Vietnam) is to approach the East humbly and in dialogue.'[103]

Thus, in spite of his own disgrace and the tragedy of 1968, Machovec refused to accept that the dialogue had ended. 'The dialogue did not die', he concluded, 'but only certain of its contemporary forms.' It had now greatly outgrown German-speaking Europe. And as Machovec observed, despite the hostility of the great powers, the fact remained that every Christian in every part of the world could, if he wished, daily meet hundreds of atheists, socialists, and Marxists and live in dialogue with them. And likewise every Marxist could daily and everywhere find Christians and attempt to find with them a mutual openness and an honest 'togetherness'—even if he had no printing press at his disposal. Finally, he wrote, 'Even those people who engaged in dialogue in the 1960s now have not only a new opportunity but also the duty of living more intensely in dialogue, or working in greater breadth and depth, and of opening up ever wider perspectives for mankind.'[104]

103. 'Zum Anfang der zweiten Phase des Dialogs', p. 277.
104. Ibid., p. 280.

9
Conclusions

The principal characters discussed in this book differed widely in temperament. Blumhardt was a man both inspiring in public utterance and introspective in private, whose style of life was that of the bourgeoisie but whose heart was identified with the proletariat. Kautsky, industrious almost to the point of appearing dry as dust, was also a man of emotion and tenderness that rarely showed itself in public. Karl Barth, mischievous and sometimes imprudent, loved an intellectual fight and battled most of his life. Ernst Bloch's tenacity in holding his opinions was passionate and occasionally even cantankerous. (At a public colloquium in 1966 he repeatedly interrupted Jürgen Moltmann, maintaining, wrongly, that Lutherans believed those in hell to be damned eternally. Moltmann failed to persuade him otherwise.)[1] Dorothee Sölle remained vulnerable to the charge that she thought with her heart rather than her head, even to the extent of sometimes ignoring uncomfortable facts in her opponents' case. And Milan Machovec, gentle and persuasive, unaggressive in his Marxism and in his leanings toward Christianity, was nonetheless prepared to accept disgrace in his own country instead of finding, as he readily could, academic reward in exile. Successively they entered into and advanced the Christian—Marxist dialogue in German-speaking Europe.

The dialogue began in response to the German Social Question and in spite of the hostility of Marxism toward religion. Blumhardt was the first leading German Christian to recognize that the churches need not go on the defensive against socialism, unlike, for example, Adolf Stöcker, for whom Marxism was a demonic response to the Social Question, or Naumann, who put his trust in liberalism. Like Naumann, Blumhardt perceived that political action was required if the church was to respond adequately to the demand for social justice; but unlike

1. *Im Gespräch mit Ernst Bloch*, p. 61.

Naumann, he was able to draw connections between his political activity and his Christian beliefs. Blumhardt's political inspiration was what he called 'the future of Jesus Christ', and he passed on both his social concern and his anti-pietistic eschatology to Karl Barth.

The First World War revealed to Barth the ease with which the unconditional truths of the Gospel could be suspended in the face of 'practical politics'. It also helped to bring about the Russian revolution of 1917, forcing men of Barth's political and theological convictions to define more precisely than had been necessary for Blumhardt where they stood with regard to Marxism as it was now put into practice. Barth saw in the success of communism a judgement on nineteenth-century and contemporary Christianity. He himself had no wish to live under a communist regime, and he called himself a socialist rather than a communist; but he was also convinced that there was no essential Christian objection to the abolition of private property and the collectivization of the means of production. He consistently refused to see communism as the chief enemy of Christianity. Communism, too, had a deep and praiseworthy social concern. And God, in any case, was judge of the West as well as the East. Because the sovereignty of God, in Barth's view, called everything into question, he was unwilling to accept some of the Promethean aspects of Marxist humanism in the way his pupil Lochman later did. Barth preached that God himself, not men, would inaugurate his kingdom; but this did not mean that Christians ought never to espouse a social programme, or even at times socialism.

Barth's judgement on nineteenth-century and contemporary Christianity was one made by orthodox Marxists, and set out in the greatest detail by Karl Kautsky. Christianity, he averred, began as a revolutionary movement and ended as an ally of the status quo. Kautsky, like all Marxists who came under the influence of Bruno Bauer, believed that nothing certain could be said about the person of Jesus (not even that he ever lived). In any case, he maintained, the noblest ideals of Christianity were socio-economic in origin. Kautsky's researches gave new prominence to the often ignored egalitarian and socialistic elements in Christian history—not only those displayed by the earliest Christians, but also those of the Franciscans, of Jan Hus and the Bohemian Brethren, of Thomas Münzer and Thomas More. But he was too much concerned to demonstrate that their form of communism or socialism was far inferior to his own. In spite of the vigour of his historical research, he often seemed to be imposing a pattern onto the past without properly encountering it. And although his account of the origins of Christianity was a learned as well as a polemical work which shaped the attitudes of later Marxists, its analysis was soon perceived to be defective. Marxists as well as Christians pointed out that he had failed to see the importance of the eschatological hopes of the early Christians, the desire for 'a victory of the future over the past' which Barth had learned from Blumhardt. Marxists too observed that Kautsky had failed to account for the continuing hold of Christianity on those who, it was thought, ought to have been emancipated from it. Kautsky, as Erich Fromm observed, did not sufficiently examine subjective springs of human action. Belief in God and Christianity, however illusory, could still give immense fantasy satisfaction to those who had little other hope in this world.

Fromm was part of the movement, connected particularly with the Frankfurt Institute of Social Research, that sought to re-think Marxism after the failure of revolutionary hopes in post-war Germany. His intention was to bring together the insights of Marx and Freud. Far more fruitful was the attempt of another man closely connected with the Frankfurt Institute, Ernst Bloch, to bring together Marxism and the prophetic and messianic elements of Christianity. Bloch saw in Christian hope the origin of the social hope of Marxism. Both Christianity and Marxism, he believed, required a point of reference in the future—whether the kingdom of God or the classless society—on which basis to criticize this present world. Bloch analysed the Exodus and the messianic parts of the Bible in the light of the concrete hope of Karl Marx. Blumhardt had discerned a moral and industrious atheism in the world. Bloch discerned atheism in the Christian tradition itself. His analysis of the principle of hope in men drew him to an examination of the metaphysical basis of Marxism, an examination in which concepts such as 'God', transcendence, and eternal life were regarded not as mystifications but as part of the debate. He enabled some Christians, even disciples of Barth, to accept in part Marxist understanding of the nature of man. Theologians began to see the future as a paradigm for divine transcendence. At the same time, Bloch made them draw some boundaries more clearly. Christians insisted that Marxism is not a complete explanation of reality. Man is not able to save himself. The kingdom of God comes as a result of God's own action and not through men. If the Marxist has hope in the future, the Christian hopes in the God of the future. In more clearly redefining their own position in debate with Bloch, Christians also sometimes modified it. Jan

Milic Lochman insisted that the God of the Old Testament who was also to reveal himself as the God and Father of Jesus Christ was by no means a God such as Zeus in *Prometheus Bound*; yet in response to Bloch, Lochman felt the need to look again at the Christian concepts of sin and grace. And as a Czech in the tradition of Hus and Comenius, Lochman in response to Bloch looked afresh at the chiliastic background of his own religious inheritance.

Bloch's atheism, ambigious though it was, remained a stumbling block between him and theologians in the Barthian tradition. Dorothee Sölle's concept of God, on the other hand, set her closer to Bloch than to Barth. The statement attributed to Jesus, 'My kingdom is not of this world' (John 18.36), did not for her imply that Christians should abandon politics. On the contrary, she believed that in some instances even the forgiveness of God could be mediated only politically. And the love of God itself, she maintained, is mediated to us in our relationships with others. Late capitalism, she argued, had brought about a false isolation of human beings which was contrary to the Scriptural view of man. In her political theology the crucifixion demonstrated God's solidarity with all who suffer. To be identified with God is to share human solidarity. This concept of solidarity made Sölle push the debate beyond the boundaries of German-speaking Europe, to wherever men and women were suffering—in Vietnam, Korea, Latin America.

As a Marxist Christian, Sölle perceived institutionalized and structural violence in the world, and she argued that sin can be collective as well as personal. She therefore developed a political theology on the basis of the Christian gospel and Marxist praxis, insisting that the privatization of Christianity negates the gospel and denies human solidarity, in spite of the fact that (as Albrecht Schönherr lamented) Marxism in practice generally regarded 'religion as a personal need, a private matter, and a middle-class private matter at that'.[2]

By this time in the debate Marxists were noting with surprise (and sometimes some cynicism) that Christians still existed.[3] Others, above all the Czech Milan Machovec, acknowledged that the Christian tradition could put valid questions against Marxism itself, and especially against revolutionary violence. Although he himself remained an atheist, he wanted Christians not to abandon Jesus but to follow him more

2. A. Schönherr, p. 5.
3. H. Marcuse, 'Gibt es noch Christen?', in *Neues Forum/Dialog*, August–September 1968, pp. 533–535.

closely, so as to avoid the reproach 'This people honours me with their lips but their heart is far from me' (Mark 7.6). At the same time, Machovec called for morally inspiring *'ideals, models, and standards of value'* in Marxism, and he looked for such in Jesus himself.[4] In the political climate of Czechoslovakia in the 1960s, it seemed that many would respond to the remarkable development in the dialogue between Christians and Marxists.

Such hopes were destroyed by the invasion of Czechoslovakia by forces of the Warsaw Pact in August 1968. The invasion could not, however, negate and efface the Christian–Marxist dialogue of the previous hundred years. In spite of the personal suffering it caused him, Machovec maintained that in some respects the ending of the debate in 1968 pointed to a new way forward. Some of the elements in the dialogue that died in 1968, such as the great 'show debates', had outlived their usefulness. Christians and Marxists had once again been reminded of their essential homelessness. And it was time for the dialogue to develop between 'ordinary' Christians and Marxists, leaving behind the 'star' debaters and professional academics. Finally, Machovec argued, the dialogue had to include new elements. Marxists and Christians needed to understand and learn from the perspectives of men and women of other faiths and traditions than those of Western Europe. The dialogue could no longer be confined to Christians and Marxists or to German-speaking Europe.

4. *Jesus für Atheisten*, pp. 254 and 25.

A Note on Translations

Wherever an accurate translation of a German text has been published, I have tried to use it. An example is T. B. Saunder's translation of Adolf Harnack's *Das Wesen des Christentums*, which is so impeccable as to reproduce a slip of the tongue by Harnack, faithfully taken down by the shorthand writer in his audience![1]

But the matter is not always so simple. For instance, many of the participants in the Christian-Marxist dialogue in German-speaking Europe wrote (and write) equally well in English and German. Thus Jan Milic Lochman originally wrote his article 'Platz für Prometheus' in English.[2] In this particular case I have preferred to translate Lochman's German, since the English version was published six years after the German,[3] the two versions differ at certain points, and the German one had most influence.

Sometimes I have refused to use an English translation because of its inaccuracy. An example is the anonymous translation of Milan Machovec's *Jesus für Atheisten*, published under the title *A Marxist Looks at Jesus*. In this translation phrases are frequently rendered in a manner that clumsily paraphrases and distorts the subtlety of the original.[4] In

1. The translation, *What is Christianity?*, p. 57, reads: 'the historian's task of distinguishing between what is traditional and what is peculiar, between kernel and husk.' The antithesis has clearly gone wrong, but Saunders is accurately translating the original, *Das Wesen des Christentums*, Leipzig 1902, p. 34: 'die Aufgabe des Historikers ... zwischen Überliefertem und Eigenem, Kern und Schale ... zu scheiden.'

2. J. M. Lochman, letter to the author, 8 December 1978.

3. J. M. Lochman, 'The Place for Prometheus. Theological Lessons from the Christian-Marxist Dialogue', in *Interpretation*, vol. 32, no. 3, July 1978, pp. 242–254.

4. For instance, 'Hromadka: Gott als letzter Grund dessen, dass der Mensch nie kapitulieren darf', and 'Buber: Gott als Gegenpol des menschlichen "Ich"', are translated as 'Hromadka who sees God as the reason why man can refuse to give in to power', and 'Buber with his I-Thou relationship': *Jesus für Atheisten*, p. 6; *A Marxist Looks at Jesus*, p. 21.

one passage, Machovec's words, 'you are no longer slaves of a law but children of God, in whom he rejoices', are puzzlingly replaced by the Revised Standard Version translation of Romans 7.6: 'But now we are discharged from the law, dead to that which held us captive, so that we serve not under the old written code but in the new life of the spirit.'[5] Among lesser errors, *notwendig* is translated as 'understandably' and *Zeitalter* as 'Kingdom'. Countless words of the original are omitted in the translation, and (because the numeration of the Psalms differs in the German and the English bibles) the cry of dereliction of the crucified Jesus and the sharing of his clothes are referred to the wrong verses of Psalm 22.[6]

I have also eschewed an execrable translation of J. Habermas's 'Ein marxistischer Schelling: zu Ernst Blochs spekulativem Materialismus'.[7]

The problem is further complicated by the fact that some translations, impeccable or not in other respects, omit important parts of the originals. The translation of Machovec's *Jesus für Atheisten* substitutes an introduction by Peter Hebblethwaite for the German introduction by Helmut Gollwitzer. The translation of Jürgen Moltmann's *Theologie der Hoffnung* omits the appendix in which he engaged the philosophy of Ernst Bloch. (This appendix was later published on its own in J. Moltmann, *Religion, Revolution and the Future*.[8]) A short section on the meeting of the World Council of Churches at Uppsala in 1968 unaccountably disappeared in David Cairns's fine translation of Helmut Gollwitzer's *Die Reichen Christen und der Arme Lazarus*. And it took S.C.M. Press thirteen years to publish a complete translation of Karl Barth's *Die Protestantische Theologie im 19. Jahrhundert*, in spite of the author's vigorous attack on the truncated version.[9]

On the other hand, translations occasionally contain useful additions to the original. Thus the French translation of G. Girardi's *Cristianesimo e marxismo* has a postface by Roger Garaudy[10] not to be found in the English or Italian version.

Finally, where several translations of a work have been published (as of Karl Kautsky's *Der Ursprung des Christentums*) I have felt free to use more than one.

5. *Jesus für Atheisten*, pp. 225f.; *A Marxist Looks at Jesus*, p. 174.
6. *A Marxist Looks at Jesus*, pp. 22, 90, and 180.
7. 'Ernst Bloch—A Marxist Romantic', in *Salmagundi*, 10/11, fall 1969–winter 1970, pp. 311–325.
8. 'Hope and Confidence. A Conversation with Ernst Bloch', pp. 148–176.
9. K. Barth, *Protestant Theology in the Nineteenth Century*, p. 7.
10. J. Girardi, *Marxisme et chrétienisme*, Paris 1968, pp. 303–314.

Bibliography

1. Manuscript Sources

Kautsky papers, International Institute of Social History, Amsterdam.

2. Unpublished Theses

H. K. Day, 'Christlicher Glaube und Gesellschaftliches Handeln: Eine Studie der Entwicklung der Theologie Helmut Gollwitzers', D.Theol. dissertation, Union Theological Seminary, New York, 1973.

J. C. Fout, 'Protestant Christian Socialism in Germany, 1848-1896, Wichern, Stoecker, Naumann: the Search for a New Social Ethic', Ph.D. thesis, University of Minnesota, 1969.

F. Gillies, 'The Eschatological Structures of Marxism', D.Phil. thesis, University of Sussex, 1975.

K. Gust, 'East German Protestantism under Communist Rule, 1945-1961', Ph.D. thesis, University of Kansas, 1966.

R. L. Massanari, 'Christianity and the Social Problem: Adolf Stöcker's Christian Socialist Alternative to Marxist Socialism in Nineteenth Century Germany', Ph.D. dissertation, Duke University, 1969.

J. D. Mote, 'Friedrich Naumann: The Course of a German Liberal', D.Phil. thesis, University of Colorado, 1971.

J. Regehr, 'The Preaching of Christoph Blumhardt', Th.D. thesis, Southern Baptist Seminary, 1970.

3. *Articles*

Anonymous, 'Der greise Marxist und der Wanderprediger der Apo', *Stern*, 18 October 1979, pp. 52-59.
—— 'Heiz Kloppenburg zum 70. Geburtstag am 10. Mai 1973', *Junge Kirche. Eine Zeitschrift europäischer Christen*, May 1973, pp. 245-249.
—— 'Marienbade Protokolle', *Neues Forum/Dialog*, March–April 1967, pp. 162f.
—— Review of V. Gardavsky *God Is Not Yet Dead*, in *Times Literary Supplement*, 26 October 1973, p. 1319.
K. L. Baker, 'The Acquisition of Partisanship in Germany', *American Journal of Political Science*, vol. xviii, no. 3, August 1974, pp. 569-582.
K. Barth, 'Die Hilfe, 1913', *Christliche Welt*, 28, 1914, cols 774-778.
—— 'Warum führt man den Kampf nicht auf der ganzen Linie?' *Frankfurter Zeitung*, 15 February 1932.
G. Benedetti, 'Blumhardts Seelsorge in der Sicht heutiger psychotherapeutischer Kenntnisse,' *Reformatio*, 1966, pp. 474-487 and 531-539.
J. Bentley, 'Christoph Blumhardt, Preacher of Hope', *Theology*, vol. 78, no. 665, November 1975, pp. 577-582.
—— 'Dorothee Sölle: political theology and the experience of Latin America', *Papers in Religion and Politics*, University of Manchester Department of Government and Faculty of Theology, no. 6, Michaelmas 1978, pp. 1-25.
—— 'Jesus for Atheists', *The Expository Times*, vol. 86, no. 2, July 1974, pp. 56f.
—— 'Karl Barth as a Christian Socialist', *Theology*, vol. 76, no. 637, July 1973, pp. 349-356.
—— 'Prometheus versus Christ in the Christian-Marxist Dialogue', *Journal of Theological Studies*, N. S. vol. XXIX, pt. 2, October 1978, pp. 483-494.
—— 'The Christian Significance of Atheist Ernst Bloch', *The Expository Times*, vol. 88, no. 2, November 1976, pp. 51-55.
—— 'Three German Marxists Look at Christianity: 1900-1930', *Journal of Church and State*, Waco, Texas, USA, vol. 22, no. 3, autumn 1980, pp. 505-517.
—— 'Vitezslav Gardavsky, Atheist and Martyr', *The Expository Times*, vol. 91, no. 9, June 1980, pp. 276f.

E. Bloch, 'Aktualität und Utopie zu Lukács Philosophie des Marxismus', *Der neue Merkur*, vii, 1924, pp. 457-477.

—— 'Der rebellierende Mensch. Gedanken über Hiob', in *Das dein Ohr auf Weisheit achte*, ed. K. H. Schröter, Berlin 1966, pp. 49-69.

—— 'Enkel der Ochrana', *Neues Forum/Dialog*, August-September 1968, p. 517.

—— 'Politisch Programme und Utopien', *Archiv für Sozialwissenschaft und Politik*, vol. 46, 1919, pp. 140-162.

—— 'Zur Rettung Georg Lukács', *Die weissen Blätter*, no. 12, 1919, pp. 529f.

C. Blumhardt, 'Lettres à un missionnaire en Chine', *Études théologiques et religieuses*, 51. année, no. 3, 1976, pp. 277-287.

F. Borkenau, Review of E. Fromm, *Die Entwicklung des Christus-dogma*, in *Zeitschrift für Sozialforschung*, Jahrgang 1, 1932, pp. 174f.

H. Braun, 'Die Problematik einer Theologie des Neuen Testaments', *Zeitschrift für Theologie und Kirche*, vol. 58, 1961, Supplement 2.

Otto Bruder, 'Johann Christoph Blumhardt als Seelsorger', *Reformatio*, 1953, pp. 621-630.

—— 'Zu den Heilungen Blumhardts', *Evangelische Theologie*, ix, 1949-50, pp. 478-480.

G. Casalis, 'Anmerkungen zur Christologie auf dem Hintergrund lateinamerikanischer Erfahrung', *Junge Kirche*, May 1973, pp. 250-255.

W. H. Chaloner and W. O. Henderson, 'Marx/Engels and Racism', *Encounter*, July 1975, pp. 18-23.

R. P. Chickering, 'The Peace Movement and the Religious Community in Germany, 1900-1914', *Church History*, vol. 38, September 1969, pp. 300-311.

H. Cox, 'Ernst Bloch and "The Pull of the Future"', in *New Theology, No. 5*, ed. M. E. Marty and D. G. Peerman, New York 1968, pp. 191-203.

G. Dehn, 'Adolf Stöcker', *Zwischen den Zeiten*, 1924, pp. 26-48.

—— 'Kirche und Völkerversöhnung', *Christliche Welt*, 45, 1931, pp. 194-204.

O. Dibelius, 'Karl Barth, A Birthday Tribute', *The Listener*, 17 May 1956, pp. 639f.

H. Diem, 'Der Sozialist in Karl Barth: Kontroverse um einen neuen

Versuch, ihn zu verstehen', *Evangelische Kommentare*, May 1972, pp. 292–296.

H. E. Du Bois, 'Karl Barth et la théologie de la révolution', *Revue de Théologie et de Philosophie*, vol. 6, 1970, pp. 401–411.

K. Farner, 'Christus oder Prometheus?' *Neue Zeit. Zeitkritische Monatsblätter*, November 1978, pp. 318–320.

—— 'Konfrontation mit dem Christentum—warum ich Marxist bleibe', *Junge Kirche*, May 1973, pp. 258–264.

—— 'Prometheische Aufgabe für Christus', *Junge Kirche*, October 1972, pp. 491–493.

E. Fischer, 'Schändung der Sowjetunion', *Neues Forum/Dialog*, August-September 1968, pp. 522f.

E. Fromm, 'Die psychoanalytische Charakterologie und ihre Bedeutung für die Sozialpsychologie', *Zeitschrift für Sozialforschung*, Jahrgang 1, 1932, pp. 253–277.

—— 'Die gesellschaftliche Bedingtheit der psychoanalytischen Therapie', *Zeitschrift für Sozialforschung*, Jahrgang 4, 1935, pp. 365–397.

—— 'Die sozialpsychologische Bedeutung der Mutterrechtstheorie', *Zeitschrift für Sozialforschung*, Jahrgang 3, 1934 (published 1935), pp. 196–227.

—— 'Robert Briffaults Werk über das Mutterrecht', *Zeitschrift für Sozialforschung*, Jahrgang 2, 1933 (published 1934), pp. 382–387.

—— 'Über Methode und Aufgabe einer analytischen Sozialpsychologie', *Zeitschrift für Sozialforschung*, Jahrgang 1, 1932, pp. 28–54.

—— 'Zum Gefühl der Ohnmacht', *Zeitschrift für Sozialforschung*, Jahrgang 6, Heft 1, 1937, pp. 95–118.

E. Fuchs, 'Von Friedrich Schleiermacher zu Karl Marx', *Zeitschrift für Religion und Sozialismus*, vol. 2, Heft 1, 1929, pp. 26–34.

R. Garaudy, 'Breschnjew, abtreten,' *Neues Forum/Dialog*, August-September 1968, p. 519.

—— 'Communists and Christians in Dialogue', in *New Theology*, No. 5, ed. M. E. Marty and D. G. Peerman, New York 1968, pp. 212–221.

—— Postface to J. Girardi, *Marxisme et chrétienisme*, Paris 1968, pp. 303–314.

D. Gerbracht, 'Aufbruch zu sittlichen Atheismus—Die Hiob-Deutung Ernst Blochs', *Evangelische Theologie*, 1975, pp. 222–227.

H. Gollwitzer, 'Muss ein Christ Sozialist sein?', in *Jenseits vom Null-Punkt*, ed. R. Weckerling *et al.*, Augsburg 1972, pp. 151–169.

—— 'Von der Religion zum Menschen', in *'Antwort'. Festschrift zum Karl Barths 70. Geburtstag*, Zürich 1956, pp. 596–709.

—— 'Zehn Thesen über "Krieg und Christentum". Vortrag von Helmut Gollwitzer auf der christlichen Friedenskonferenz 1959', *Junge Kirche*, 1959, pp. 228ff.

R. A. Graham, 'The Vatican's East-West Policy Since Pope John XXIII', *The Vatican and World Peace*, ed. F. Sweeney, 1970, pp. 51–78.

J. Habermas, 'Ein marxistischer Schelling. Zu Ernst Blochs spekulativem Materialismus', *Merkur. Deutsche Zeitschrift für europäisches Denken*, vol. 15, 1960, pp. 1078–1091.

—— 'Ernst Bloch – A Marxist Romantic', *Salmagundi*, fall 1969–winter 1970, pp. 311–325.

A. Ham, 'Introduction to the Theology of Liberation', *Communio Viatorum*, vol. 16, no. 3, summer 1973, pp. 113–120.

J. Hellman, 'French "Left Catholics" and Communism in the Nineteen Thirties', *Church History*, vol. 45, December 1976, pp. 507–523.

S. Hook, 'The Enlightenment and Marxism', *Journal of the History of Ideas*, vol. 29, January-March 1968, pp. 93–108.

J. L. Hromadka, 'Gemeinsames Unglück', *Neues Forum/Dialog*, August-September 1968, p. 517.

—— 'The Situation in Czechoslovakia', in *The World Year Book of Religion: The Religious Situation*, ed. D. R. Luther, 1970, II.44–61.

A. von Jäcken, 'Der Faschismus nackt', *Zeitschrift für Religion und Sozialismus*, Band III, Heft 5, 1931, pp. 347–354.

K. Kautsky, 'Bauernagitation in Amerika', *Die Neue Zeit. Wochenschrift der deutschen Sozialdemokratie*, Jahrgang 20, 1902, pp. 453–463.

—— 'Das neueste Leben Jesu', *Die Neue Zeit*, Jahrgang 29, 1911, pp. 35–46.

—— 'Der deutsche Bauernkrieg', *Die Neue Rheinische Zeitung*, nos 5 and 6, Hamburg 1860.

—— 'Die Entstehung des Christentums', *Die Neue Zeit*, Jahrgang 3, 1885, pp. 481–499 and 529–545.

—— 'Der Heilige Franz von Assisi', *Die Neue Zeit*, Jahrgang 21, 1904, pp. 260–267.

—— 'Ein sozial-demokratischer Katechismus', *Die Neue Zeit*, Jahrgang 12/1, 1893, pp. 368f.

—— 'Kant und der Sozialismus', *Die Neue Zeit*, Jahrgang 18, 1900, pp. 1-4.

—— 'Utopischer und materialistischer Marxismus', *Die Neue Zeit*, Jahrgang 15, 1897, pp. 716-727.

—— Review of A. Deissmann, *Das Urchristentum und die unteren Schichten*, in *Die Neue Zeit*, Jahrgang 17, 1/2, 1909, pp. 649f.

A. Kenny, 'German Philosophy Today', *The Listener*, 20 May 1976, pp. 640f.

G. D. Kilpatrick, 'The New Testament and History', *St Mark's Review*, no. 85, September 1975, pp. 4-11.

J. L. Klaiber, 'The Non-Communist Left in Latin America', *Journal of the History of Ideas*, vol. 32, October-December 1971, pp. 607-616.

L. Kolakowski (in discussion with S. Hampshire and C. Taylor), 'Is Marxism Alive and Well?', *The Listener*, 4 May 1972, pp. 583-585.

—— 'Jesus Christus – Prophet und Reformator', in *Almanach 1 für Literatur und Theologie*, ed. D. Sölle *et al.*, Wuppertal 1967, pp. 141-157.

K. Kyle, 'The Fall of Prague', *The Listener*, 24 August 1978, pp. 226-228.

G. Lichtheim, 'Dialectical Methodology', *Times Literary Supplement*, 12 March 1970, pp. 269-272 (published anonymously).

H. Lloyd-Jones, 'Zeus in Aeschylus', *Journal of Hellenic Studies*, vol. 76, 1956, pp. 54-66.

J. M. Lochman, 'Ecumenical Theology of Revolution', in *New Theology, No. 6*, ed. M. E. Marty and D. G. Peerman, New York 1969, pp. 103-122.

—— 'Gardavskys Wandlung von Jakob zu Jeremia', *Orientierung. Katholische Blätter für Weltanschauliche Information*, no. 10, 1978, pp. 110f.

—— 'Konrad Farners aufrechter Gang', *Neue Zeit. Zeitkritische Monatsblätter*, November 1978, pp. 318-320.

—— 'Marxism, Liberalism and Religion, an East European Perspective', in *Marxism and Radical Religion*, ed. J. C. Raines and T. Dean, Philadelphia 1970, pp. 11-25.

—— 'Platz für Prometheus', *Evangelische Kommentare*, March 1972, pp. 136-141.

—— 'The Gospel for Atheists', *Concurrence*, no. 3, autumn 1969, pp. 233-241.

—— 'The Just Revolution', *Christianity and Crisis*, no. 32, 1972, pp. 163f.

—— 'The Place for Prometheus. Theological Lessons from the Christian-Marxist Dialogue,' *Interpretation*, vol. 32, no. 3, July 1978, pp. 242-254.

—— 'Towards an Ecumenical Account of Hope', *Ecumenical Review*, vol. 31, no. 1, January 1979, pp. 13-22.

—— 'Zur Frage der Geschichtsphilosophie J. L. Hromadkas', *Evangelische Theologie*, 1965, pp. 413-428.

M. McHaffie, 'Prometheus and Viktor: Carl Spitteler's "Imago"', *German Life and Letters*, N. S. vol. 31, no. 1, October 1977, pp. 67-77.

M. Machovec, 'Aufgabe des Dialogs. Gespräch zwischen Helmut Gollwitzer und Milan Machovec', in *Partner von Morgen. Das Gespräch zwischen Christen und Marxisten*, Stuttgart 1968, pp. 61-78.

—— 'Panzersozialismus', *Neues Forum/Dialog*, August-September 1968, pp. 520f.

—— 'Zum Anfang der zweiten Phase des Dialogs', *Junge Kirche*, May 1973, pp. 275-280.

J. Macquarrie, 'Liberal and Radical Theologies: An Historical Comparison', *The Modern Churchman*, N.S., vol. 15, no. 4, July 1972, pp. 214-223.

—— 'Theologies of Hope', *The Expository Times*, January 1971, pp. 100-105.

H. Marcuse, 'Gibt es noch Christen?', *Neues Forum/Dialog*, August-September 1968, pp. 533-535.

F.-W. Marquardt, 'Exegese und Dogmatik in Karl Barths Theologie', in Karl Barth, *Die Kirchliche Dogmatik: Register*, ed. H. Krause, Zürich 1970.

—— 'Sozialismus bei Karl Barth', *Junge Kirche*, January 1972, pp. 2-15.

—— 'Theologie und politische Motivation Karl Barths im Kirchenkampf', *Junge Kirche*, May 1973, pp. 283-303.

W.-D. Marsch, 'Theologische Legitimisierung revolutionärer Praxis', *Evangelische Kommentare*, June 1969, pp. 517-521.

D. Martin, 'Revs and Revolutions: Church Trends and Fashionable Theologians', *Encounter*, January 1969, pp. 10-19.

R. L. Massanari, 'True and False Socialism: Adolf Stoecker's Critique of Marxism From a Christian Socialist Perspective', *Church History*, vol. 41, December 1972, pp. 487-496.

J. Moltmann, 'Die Zukunft als neues Paradigma der Transzendenz', *Internationale Dialog Zeitschrift*, ii/i, 1969, pp. 2-13.

—— 'Existenzgeschichte und Weltgeschichte', *Evangelische Kommentare*, January 1968, pp. 13-20.

G. Nenning, 'Konsequenzen aus der Aggression', *Neues Forum/Dialog*, August-September 1968, pp. 513-515.

T. Perlini, 'Metafisica e utopia in Bloch', *Aut Aut*, vol. 125, September-October 1971, pp. 61-82.

R. Puffert, 'Kirchliches Leben in der CSSR', *Evangelische Kommentare*, June 1969, pp. 345-349.

B. Rigaux, 'La redécouverte de la dimension eschatologique de l'Évangile', *Revue d'Histoire de Philosophie Religieuse*, 1967, pp. 3-27.

E. G. Rüsch, 'Dämonenaustreibung in der Gallus-Vita und bei Blumhardt dem Älteren', *Theologische Zeitschrift*, March-April 1978, pp. 86-94.

A. Schönherr, 'The Christian's Place in East German Society as Illuminated by Aspects of Bonhoeffer's Theology', duplicated copy of the lecture delivered at the University of Durham, 15 November 1972.

H. Skolimowski, 'Analytical Linguistic Marxism in Poland', *Journal of the History of Ideas*, vol. 26, 1965, pp. 242-245.

D. Sölle, 'Christus oder Prometheus. Eine Auseinandersetzung mit Helmut Gollwitzer', *Merkur*, July 1972, pp. 701-708.

—— 'Gott und die Revolution', in *Almanach 1 für Literatur und Theologie*, ed. D. Sölle *et al.*, Wuppertal 1967, pp. 126-136.

—— 'How Homeless Is the Christian Left', in *Jenseits vom Null-Punkt*, ed. R. Weckerling *et al.*, Augsburg 1972, pp. 249-256.

—— 'Liebe Deinen Nächsten wie Dich,' *Merkur*, April 1977, pp. 333-339.

—— 'The Role of Political Theology in Relation to the Liberation of Men', in *Religion and the Humanization of Man*, ed. J. M. Robinson, Ontario 1972, pp. 131-142.

—— 'Zum Dialog zwischen Theologie und Literaturwissenschaft', *Internationale Dialog Zeitschrift*, 4, 1969, pp. 299ff.

W. J. C. Thompson, 'Martin Luther and the "Two Kingdoms"', in *Political Ideas*, ed. D. Thomson, 1966.

E. Thurneysen, 'Politische Gemeinde', an interview with W.-D. Zimmermann, *Evangelische Kommentare*, April 1972, pp. 489f.

P. A. Toma and M. J. Reban, 'Church-State Schism in Czechoslovakia', in *Religion and Atheism in the USSR and Eastern Europe*, ed. B. R. Bociurwic and J. W. Strong, 1967, pp. 273-291.

M. Del Verme, 'La Comunione dei beni nella Comunità di Gerusalemme', *Rivista Biblica*, October-December 1975, pp. 353-382.

W. R. Ward, 'The Socialist Commitment in Karl Barth', in *Religious Motivation, Studies in Church History*, ed. D. Baker, 1978, pp. 455-459.

J. Werner, 'Thomas Münzers Regenbogenfahne', *Theologische Zeitschrift*, January-February 1975, pp. 32-37.

G. Wünsch, 'Christliche und marxistische Eschatologie', *Zeitschrift für Religion und Sozialismus*, Band IV, Heft 4, 1932, pp. 231-237.

4. Books

Anonymous, *Histoire des Anabaptistes*, Amsterdam 1702.

—— *Kritische Geschichte des Chiliasmus*, Frankfurt and Leipzig 1781-1783.

—— *Ordnung und Berechnung des Teutschenampts zu Alstadt*, Alddorf 1523.

T.-W. Adorno, *Minima Moralia*, tr. E. F. W. Jephcott, London 1974.

—— *Noten zur Literatur*, II, Frankfurt am Main 1961.

L. Althusser, *For Marx*, London 1977.

T. J. J. Altizer and W. Hamilton, *Radical Theology and the Death of God*, 1968.

T. J. J. Altizer, *The Gospel of Christian Atheism*, 1967.

J. B. Barra and H. M. Waddams, *Communism and the Churches, A Documentation*, 1950.

K. Barth, *Against the Stream, Shorter Post-War Writings, 1948-1951*, 1954.

—— and E. Thurneysen, *Briefwechsel, Band II, 1921-1930*, Zürich 1974.

—— *Brief an einen Pfarrer in der DDR*, Zürich 1958.

—— *Church Dogmatics*, I/i, revised edition 1975 (first translated 1936); II/i, 1957; III/ii, 1960; III/iv, 1961; IV/i and iii, 1st half, 1961; IV/iii, 2nd half, 1962.

—— *Der Römerbrief*, 1st edition, Bern 1919.

—— *Eine Schweizer Stimme, 1938-1945*, Zürich 1945.

—— *Fragments Grave and Gay*, ed. M. Rumscheidt, tr. E. W. Mosbacher, 1972.

—— *God's Search for Man*, tr. G. W. Richards *et al.*, Edinburgh 1935.

—— *How I Changed My Mind*, Edinburgh 1969.

—— and J. Hamel, *How to Serve God in a Marxist Land*, New York 1959.

—— *Letzte Zeugnisse*, Zürich 1969.

—— *Protestant Theology in the Nineteenth Century*, tr. J. Cozens, J. Bowden, *et al.*, 1972.

—— *The Church and the Political Problems of Our Day*, 1939.

—— *The Epistle to the Romans*, tr. E. C. Hoskyns, 1968 edition.

—— *The German Church Conflict*, ed. A. M. Allchin, M. E. Marty and T. H. L. Parker, 1964.

—— *The Word of God and the Word of Man*, 1928.

—— *Theological Existence Today*, tr. R. B. Hoyle, 1933.

—— *Theology and the Church*, tr. L. P. Smith, New York 1962.

—— *Trouble and Promise in the Struggle of the Church in Germany*, Oxford 1938.

B. Bauer, *Christus und die Caesaren. Der Ursprung des Christentums aus dem römischen Griechentum*, 2nd edn, Berlin 1875.

—— *Kritik der evangelischen Geschichte der Synoptiker*. 3 vols, Leipzig 1841–1842.

—— *Kritik der evangelischen Geschichte des Johannes*, Bremen 1840.

T. Beeson, *Discretion and Valour*, 1974.

E. Bernstein, *Evolutionary Socialism*, tr. E. C. Harvey, 1909.

P. L. Berger, *Pyramids of Sacrifice. Political Ethics and Social Change*, 1974.

I. Berlin, *Against the Current. Essays in the History of Ideas*, 1979.

F. Blackaby, ed., *De-Industrialization*, 1979.

E. Bloch, G. Lukács, B. Brecht, W. Benjamin and T.-W. Adorno, *Aesthetics and Politics*, London 1977.

E. Bloch, *Atheismus im Christentum*, Frankfurt am Main, 1968.

—— *Das Materialismusproblem, seine Geschichte und Substanz*, Frankfurt am Main 1972.

—— *Das Prinzip Hoffnung*, 3 vols, Frankfurt am Main 1959.

—— *Freiheit und Ordnung*, ed. E. Grassi, Munich 1969.

—— *Geist der Utopie*, Leipzig 1918.

—— *Gespräche mit Ernst Bloch*, ed. R. Traub and H. Wieser, Frankfurt am Main 1975.

—— *Karl Marx*, tr. L. Tosti, Bologna 1972.

—— *Naturrecht und menschliche Würde*, Frankfurt am Main 1961.

—— *Philosophische Aufsätze zur objektiven Phantasie*, Frankfurt am Main 1969.

—— *Politische Messungen, Pestzeit, Vormärz*, Frankfurt am Main 1976.

—— *Recht, Moral, Staat*, Frankfurt am Main 1976.

—— *Spuren*, Frankfurt am Main 1959.

—— *Tendenz-Latenz-Utopie*, Frankfurt am Main 1978.

—— *Thomas Münzer als Theologe der Revolution*, Berlin 1960.

—— *Tübinger Einleitung in die Philosophie*, Frankfurt am Main 1970.

W. Blumenberg, *Karl Kautskys literarisches Werk*, 'S-Gravenhage 1960.

C. Blumhardt, *Gottes Reich kommt! Predigten und Andachten aus den Jahren 1906 bis 1919*, Zürich 1932.

—— *Ihr Menschen seid Gottes! Predigten und Andachten aus den Jahren 1896 bis 1906*, Zürich 1936.

—— *Jesus ist Sieger! Predigten und Andachten aus den Jahren 1880 bis 1888*, Zürich 1937.

—— *Sterbet, so wird Jesus leben! Predigten und Andachten aus den Jahren 1888 bis 1896*, Zürich 1925.

J. C. Blumhardt, *Ausgewählte Schriften*, Zürich 1947.

D. Bonhoeffer, *Fragmente aus Tegel*, Munich 1978.

—— *Gesammelte Schriften*, Munich 1968.

—— *Letters and Papers from Prison, The Enlarged Edition*, ed. E. Bethge, tr. R. H. Fuller *et al.*, 1967.

J. M. Bonino, *Christians and Marxists. The Mutual Challenge to Revolution*, 1976.

G. Brakelmann, *Kirche und Sozialismus in 19. Jahrhundert. Die Analyse des Sozialismus und Kommunismus bei Johann Hinrich Wichern und bei Rudolf Todt*, Witten 1966.

B. Brecht, *Poems, part 3, 1938–1958*, ed. J. Willett and T. Manheim, 1976.

H. D. Brunotte, *Die evangelische Kirche in Deutschland*, Hanover 1959.

M. Buber, *I and Thou*, tr. W. Kaufmann, Edinburgh 1970.

R. Bultmann, *Glauben und Verstehen*, Tübingen 1933.

—— *History and Eschatology: The Presence of Eternity*, New York 1962.

—— *Jesus Christ and Mythology*, 1960.

—— *Jesus and the Word*, tr. L. P. Smith and E. H. Lantero, 1958.

—— *Kerygma and Myth*, vol. 1, tr. R. H. Fuller, 1953.

E. Busch, *Karl Barth. His life from Letters and Autobiographical Texts*, tr. J. Bowden 1976.

E. Cardenal, *Love in Practice: The Gospel in Solentiname*, tr. G. D. Walsh, 1975.

—— *Marilyn Monroe and Other Poems*, ed. R. Pring-Mill, 1975.

—— *Zerschneide den Stracheldraht*, Wuppertal 1967.

T. Carlyle, *Chartism*, 2nd edn, 1870.

H. Chadwick, *Some Reflections on Conscience: Greek, Jewish, and Christian*, 1968.

O. Chadwick, *The Secularization of the European Mind in the Nineteenth Century*, 1975.

A. B. Come, *An Introduction to Barth's Dogmatics for Preachers*, 1963.

B. L. Cordingley, *Theology and Politics*, Manchester 1978.

E. H. Cousins, ed., *Hope and the Future of Man*, 1973.

E. Crankshaw, *The Shadow of the Winter Palace. The Drift to Revolution, 1825-1917*, 1978.

G. F. Daumen, *Die Geheimnisse des christlichen Altertums*, 2 vols, Hamburg 1847.

A. Deissmann, *Das Urchristentum und die unteren Schichten*, Stuttgart 1910.

Dictionnaire de Théologie Catholique, Paris 1848.

Die Religion in Geschichte und Gegenwart, 3rd edn, Tübingen 1957.

A. Drews, *Die Christusmythe. Verbesserte und erweiterte Ausgabe*, 2 vols, Jena 1910.

G. Ebers, *Aegypten und die Bücher Moses*, Leipzig 1868.

—— *Durch Gosen zum Sinai*, Leipzig 1872.

D. Erasmus, *Epigrammatica Des. Erasmi Roterdami*, Basel 1519.

K. Farner, *Für die Erde: geeint – Für den Himmel: entzweit*, Zürich 1973.

—— *Marxistiches Salz für christliche Erde – Christliches Salz für marxistische Erde*, Zürich 1972.

E. Feil and R. Weth, eds., *Diskussion zur Theologie der Revolution*, Munich 1969.

L. Feuerbach, *The Essence of Christianity*, tr. G. Eliot, New York 1957.

F. Flückiger, *Theologie der Geschichte. Die biblische Rede von Gott und die neuere Geschichtstheologie*, Wuppertal 1970.

S. Franck, *Chronica*, Strassburg 1531.

W. Frank, *Hofprediger Adolf Stöcker und die christlichsoziale Bewegung*, 2nd edn, Hamburg 1935.

E. Fromm, *Beyond the Chains of Illusion*, New York 1962.

—— *The Dogma of Christ and Other Essays*, tr. J. L. Adams, 1953.

J. A. Froude, *History of England*, 2 vols, 1876.

E. Fuchs, *Christliche und marxistische Ethik*, 2 vols, Leipzig 1959.

—— *Marxismus und Christenglaube*, Leipzig 1953.

M. Furlong, *Merton. A Biography*, 1980.

V. Gardavsky, *Hoffnung aus der Skepsis*, tr. D. Neumärker, Munich 1970.

—— *God Is Not Yet Dead*, tr. V. Menkes, 1973.

R. Garaudy, *Marxism in the Twentieth Century*, tr. R. Hague, 1970.

M. Gerhardt, *Johann Hinrich Wichern. Ein Lebensbild*, vol. 1, Hamburg 1929.

A. Gindely, *Geschichte der böhmischen Brüder*, Prague 1857.

G. Girardi, *Marxism and Christianity*, Dublin 1968.

—— *Marxisme et chrétienisme*, Paris 1968.

J. Glenthøg, ed., *Die Mündige Welt V*, Munich 1969.

E. Goldstücker, *et al.*, eds., *Franz Kafka in Prager Sicht*, Prague 1963.

H. Gollwitzer, *Das Recht ein anderer zu werden*, Neuwied and Berlin 1971.

—— *Die Reichen Christen und der Arme Lazarus*, Munich 1968.

—— *Karl Barth, Kirchliche Dogmatik. Auswahl und Einleitung von Helmut Gollwitzer*, Frankfurt am Main 1965.

—— *Krummes Holz - aufrechter Gang. Zur Frage nach dem Sinn des Lebens*, Munich 1970.

—— *Reich Gottes und Sozialismus bei Karl Barth*, Munich 1972.

—— *The Christian Faith and the Marxist Critique of Religion*, tr. D. Cairns, Edinburgh 1970.

—— *The Existence of God as Confessed by Faith*, tr. J. W. Leitch, 1965.

—— *The Rich Christians and Poor Lazarus*, tr. D. Cairns, Edinburgh 1970.

R. O. Grupp, ed., *Ernst Bloch zum 70. Geburtstag*, Berlin 1955.

G. Gutiérrez, *A Theology of Revolution*, 1974.

J. Hamer, *Karl Barth*, 1962.

A. Harnack, *Das Wesen des Christentums*, Siebenstern-Taschenbuch edition, Munich 1960, with a preface by Rudolf Bultmann.

—— *Aus Wissenschaft und Leben*, vol. 2, Giessen 1911.

—— *What is Christianity?* tr. T. B. Saunders, 3rd and revised edn, 1904.

P. Hebblethwaite, *The Christian-Marxist Dialogue and Beyond*, 1977.

J. A. Hebly, *The Russians and the World Council of Churches*, Belfast 1978.

M. Hengel, *Property and Riches in the Early Church*, tr. J. Bowden 1975.

O. W. Heick, *A History of Christian Thought*, vol. 2, Philadelphia 1966.

K. Heuss, *Kompendium der Kirchengeschichte*, 12th edn, Tübingen 1960.

T. Heuss, *Friedrich Naumann. Der Mann, Das Werk, Die Zeit*, 2nd edn, Stuttgart 1949.

S. H. Hook, *Marx and the Marxists: The Ambiguous Legacy*, New York 1955.

J. L. Hromadka, *Evangelium für Atheisten*, Berlin 1957.

—— *Thoughts of a Czech Pastor*, 1970.

G. Hunsinger, *Karl Barth and Radical Politics*, Philadelphia 1976.

E. Jackh, *Christoph Blumhardt. Ein Zeuge des Reich Gottes*, Stuttgart 1950.

R. Jakoby, *Social Amnesia. A Critique of Conformist Psychology from Adler to Laing*, Hassocks 1975.

J. Joll, *Europe Since 1870. An International History*, 1973.

—— *Three Intellectuals in Politics*, New York 1965.

E. Jones, *Zur Psychoanalyse der christlichen Religion*, Berlin 1913.

K. Kautsky, *Das Erfurter Programm*, Stuttgart 1892.

—— *Die soziale Revolution*, Berlin 1907.

—— *Die Vorläufer des Neueren Sozialismus*, Stuttgart 1895.

—— *Ethics and the Materialist Conception of History*, tr. J. B. Askew, Chicago 1918.

—— *Rosa Luxemburg, Karl Liebknecht, Leo Jogiches. Ihre Bedeutung für die deutsche Sozialdemokratie*, Berlin 1921.

—— *The Dictatorship of the Proletariat*, tr. H. J. Stenning, 1920.

—— *The Foundations of Christianity*, 1925.

—— *Thomas More and His Utopia*, tr. H. J. Stenning, 1927.

A. Kalthoff, *An der Wende des Jahrhunderts. Kanzelreden über die sozialen Kämpfe unserer Zeit*, Braunschweig 1898.

—— *Christusproblem. Grundlinien zu einer Sozialtheologie*, Jena 1902.

—— *Die religiösen Probleme in Goethes Faust*. Braunschweig 1901.

—— *Friedrich Nietzsche und die Kulturprobleme unserer Zeit*, Berlin 1900.

—— *Modernes Christentum*, Berlin n.d. (1906).

—— *The Rise of Christianity*, tr. J. McCabe, 1907.

—— *Zarathustrapredigten*, Jena 1904.

—— *Zukunftsideale, mit einer Lebensskizze von Friedrich Steudel*, Jena 1907.

S. Kierkegaard, *Either/Or*, tr. D. F. Swenson and L. M. Swenson, 1944.

H. Küng, *On Being a Christian*, tr. E. Quinn, 1977.

K. Kupisch, *Durch den Zaun der Geschichte*, Berlin 1964.

—— *Quellen zur Geschichte des deutschen Protestantismus, 1871–1945*, Siebenstern-Taschenbuch, Munich 1965.

L. Labedz, ed., *Revisionism. Essays on the History of Marxist Ideas*, 1962.

K. S. Latourette, *Christianity in a Revolutionary Age*, vol. 2, 1960.

A. Th. van Leeuwen, *Critique of Heaven*, 1972.

J. Leidmann, *Thomas Münzer, seine Biographie*, Leipzig 1842.

R. Lejeune, ed., *Christoph Blumhardt und seine Botschaft*, Erlangen-bach 1968.

V. Lenin, *The Proletarian Revolution and Kautsky the Renegade*, 1920.

G. E. Lessing, *Lessing's Theological Writings*, ed. H. Chadwick, 1956.

G. Lichtheim, *From Marx to Hegel*, 1971.

J. Lingard, *History of England*, 5th edn 1849.

J. M. Lochman, *Christus oder Prometheus? Die Kernfrage des christlich-marxistischen Dialogs und die Christologie*, Hamburg 1972.

—— *Church in a Marxist Society. A Czechoslovak View*, 1970.

—— *Das radikale Erbe. Versuche einer theologischer Orientierung im Ost und West*, Zürich 1973.

—— *Die Not der Versöhnung*, Hamburg 1963.

—— with F. Buri and H. Ott, *Dogmatik in Dialog*, 2 vols, Gütersloh 1973 and 1974.

—— *Encountering Marx*, tr. E. Robertson, Belfast 1977.

—— *Reconciliation and Liberation*, tr. D. Lewis, Belfast 1980.

H. Ludwig, *Die Entstehung des Darmstädter Wortes*, Bremen 1977.

G. Lukács, *History and Class Consciousness. Studies in Marxist Dialectics*, tr. R. Livingstone, 1971.

—— *Lenin, a Study on the Unity of His Thought*, tr. N. Jacobs, London 1972.

J. R. Lumby, ed., *Utopia and Roper's More*, 1879.

R. Luxemburg, *Ausgewählte Reden und Schriften*, vol. 2, Berlin 1951.

W. L. McBride, *The Philosophy of Marx*, 1977.

M. Machovec, *A Marxist Looks at Jesus*, 1976.

—— *Jesus für Atheisten*, 3rd edn, Stuttgart 1973.

—— *Marxismus und dialektische Theologie. Barth, Bonhoeffer und Hromadka in atheistisch-kommunistischer Sicht*, tr. D. Neumärker, Zürich 1965.

D. B. McKown, *The Classical Marxist Critiques of Religion: Marx, Engels, Lenin, Kautsky*, The Hague 1975.

D. M. McLellan, *Karl Marx, His Life and Thought*, 1973.

—— *Marx*, 1974.

T. H. Mandel, *Der Sieg von Möttlingen im Lichte des Glaubens und der Wissenschaft*, Leipzig 1895.

G. Mann, *The History of Germany Since 1789*, tr. M. Jackson, 1974.

K. Mannheim, *Ideology and Utopia*, 1936.

F. E. Manuel and F. P. Manuel, *Utopian Thought in the Western World*, 1979.

H. Marcuse, *Studies in Critical Philosophy*, tr. J. de Bres, London 1972.

F.-W. Marquardt, *Theologie und Sozialismus. Das Beispiel Karl Barths*, 2nd edn, Munich 1972.

R. Marquez, ed., *Latin American Revolutionary Poetry*, New York 1974.

K. Marx, *Capital* Volume 1, Harmondsworth 1975.

—— *Die Frühschriften*, ed. S. Landshut and J. Mayer, Stuttgart 1932.

—— *Early Texts*, ed. D. M. McLellan, 1971.

—— *Grundrisse*, tr. M. Nicolaus, Harmondsworth 1973.

—— and F. Engels, *Collected Works*, vol. 1, 1975.

—— and F. Engels, *Historisch-Kritische Gesamtausgabe*, ed. D. Rjazonov, vol. I, Frankfurt am Main 1927.

—— and F. Engels, *On Religion*, Moscow 1957.

—— and F. Engels, *Werke*, vol. 35, Berlin 1967.

E. Matthias, *Das Ende der Parteien*, Düsseldorf 1960.

C. E. Maurice, *The Lives of English Popular Leaders in the Middle Ages*, 1875.

C. Merivale, *The Romans under the Empire*, vol. 7, 1862.

T. Merton, *Contemplative Prayer*, 1973.

—— *Elected Silence*, 1949.

—— *The Secular Journal*, 1977.

J. Messner, *Die Soziale Frage*, Vienna 1964.

J. B. Metz, *Zur Theologie der Welt*, Mainz/Munich 1968.

J. Miranda, *Marx and the Bible. A Critique of the Philosophy of Oppression*, New York 1974.

W. Mittenzwei, *Exil in der Schweiz*, Leipzig 1978.

J. Moltmann, *Hope and Planning*, tr. M. Clarkson, 1973.

—— *Im Gespräch mit Ernst Bloch. Eine theologische Wegbegleitung*, Munich 1976.

—— *The Crucified God*, tr. R. A. Wilson and J. Bowden, 1974.

—— *Theology of Hope*, tr. J. W. Leitch, 1967.

T. More, *Sir Thomas More, a Selection From His Works*, ed. W. J. Walter, Baltimore 1841.

—— *The Works of Sir Thomas More, Knight*, 1557.

R. Morgan, *The German Social Democrats and the First International, 1864–1873*, 1965.

G. L. Mosse, *Germans and Jews*, 1971.

T. Münzer, *Protestation odder empietung Tome Müntzers von Stolberg*, Altstedt 1524.

F. Naumann, *Was heisst Christlich-sozial?*, vol. 1, 2nd edn, Leipzig 1896.

—— Ibid., vol. 2, Leipzig 1896.

—— *Werke*, ed. W. Usahdel and T. Scheider, Cologne 1964.

S. Neill, *The Interpretation of the New Testament, 1861–1961*, 1966.

J. P. Nettl, *Rosa Luxemburg*, 1966.

R. Niebuhr, *Essays in Applied Christianity*, ed. D. B. Robertson, New York 1959.

D. Nisard, *Renaissance et Réforme, Erasme, Thomas Morus, Melanchthon*, 2nd edn, Paris 1871.

C. Ordnung, *Christen im Ringen um eine bessere Welt. Zum Selbstverständniss der christlichen Friedenskonferenz*, Prague 1969.

W. Pannenberg, *Basic Questions in Theology*, vol. 2, 1971.

—— *Jesus – God and Man*, 1968.

J. Pelikan, ed. *Twentieth Century Theology in the Making, vol. 2: The Theological Dialogue: Issues and Resources*, tr. R. A. Wilson, 1970.

J. Pelikan, *The Secret Visocany Congress*, 1971.

H. Peukert, ed., *Diskussion zur 'Politische Theologie'*, Mainz/Munich 1961.

O. Pfleiderer, *Das Urchristentum, seine Schriften und Lehren in geschichtlichem Zusammenhang beschrieben*, 2nd edn, 2 vols, Berlin 1902.

K. E. Pollmann, *Landes-herrliches Kirchenregiment und Soziale Frage*, Berlin 1974.

G. von Rad, *Theologie des Alten Testaments*, vol. 1, Munich 1957.

L. Ragaz, *Der Kampf um das Reich Gottes in Blumhardt, Vater und Sohn – und weiter!*, Zürich 1922.

K. Rahner, *Theological Investigations*, vol. 6, 1966.

G. Raulet, ed., *Utopie – marxisme selon Ernst Bloch*, Paris 1976.

A. J. Rasker and M. Machovec, *Theologie und Revolution. Ein west-östlichen Dialog*, Hamburg 1969.

J. M. Robinson, ed., *The Beginnings of Dialectical Theology*, vol. 1, Richmond, Virginia, 1968.

G. T. Rudhart, *Tomas Morus. Aus den Quellen bearbeitet*, Nuremberg 1829.

R. Ruether, *The Radical Kingdom. The Western Experience of Messianic Hope*, New York 1970.

H. M. Rumscheidt, *Revolution and Theology. An analysis of the Barth-Harnack Correspondence of 1932*, 1972.

A. Ruge, *Briefwechsel und Tageblätter*, vol. 1, Berlin 1866.

E. Sarkisyanz, *Russland und der Messianismus des Orients*, Tübingen 1955.

E. Schappler, ed., *Quellen zur Geschichte der sozialen Frage in Deutschland*, 2nd edn, 2 vols, Göttingen 1960 and 1964.

L. Schneider, ed., *Religion, Culture and Society*, New York 1964.

M. Schneider, *Neurose und Klassenkampf*, Hamburg 1973.

A. Schweitzer, *Die Messianitäts- und Leidensgeheimnisse*, 3rd edn, Tübingen 1956.

―― *The Quest of the Historical Jesus*, tr. W. Montgomery, 1910.

F. Seebohm, *The Oxford Reformers of 1498*, 1867.

Ota Šik, *The Third Way*, 1976.

H. G. Skilling, *Czechoslovakia's Interrupted Revolution*, Princeton 1976.

D. Sölle, *Atheistisch an Gott glauben*, Stuttgart 1968.

―― *Christ the Representative. An Essay in Theology After the 'Death of God'*, tr. D. Lewis, 1967.

―― *Die Wahrheit ist konkret*, Olten 1967.

―― *Herausforderung durch die Zeit*, Stuttgart 1970.

―― and F. Steffenski, *Politisches Nachtgebet in Köln*, 2 vols, Stuttgart 1969 and 1971.

―― *Politische Theologie. Auseinandersetzung mit Rudolf Bultmann*, Stuttgart 1971.

―― *Suffering*, tr. E. R. Kalin, 1975.

T. Stapleton, *Histoire de Thomas More*, Paris 1879.

J. Steele, *Socialism with a German Face*, 1977.

L. Stein, *Die Soziale Frage im Licht der Philosophie*, Stuttgart 1897.

A. Stöcker, *Christlich-Sozial. Reden und Aufsätze*, 2nd edn, Berlin 1890.

―― *Dreizehn Jahre Hofprediger und Politiker*, Berlin 1895.

D. F. Strauss, *Das Leben Jesu kritisch bearbeitet*, 4th edn, 2 vols, Tübingen 1840.

G. T. Strobel, *Leben, Schriften und Lehren Thomas Müntzers*, Altdorf 1795.

H. Thielicke, *Between Heaven and Earth*, tr. J. W. Doberstein, 1967.

—— *Theological Ethics, vol. 2: Politics*, W. H. Lazareth, ed., 1979.

E. Thurneysen, *Christoph Blumhardt*, 2nd edn, Stuttgart 1962.

—— *Karl Barth. 'Theologie und Sozialismus' in den Briefen seiner Frühzeit*, Zürich 1973.

.P. Tillich, *Auf der Grenze*, Stuttgart 1962.

—— *Perspectives on Nineteenth and Twentieth Century Theology*, ed. C. E. Braaten, 1967.

—— *Systematic Theology*, vol. 1, 1953.

—— *The Boundaries of our Being*, 1973.

—— *The Religious Situation*, tr. H. R. Niebuhr, New York 1956.

—— *The Socialist Decision*, tr. F. Sherman, New York 1977.

R. Todt, *Der radikale deutsche Sozialismus und die christliche Gesellschaft*, 2nd edn, Wittenberg 1878.

T. F. Torrance, *Karl Barth. An Introduction to His Early Theology, 1910–1931*, 1962.

A. Toynbee, *A Study of History, vol. 12: Reconsiderations*, 1961.

W. Treue, *Deutsche Parteiprogramme, 1861–1961*, 3rd edn, Göttingen 1961.

C. Troebst, *Aussenseiter oder Wegbereiter. Christoph Blumhardt, der Prediger zwischen den Fronten*, Bad Boll n.d.

E. Troeltsch, *Die Soziallehren der christlichen Kirchen und Gruppen*, Tübingen 1922.

—— *Zur religiösen Lage, Religionsphilosophie, und Ethik*, Tübingen 1922.

L. Trotsky, *The Defence of Terrorism. Terrorism and Communism, A Reply to Karl Kautsky*, 1935.

—— *The Struggle Against Fascism in Germany*, 1975.

G. Tyrrell, *Christianity at the Crossroads*, edition of 1963.

S. Unseld, ed., *Ernst Bloch zu ehren*, Frankfurt am Main 1965.

J. Wade, *History of the Middle and Working Classes*, vol. 10, 1835.

G. Walter, *Les origines du communisme*, 2nd edn, Paris 1975.

M. Weber, *Gesammelte Ausätze zur Religionssoziologie*, vol. 1, Tübingen 1920.

J. Weiss, *Jesus von Nazareth, Mythus oder Geschichte? Eine Auseinandersetzung mit Kalthoff, Drews, Jensen*, Tübingen 1910.

—— *Die Predigt vom Reich Gottes*, Göttingen 1892.

J. Wellhausen, *Geschichte Israels*, vol. 1, Berlin 1878.

C. C. West, *Communism and the Theologians*, 1958.

H. J. Wetzer and B. Welte, eds., *Kirchenlexikon oder Encyklopädie der katholischen Theologie*, Freiburg im Briesgau 1853.

J. H. Wichern, *Sämtliche Werke*, ed. P. Meinhold, vol. 1, Berlin and Hamburg 1958.

B. Wielanga, *Lenins Weg zur Revolution*, Munich 1971.

J. R. C. Wright, '*Above Parties*'. *The Political Attitudes of the German Protestant Church Leadership, 1918–1933*, 1974.

A. Wünsche, *Die Lehre der zwölf Apostel*, 2nd edn, Leipzig 1884.

H. Zahrnt, *Die Sache mit Gott*, Munich 1972.

E. Zellweger, *Der jüngere Blumhardt. Was denken wir von ihm?* Basle 1945.

F. Zündel, *Pfarrer Johann Christoph Blumhardt. Ein Lebensbild*, Heilbronn 1880.

N. Zernov, *The Russians and Their Church*, 3rd edn 1978.

S. Zweig, *Die Welt von Gestern*, Frankfurt am Main 1970.

5. Interviews and Correspondence

Dr E. Bethge.
Sir Robert Birley.
Professor Eduard Goldstücker.
Professor Helmut Gollwitzer.
Professor J. M. Lochman.
Professor F.-W. Marquardt.
Professor Jürgen Moltmann.
Bishop Albrecht Schönherr.
Dr Christian Troebst.
Dr Visser 't Hooft.

Index